First World War
and Army of Occupation
War Diary
France, Belgium and Germany

42 DIVISION
126 Infantry Brigade
Manchester Regiment
1/10th Battalion
1 March 1917 - 4 April 1919

WO95/2658/2

The Naval & Military Press Ltd
www.nmarchive.com
Published in association with The National Archives

Published by

The Naval & Military Press Ltd

Unit 10 Ridgewood Industrial Park,

Uckfield, East Sussex,

TN22 5QE England

Tel: +44 (0) 1825 749494

www.naval-military-press.com

www.nmarchive.com

This diary has been reprinted in facsimile from the original. Any imperfections are inevitably reproduced and the quality may fall short of modern type and cartographic standards.

© **Crown Copyright**
Images reproduced by permission of The National Archives, London, England, 2015.

Contents

Document type	Place/Title	Date From	Date To
Heading	WO95/2658 1/10 Manchester R Mar 17-Apr19		
Heading	42nd Division 126th Infy Bde 1-10th Bn Manchester Regt Mar 1917-Apr 1919		
Heading	War Diary Of OC. 1/10th Manchester Regt From March 1st To 31st/1917 Volume XIX		
War Diary	At Sea	01/03/1917	05/03/1917
War Diary	Aqrseilles	06/03/1917	06/03/1917
War Diary	On Train	07/03/1917	07/03/1917
War Diary	Pont Remy	08/03/1917	08/03/1917
War Diary	Huppy	09/03/1917	30/03/1917
War Diary	Liercourt	31/03/1917	31/03/1917
Heading	War Diary of O.C. 1/10 Manchester Regiment Left by Lieut J.C.S. Rowbotham the officer Detailed by line for that Purpose from April 1st to April 30/1917 Volume XX		
War Diary	Liercourt	01/04/1917	07/04/1917
War Diary	Morcourt.	08/04/1917	10/04/1917
War Diary	Flaucourt	11/04/1917	15/04/1917
War Diary	Longavesnes	16/04/1917	21/04/1917
War Diary	Peziere	22/04/1917	29/04/1917
War Diary	Villers Faucon	30/04/1917	30/04/1917
Heading	War Diary of Officer Commanding 1/10R Manchester Regt Kept by Lieut J.C.S. Rowbotham (Adjutant) (The Officer Detailed by Him for that Purpose) from May 1st 1917 To May 31st 1917 Volume 21		
War Diary	Villers Faucon	01/05/1917	03/05/1917
War Diary	Lempire	04/05/1917	09/05/1917
War Diary	St Emilie	10/05/1917	13/05/1917
War Diary	Lempire	14/05/1917	17/05/1917
War Diary	Villers Faucon	18/05/1917	18/05/1917
War Diary	Equan Court	19/05/1917	19/05/1917
War Diary	Ytres	20/05/1917	20/05/1917
War Diary	Havrincourt Wood	21/05/1917	31/05/1917
Heading	War Diary Of OC 1/10R Manchester Regiment kept by Lieut J.C.S. Rowbotham (Adjutants) From 1st June 1917 to 30th June 1917 Volume 22		
War Diary	Havrincourt Wood	01/06/1917	04/06/1917
War Diary	Ytres	05/06/1917	21/06/1917
War Diary	Havrincourt Wood	22/06/1917	30/06/1917
Heading	War Diary of O.C 1/10th Manchester Regiment From July 1/1917 to July 31/1917 Volume 23.		
War Diary	Haurincourt	01/07/1917	04/07/1917
War Diary	Havrincourt Wood	05/07/1917	06/07/1917
War Diary	Bus (0.16 57c NE)	07/07/1917	08/07/1917
War Diary	Bihucourt 54/C 1/40000 G.II	09/07/1917	10/07/1917
War Diary	Courcelles Map 54/C 1/40000 A 15 & 16	11/07/1917	31/07/1917
Heading	War Diary of Officer Commanding 1/10th Manchester Regiment Kept by 2/Lieut O.M. Harry (Intelligence Officer) the Officer Detailed by him for that Purpose From August 1st To August 31st 1917 Volume XXIV		

War Diary	Courcelles	01/08/1917	20/08/1917
War Diary	Forceville	21/08/1917	21/08/1917
War Diary	Proven & Watou	22/08/1917	22/08/1917
War Diary	Watou	23/08/1917	31/08/1917
Operation(al) Order(s)	1/10th Manchester Regiment Operation Order No 17	20/08/1917	20/08/1917
Operation(al) Order(s)	Administrative Instructions Issued With Operation Order No. 17.		
Operation(al) Order(s)	1/10th Manchester Regiment Operation Order No. 20	29/08/1917	29/08/1917
Operation(al) Order(s)	1/10th Manchester Regiment. Preliminary Administrative Instructions To Operation Order No. 20	29/08/1917	29/08/1917
Operation(al) Order(s)	Addendum No. 1 To Administrative Instructions Issued In Conjunctions With Operation Order No. 20.	29/08/1917	29/08/1917
Operation(al) Order(s)	Administrative Instructions issued With Addendum No. 2 (Operation Order No. 20	29/08/1917	29/08/1917
Operation(al) Order(s)	Addendum No 1. To Administrative Instructions Issued In Conjunction With Operation Order No 20	29/08/1917	29/08/1917
Heading	War Diary Of the 1/10 Manchester Regiment Kept by 2/Lieut O M Harry the Officers detailed by the Commanding officer Vol XXV		
War Diary	Ypres	01/09/1917	20/09/1917
War Diary	Winnezeele	21/09/1917	24/09/1917
War Diary	La Panne	25/09/1917	30/09/1917
Operation(al) Order(s)	Addendum To Operation Order No 21	05/09/1917	05/09/1917
Miscellaneous	S Will Lt. RAMC		
Operation(al) Order(s)	Operation Order No 25. by Major J.H.Allan. Commanding 1/10th Manchester Regiment.	09/09/1917	09/09/1917
Miscellaneous	1/10th Manchester Regiment Battalion Operation Order No 27 by Major J.R Paul D.S.O., Commanding.	15/09/1917	15/09/1917
Heading	War Diary		
Miscellaneous	Warning Order. by Major W.R. Peel D.S.O. Commanding 1/10th Manchester Regiment.	16/09/1917	16/09/1917
Operation(al) Order(s)	Operation Order No. 28 by Major W.R. Peel. D.S.O. Commanding 1/10th Manchester Regiment.	16/09/1917	16/09/1917
Operation(al) Order(s)	Addendum No. 1 to Administrative Instructions issued in accordance with Battalion Operation Order No. 28	18/09/1917	18/09/1917
Operation(al) Order(s)	Administrative Instructions in accordance with Operation Order No. 28	16/09/1917	16/09/1917
Heading	War Diary		
Operation(al) Order(s)	Operation Order No 29 by Major W.R. Peel D.S.O. Commanding 1/10th Manchester Regiment.	18/09/1917	18/09/1917
Operation(al) Order(s)	Administrative Instructions To Battalion Operation Order Number 29	18/09/1917	18/09/1917
Operation(al) Order(s)	Operation Order No 30 by Major W.R. Peel D.S.O. Commanding 1/10th Manchester Regiment.	29/09/1917	29/09/1917
Operation(al) Order(s)	Administrative Instructions with Operation Order No 30	29/09/1917	29/09/1917
Miscellaneous	1/10th Manchester Regiment Warning Order.	23/09/1917	23/09/1917
Operation(al) Order(s)	Operation Order No 31 by Major W.R. Peel D.S.O. Commanding 1/10th Manchester Regiment.	21/09/1917	21/09/1917
Operation(al) Order(s)	Operation Order No 31 (Administrative Instructions) by Major W.R. Peel D.S.O. Commanding 1/10th Manchester Regiment.		
Operation(al) Order(s)	Operation Order No 33 by Major W.R. Peel D.S.O. Commanding 1/10th Manchester Regiment.	23/09/1917	23/09/1917
Operation(al) Order(s)	Administrative Instructions Issued To Accompany Operation Order No. 35 Dated 23/9/17	23/09/1917	23/09/1917
Heading	1/10 Manchester Vol 9		

Heading	D.A.G. 3rd Echelon Rouen		
Heading	War Diary of 1/10th Manchester Regiment Kept by Lieut F. Howarth (Intelligence officer) the officer detailed by the O.C. for that Purpose From October 1st to 31st 1917 Vol XXV		
War Diary	La Panne	01/10/1917	06/10/1917
War Diary	Coxyde	07/10/1917	07/10/1917
War Diary	Nieuport	08/10/1917	11/10/1917
War Diary	Cost Dunkerke	12/10/1917	15/10/1917
War Diary	Nieuport	16/10/1917	18/10/1917
War Diary	Wulpen	19/10/1917	22/10/1917
War Diary	Nieuport	23/10/1917	26/10/1917
War Diary	Cost Donkerke	27/10/1917	29/10/1917
War Diary	Nieuport	30/10/1917	31/10/1917
Operation(al) Order(s)	Operation Order No.34 by Lieut Colonel W.R. Peel D.S.O. Commanding 1/10th Manchester Regiment.	05/10/1917	05/10/1917
Miscellaneous	1/10th Manchester Regiment. Addendum No 1. to Administrative Instructions.	05/10/1917	05/10/1917
Operation(al) Order(s)	1/10th Manchester Regiment. Addendum No. 2 to Operation Order No. 34	05/10/1917	05/10/1917
Miscellaneous			
Operation(al) Order(s)	Administrative Orders In Accordance With Operation Orders No. 34.	05/10/1917	05/10/1917
Operation(al) Order(s)	Operation Order No 35 by Lieut, Colonel W.R. Peel D.S.O. Commanding 1/10th Manchester Regiment.	05/10/1917	05/10/1917
Miscellaneous	1/10th. Battalion Manchester Regiment.	07/10/1917	07/10/1917
Miscellaneous	1/10th. Manchester Regiment.	07/10/1917	07/10/1917
Miscellaneous	B.M. 80/135	08/10/1917	08/10/1917
Miscellaneous	1/10th Manchester Regiment. Warning Order	09/10/1917	09/10/1917
Miscellaneous	Reference Operation Order No. 36. by Lieut-Col. W.R. Peel. Commanding 1/10th Battalion Manchester Regiment.	10/10/1917	10/10/1917
Miscellaneous	Lieut B.E.H. Hughes		
Operation(al) Order(s)	Operation Order No 37 Lieut Col. W.R. Peel D.S.O. Commanding 1/10th Manchester Regiment.	10/10/1917	10/10/1917
Operation(al) Order(s)	Operation Order No. 38. by Lieut-Colonel W.R. Peel D.S.O. Commanding 1/10th. Manchester Regiment.	17/10/1917	17/10/1917
Operation(al) Order(s)	Operation Order No 37 by Lt-Col W.R. Peel D.S.O. Commanding 1/10th. Battalion Manchester Regiment.	13/10/1917	13/10/1917
Miscellaneous	1/10th. Battalion Manchester Regiment.	21/10/1917	21/10/1917
Miscellaneous	1/10th. Battalion Manchester Regt.	19/10/1917	19/10/1917
Operation(al) Order(s)	Operation Order No 39. by Lieut-Colonel W.R. Peel, D.S.O. Commanding 1/10th. Battalion Manchester Regiment.	21/10/1917	21/10/1917
Operation(al) Order(s)	Operation Order No. 40 by Lieut-Colonel W.R. Peel, D.S.O. Commanding 1/10th. Battalion Manchester Regiment.	25/10/1917	25/10/1917
Operation(al) Order(s)	Addendum No. 1. to Operation Order No, 39.1/10th. Manchester Regiment.	22/10/1917	22/10/1917
Miscellaneous		25/10/1917	25/10/1917
Heading	War Diary of 1/10 Manchester Regt Kept by Lieut O.M. Harry the Officer detailed to do so by the Commanding Officer Vol XXVI		
Miscellaneous			
War Diary		01/11/1917	30/11/1917

Operation(al) Order(s)	Operation Order No 44 by Major C.E. Higham, Commanding 1/10th. Battalion Manchester Regiment.	06/11/1917	06/11/1917
Operation(al) Order(s)	Operation Orders No 42 by Major C.E. Higham, Commanding 1/10th Manchester Regiment.	02/11/1917	02/11/1917
Heading	War Diary of Officer Commanding 1/10th Manchester Regiment Kept by Lieut O.M. Harry (Intelligence Officer) (the officer detailed by him for that Purpose) From December 1st 1917 To December 31st 1917		
War Diary	Beuvry	01/12/1917	09/12/1917
War Diary	Guinchy	10/12/1917	15/12/1917
War Diary	Le Preol	16/12/1917	21/12/1917
War Diary	Guinchy	22/12/1917	31/12/1917
Operation(al) Order(s)	Operation Orders No. 60 by Lieut Col. W.R. Peel D.S.O. Commanding 1/10th Manchester Regiment.	27/10/1917	27/10/1917
Miscellaneous	Preliminary Order.by Lieut Col W.R. Peel D.S.O. Commanding 1/10th. Manchester Regiment.	26/12/1917	26/12/1917
Operation(al) Order(s)	Operation Order No 57 by Lieut Col.W.R. Peel D.S.O. Commanding 1/10th Manchester Regiment	21/12/1917	21/12/1917
Operation(al) Order(s)	Operation Order No 58. by Lieut Col W.R. Peel. D.S.O. Commanding 1/10th. Manchester Regiment	22/12/1917	22/12/1917
Miscellaneous			
Operation(al) Order(s)	1/10th. Manchester Regiment. Operation Order No 58 by Lieut Col W.R. Peel D.S.O. Commanding 1/10th. Manchester Regiment.	16/12/1917	16/12/1917
Operation(al) Order(s)	Operation Order No 54 by Lieut. Col W.R. Peel. D.S.O. Commanding 1/10th. Manchester Regiment.	12/12/1917	12/12/1917
Operation(al) Order(s)	Operation Order No. 55 by Lieut: Col: W.R. Peel D.S.O. Commanding 1/10th. Manchester Regiment.	14/12/1917	14/12/1917
Miscellaneous	1/10th. Manchester Regiment.	08/12/1917	08/12/1917
Miscellaneous	Addendum To Para 8.		
Miscellaneous	1/10th Manchester Regiment. Reference Operation Order No. 59.	24/12/1917	24/12/1917
Operation(al) Order(s)	1/10th Manchester Regiment. Operation Order No 59	23/12/1917	23/12/1917
Heading	War Diary of Officer Commanding 1/10th Battn Manchester Regt From January 1st 1918 To January 31st 1918 Vol 12		
War Diary	Cuinchy	01/01/1918	02/01/1918
War Diary	Hingette	03/01/1918	17/01/1918
War Diary	Givenchy	18/01/1918	23/01/1918
War Diary	Windy Corner	23/01/1918	29/01/1918
War Diary	Givenchy	29/01/1918	31/01/1918
Operation(al) Order(s)	Operation Orders No. 61 by Lieut Col W.R. Peel D.S.O. Commanding 1/10th. Manchester Regiment.	01/01/1918	01/01/1918
Miscellaneous	1/10th. Manchester Regiment.	02/01/1918	02/01/1918
Operation(al) Order(s)	Operation Order No. 64 by Lieut: Col W.R. Peel, D.S.O. Commanding 1/10th Manchester Regiment	22/01/1918	22/01/1918
Operation(al) Order(s)	Operation Orders No. 63 by Lieut : Col: W.R. Peel. D.S.O. Commanding 1/10th Manchester Regiment.	16/01/1918	16/01/1918
Miscellaneous	1/10th. Manchester Regiment.	12/01/1918	12/01/1918
Operation(al) Order(s)	Operation Order No. 62. by Lieut: Col : W.R. Peel. D.S.O. Commanding 1/10th. Manchester Regt.	15/01/1918	15/01/1918
Operation(al) Order(s)	Operation Order No. 65 by Lieut: Col : W.R. Peel. D.S.O. Commanding 1/10th. Manchester Regiment.	27/01/1918	27/01/1918

Heading	War Diary of Officer Commanding 1/10th Battn Manchester Regt Kept By Capt J.C.S. Rowbotham (Adjutant) From Feby 1st 1918 To Feby 28th 1918 Vol 13		
War Diary	Givenchy	01/02/1918	03/02/1918
War Diary	Gorre	04/02/1918	09/02/1918
War Diary	Givenchy	10/02/1918	13/02/1918
War Diary	Busnes	14/02/1918	21/02/1918
War Diary	Hingette	22/02/1918	28/02/1918
Operation(al) Order(s)	Operation Order No. 66. by Lieut: Col: W.R. Peel. D.S.O. Commanding 1/10th. Manchester Regiment.	02/02/1918	02/02/1918
Miscellaneous			
Operation(al) Order(s)	Operation Order No 67. Lieut :Col: W.R. Peel. D.S.O. Commanding 1/10th. Manchester Regiment.	02/02/1918	02/02/1918
Operation(al) Order(s)	Operation Order No. 68. by Lieut. Col.W.R.Peel. D.S.O. Commanding 1/10th. Manchester Regiment.	12/02/1918	12/02/1918
Operation(al) Order(s)	Addendum No. 1 To Operation Order No. 68	12/02/1918	12/02/1918
Operation(al) Order(s)	Operation Order No. 69 by Lieut. Col. W.R. Peel. D.S.O. Commanding 1/10th. Manchester Regiment.	13/02/1918	13/02/1918
Operation(al) Order(s)	Operation Order No. 70 by Lieut. Col. W.R. Peel. D.S.O. Commanding 1/10th. Batt. Manchester Regiment.	21/02/1918	21/02/1918
Heading	42nd Division. 126th Infantry Brigade 1/10th Battalion Manchester Regiment March 1918		
Miscellaneous	1/10 Manchester Regiment	01/04/1918	01/04/1918
Heading	War Diary Of OC 1/10 Manchester Regt. (kept by Lieut W.A. Haslewood The officer detailed by him for that Purpose) From March 1st to 31st 1918 Inclusive Vol XXV		
War Diary	Hingette	01/03/1918	04/03/1918
War Diary	Lapugnoy	05/03/1918	23/03/1918
War Diary	Adinfer	24/03/1918	31/03/1918
Heading	Appendices I & II		
Operation(al) Order(s)	Operation Order No. 72. by Major F.E. Tetley. D.S.O. Commanding 1/10th. Battalion Manchester Regiment.	03/03/1918	03/03/1918
Miscellaneous	Appendix II		
Operation(al) Order(s)	Operation Order No. 1. by Lieut. Col: W.R. Peel. D.S.O.Commanding 1/10th. Batt: Manchester Regt	19/03/1918	19/03/1918
Heading	126th Inf. Bde. 42nd Div. War Diary 1/10th Battn. The Manchester Regiment. April 1918		
Heading	War Diary Of Officer Commanding 1/10th Manchester Regt From April 1st 1918 To April 30th 1918 Volume 15		
War Diary	Essarts	01/04/1918	06/04/1918
War Diary	Souastre Pas.	07/04/1918	30/04/1918
Heading	Appendices 1 to II.		
Operation(al) Order(s)	Operation Order No. 10	04/04/1918	04/04/1918
Operation(al) Order(s)	Operation Order No. 11	06/04/1918	06/04/1918
Operation(al) Order(s)	Operation Order No. 15 Lieut Col W.R Peel D.S.O. Commanding	07/04/1918	07/04/1918
Operation(al) Order(s)	Operation Order No. 76.by Lieut. Col.W.R. Peel. D.S.O. Commanding 1/10th Batt: Manchester Regt.	12/04/1918	12/04/1918
Operation(al) Order(s)	Operation Order No.77.by Lieut. Colonel. W.R. Peel. D.S.O. Commanding	13/04/1918	13/04/1918
Operation(al) Order(s)	Operation Order No. 78 By Lieut. Col. W.R.Peel D.S.O. Commanding	15/04/1918	15/04/1918

Type	Description	Date From	Date To
Operation(al) Order(s)	Operation Order 79	17/04/1918	17/04/1918
Operation(al) Order(s)	Addenda To Operation Order No. 79	17/04/1918	17/04/1918
Operation(al) Order(s)	Operation Order No. 80	19/04/1918	19/04/1918
Operation(al) Order(s)	Operation Order No. 81	23/04/1918	23/04/1918
Miscellaneous	Reference Operation Order No. 81	23/04/1918	23/04/1918
Operation(al) Order(s)	Operation Order No. 82. By Lieut Col W.R.Peel D.S.O. Commanding	24/04/1918	24/04/1918
Operation(al) Order(s)	Operation Order No. 83 By Lieut Col W.R.Peel D.S.O. Commanding	25/04/1918	25/04/1918
Heading	1/10 Battn Manchester Regiment War Diary Of OC 1/10 Manchester Regiment May 1st To 31st 1918 Volume 34		
War Diary	Fonquevillers	01/05/1918	02/05/1918
War Diary	J 6d	03/05/1918	03/05/1918
War Diary	Beer Trench	04/05/1918	06/05/1918
War Diary	Pas	07/05/1918	31/05/1918
Miscellaneous	Appendix III		
Operation(al) Order(s)	Operation Order No. 85	05/05/1918	05/05/1918
Miscellaneous			
Operation(al) Order(s)	Operation Order No 86 By Lt Col W.R Peel D.S.O. Commanding	03/05/1918	03/05/1918
Miscellaneous			
Miscellaneous	D Coy At 4-30am		
Heading	1/10th Battalion Manchester Regiment War Diary June 1st To June 30th 1918 Volume No. 35		
War Diary		01/06/1918	30/06/1918
Miscellaneous	Warning Order	04/05/1918	04/05/1918
Miscellaneous	1/10th Manchester Regiment	04/06/1918	04/06/1918
Miscellaneous	Administrative Instructions No. 88 by Lieut. Colonel. W.R. Peel. D.S.O. Commanding.	06/06/1918	06/06/1918
Miscellaneous	1/10th. Battalion Manchester Regiment. Reference Operation Order No. 88	07/06/1918	07/06/1918
Operation(al) Order(s)	Operation Order No. 88.by Lieut. Colonel. W.R. Peel. D.S.O. Commanding	06/06/1918	06/06/1918
Operation(al) Order(s)	Operation Order No. 93 by Major L. C. Wilde. D.S.O. Commanding	20/06/1918	20/06/1918
Operation(al) Order(s)	Operation Order No. 89 by Lt Col W.R Peel D.S.O. Commanding	11/06/1918	11/06/1918
Operation(al) Order(s)	Operation Order No. 90 by Lieut. Col W.R. Peel D.S.O. Comdg	15/06/1918	15/06/1918
Miscellaneous	Real		
Operation(al) Order(s)	Operation Order No. 91. by Lt. Col.W.R. Peel D.S.O. Commanding.	18/06/1918	18/06/1918
Miscellaneous	Ref. Operation Order No. 91	18/06/1918	18/06/1918
Operation(al) Order(s)	Operation Order No. 92 by Major L.C. Week D.S.O. Comdg.	21/06/1918	21/06/1918
War Diary	Colincamps & Bertrancourt.	01/07/1918	02/07/1918
War Diary	Ref Sheets 57 D N E and 57 D S E	04/07/1918	31/07/1918
Operation(al) Order(s)	Operation Order No.93 by Major H.C Wilds. D.S.O. Commanding	30/06/1918	30/06/1918
Operation(al) Order(s)	Operation Order No. 94.by Major D.G. Wilds. D.S.O. Commanding.	05/06/1918	05/06/1918
Miscellaneous	Amendment To Operation Order No. 95 By Major L.G. Wilds. D.S.O. Commanding.	10/07/1918	10/07/1918
Operation(al) Order(s)	Operation Order No. 98 by Lieut. Col. W.R. Peel. D.S.O. Commanding.	13/07/1918	13/07/1918

Type	Description	Start	End
Miscellaneous		25/07/1918	25/07/1918
Heading	War Diary Of Officer Commanding 1/10th Manchester Regiment From August 1st 1918 To August 31st 1918 Volume 37		
War Diary	Colincamps	01/08/1918	12/08/1918
War Diary	Bertrancourt	13/08/1918	15/08/1918
War Diary	Colincamps	15/08/1918	20/08/1918
War Diary	K 27-K 26 and K 25 (Sheet 57 D N E)	21/08/1918	24/08/1918
War Diary	Pys.	24/08/1918	26/08/1918
War Diary	Warlincourt.	27/08/1918	29/08/1918
War Diary	East Of Thilloy	30/08/1918	31/08/1918
Operation(al) Order(s)	Operation Order No. 105 by Lt Col W.R. Peel D.S.O. Comdg.	25/08/1918	25/08/1918
Operation(al) Order(s)	Operation Order No. 106 by Lt Col W.R Peel D.S.O. Comdg.	31/08/1918	31/08/1918
Operation(al) Order(s)	Operation Order No. 107 by Lieut. Col. W.R. Peel. D.S.O. Commanding.	15/08/1918	15/08/1918
Operation(al) Order(s)	Operation Order No. 103 by Lieut. Col. W.R. Peel. D.S.O. Commanding.	12/08/1918	12/08/1918
Operation(al) Order(s)	Operation Order No. 102 by Lt. Col W.R. Peel D.S.O. Comdg.	08/08/1918	08/08/1918
Operation(al) Order(s)	Operation Order No. 101 by Lieut. Col. W.R. Peel, D.S.O. Commanding.	06/08/1918	06/08/1918
Miscellaneous		02/03/1918	02/03/1918
Operation(al) Order(s)	Operation Order No.100 by Major L.G. Wilds, D.S.O. Commanding		
Heading	1/10th Battalion Manchester Regiment. War Diary Volume No. 38 Sept 1918		
War Diary		01/09/1918	30/09/1918
Operation(al) Order(s)	Provisional Defence Order No.2. by Lieut. Col. W.R. Peel. D.S.O. Commanding.	17/09/1918	17/09/1918
Operation(al) Order(s)	Operation Order No. 109 by Lt. Col. W.R. Peel D.S.O. Comdg.	04/09/1918	04/09/1918
Operation(al) Order(s)	Operation Order No. 109 by Lt. Col W.R. Peel D.S.O. Comdg.	31/08/1918	31/08/1918
Operation(al) Order(s)	Operation Order No.110 by Lt. Col. W.R. Peel D.S.O. Comdg.	05/09/1918	05/09/1918
Operation(al) Order(s)	Administrative Instructions No. 115 issued in Conjunction With O.O. 115 by Major T.J. Kelly. M.C. Commanding.	26/09/1918	26/09/1918
Heading	War Diary		
Operation(al) Order(s)	Provisional Operation Order No. 3 by Major T.T. Kelly M.C. Commanding.	27/09/1918	27/09/1918
Heading	War Diary		
Operation(al) Order(s)	Operation Order No. 115 by Major T.T. Kelly M.C. Commanding	26/09/1918	26/09/1918
Heading	War Diary		
Miscellaneous		05/09/1918	05/09/1918
Operation(al) Order(s)	Addendum To Operation Order No 114 by Major Kelly M.C. Commanding	24/09/1918	24/09/1918
Operation(al) Order(s)	Operation Order No. 114 by Major Kelly. M.C. Commanding.	24/09/1918	24/09/1918
Operation(al) Order(s)	Operation Order No. 116 by Major T.T. Kelly M.C. Commanding.	28/09/1918	28/09/1918
Heading	War Diary		
Operation(al) Order(s)	Operation Order 111		

Operation(al) Order(s)	Operation Order No. 113. by Lieut. Col. W.R. Peel. D.S.O. Commanding.	21/09/1918	21/09/1918
Operation(al) Order(s)	Provisional Defence Order No. 2 by Lt. Col. W.R. Peel D.S.O. Commanding.	20/09/1918	20/09/1918
Miscellaneous	1/10th. Battalion Manchester Regiment Warning Order.	18/09/1918	18/09/1918
Operation(al) Order(s)	Operation Order No. 112 by Lieut. Col. W.R. Peel. D.S.O. Commanding.	19/09/1918	19/09/1918
Operation(al) Order(s)	Administrative Instructions No. 112 Issued In connection With Operation Order No. 112 by Lieut. Col. W.R. Peel. D.S.O. Commanding.	19/09/1918	19/09/1918
Heading	War Diary Of Officer Commanding (Lt Col W.R. Peel D.S.O.) 1/10th Battalion Manchester Regiment. From October 1st 1918 To October 31st 1918 Volume 39		
War Diary	Havrincourt Wood	01/10/1918	07/10/1918
War Diary	Hindenburg Support Line (Sheet 57c SE)	08/10/1918	08/10/1918
War Diary	Briseux Wood (Sheet 57 B)	09/10/1918	10/10/1918
War Diary	Fontaine-Au Pire	11/10/1918	11/10/1918
War Diary	Herpigny Farm	12/10/1918	17/10/1918
War Diary	Briastre (East Of)	18/10/1918	21/10/1918
War Diary	Herpigny Farm	22/10/1918	23/10/1918
War Diary	Beauvois-En-Cambresis	24/10/1918	31/10/1918
Heading	War Diary of The 1/10 Manchester Regt. Nov 1st to 30th 1918 Vol 40		
War Diary	Beauvois	01/11/1918	03/11/1918
War Diary	Solesmes	04/11/1918	08/11/1918
War Diary	Hautmont	09/11/1918	30/11/1918
Heading	War Diary Of OC. 1/10th Manchester Regiments From December 1st to 31st 1918 Volume 41		
War Diary	Hautmont	01/12/1918	18/12/1918
War Diary	Gilly	19/12/1918	31/12/1918
Heading	1/10th Battalion Manchester Regiment War Diary For January 1919 Volume No. 42		
War Diary	Gilly	01/01/1919	31/01/1919
Heading	1/10th Battalion Manchester Regiment War Diary For February 1919 Volume No 42		
War Diary	Gilly	01/02/1919	28/02/1919
Heading	1/10th Manchester Regiment. War Diary For March 1919 Volume No 44		
War Diary	Gilly	01/03/1919	31/03/1919
Heading	1/10th Battalion Manchester Regiment War Diary For April 1919 Volume No.45		
War Diary	Gilly	01/04/1919	02/04/1919
War Diary	Antwerp	03/04/1919	04/04/1919

WO95/2658 (2)

1/10 Manchester R.
Mar '17 - Apr '19

42ND DIVISION
126TH INFY BDE

1-10TH BN MANCHESTER REGT
MAR 1917 - APR 1919

42ND DIVISION
126TH INFY BDE

Confidential
Vol 2

War Diary
of
Obs. 1/10th Manchester Regt.

From March 1st to 31st/1917.

VOLUME XIX

Army Form C. 2118.

WAR DIARY
or
INTELLIGENCE SUMMARY
(Erase heading not required.)

Instructions regarding War Diaries and Intelligence Summaries are contained in F. S. Regs., Part II. and the Staff Manual respectively. Title pages will be prepared in manuscript.

Place	Date 1917.	Hour	Summary of Events and Information	Remarks and references to Appendices
At Sea	March 1st		Physical Exercises. Nothing of interest to report.	LCW
–ditto–	2nd		Physical Exercises – ditto –	LCW
–ditto–	3rd		Physical Exercises – ditto –	LCW
–ditto–	4th		Physical Exercises – ditto –	LCW
–ditto–	5th		Physical Exercises – ditto –	LCW
MARSEILLES	6th	8 AM	Arrived MARSEILLES. Orders to entrain at 5 PM subsequently varied to entrain at 2 PM. Disembarkation of troops completed by 12 P.M. Difficulties in unloading Baggage owing to no facilities provided. Entrainment completed by 2.30 p.m. Departed 3 PM. Halted at ORANGE for 1 Hour.	LCW
ON TRAIN.	7th		On Train. Halt at MACON.	LCW
PONT REMY	8th	11 PM	On Train. Long halt at JUVISY. Arrived PONT REMY. Commenced march to HUPPY.	Ref Map. ABBEVILLE/14 1/100000 LCW
HUPPY	9th	3 AM	Arrived HUPPY. Battalion proceeded into Billets.	LCW
HUPPY	10th		Company marched to PONT REMY to draw rifles, bayonets, steel helmets, gas masks & 2nd Bandoliers.	LCW
HUPPY	11th		Voluntary Divine Service.	LCW

Army Form C. 2118.

WAR DIARY
or
INTELLIGENCE SUMMARY
(Erase heading not required.)

Instructions regarding War Diaries and Intelligence Summaries are contained in F. S. Regs., Part II. and the Staff Manual respectively. Title pages will be prepared in manuscript.

Place	Date 1917	Hour	Summary of Events and Information	Remarks and references to Appendices
HUPPY	MARCH 12th	Morning Afternoon	Lieut Col G.W. ROBINSON C.B. assumed temporary command of 120th Infantry Brigade. Major L.C. WILDE assumed temporary command of Battalion. Training. Route March. Specialist training.	LCW
HUPPY	13th	Morning Afternoon	Companies engaged in fitting steel helmets. Specialist Training.	LCW
HUPPY	14th	Morning Afternoon	Kit Inspection. Parade in "fighting order". Inspection of Battalion in "fighting order" by Brigade Commander. Inspection of Transport by Brigade Commander.	LCW
HUPPY	15th	Morning Afternoon	Battalion Training & Route March. Specialist Training.	LCW
HUPPY	16th		"C" Coy dug a Cruciform Post. Battalion Training for remainder. Battalion Grenade Course conducted.	LCW
HUPPY	17th	Morning Afternoon	Battalion Route March. "D" Coy dug a Cruciform Post. Bath Training for remainder.	LCW
HUPPY	18th		Divine Services.	LCW
HUPPY	19th		"B" Coy dug a Cruciform Post. Battalion Training for remainder.	LCW
HUPPY	20th		"A" Coy dug a Cruciform Post. Specialist Training for remainder.	LCW
HUPPY	21st	Morning aft.	Batt. Route march. Specialist Training.	LCW

Army Form C. 2118.

WAR DIARY
or
INTELLIGENCE SUMMARY.
(Erase heading not required.)

Instructions regarding War Diaries and Intelligence Summaries are contained in F.S. Regs., Part II. and the Staff Manual respectively. Title pages will be prepared in manuscript.

Place	Date 1917	Hour	Summary of Events and Information	Remarks and references to Appendices
HUPPY	Sept. 22		Day devoted to Specialist Training.	LCW
HUPPY	23rd		Lieut Col G.W. ROBINSON C.B. returned & resumed command of the Battalion. Specialist Training. Gas Below.	LCW
HUPPY	24th		Battalion Training. Lieut Col G.W. ROBINSON C.B. proceeded on leave to ENGLAND. Major L.C. WILDE assumed command of Battalion.	LCW
HUPPY	25th		Divine Service.	LCW
HUPPY	26th		Reorganisation for Attack Formations. Wiring.	LCW
HUPPY	27th		Lecture on Gas by Divisional Gas Officer. Battalion fitted with Gas Helmets. Battn Training.	LCW
HUPPY	28th		Battalion Specialist Training & reorganisation. "D" Coy proceeded to ERONDELLE for Musketry Training. 100 Wood Shots proceeded to PONT REMY for Musketry Training.	LCW
HUPPY	29th		"A" Coy proceeded to LIERCOURT to take up Divisional outer permanence of Battalion engaged in rifles & fitting of Trench dug by the mend & by 1/4 R. West Lancs Regt. Preparation for move to LIERCOURT.	Reg Maps. ABBEVILLE 14 Scale 1/100000. LCW
HUPPY	30th		Battn (less 2 Coys) march to LIERCOURT & billets here remainder of day spent in settling the men in billets etc.	LCW
LIERCOURT	31st		Battn Training. Physical Training before breakfast, Practice in New Formations, Bayonet fighting, Close Order Drill, & Musketry. No parade in afternoon. The weather has been remarkably cold & wet since our arrival in FRANCE.	LCW

L.C. Wilde Major.
Commandg 1/10 R Lancashire Regt.

Army Form C. 2118.

WAR DIARY
or
INTELLIGENCE SUMMARY
(Erase heading not required.)

Vol 3

War Diary
of
O/C 1/10th Manchester Regiment

Written by Lieut J.B. McRowbotham, the Officer detailed by him for that purpose.

From April 1st to April 30/1917

Volume XX

Army Form C. 2118.

WAR DIARY
or
INTELLIGENCE SUMMARY
(Erase heading not required.)

Instructions regarding War Diaries and Intelligence Summaries are contained in F. S. Regs., Part II. and the Staff Manual respectively. Title Pages will be prepared in manuscript.

Place	Date	Hour	Summary of Events and Information	Remarks and references to Appendices
LIERCOURT	April 1st 1917		Battalion on Divisional Fatigue. Voluntary Church Parade.	
-do-	2nd		A & B Coy range firing at PONT REMY. Divisional Fatigue. Brigade Commander inspects Battalion billets.	
-do-	3rd		Divisional Fatigue. Battalion Training on new scheme, 1 Coy on fatigue, 1 Coy under Coy Commanders, one on Specialist training and one detailed at ERONDELLE.	
-do-	4th		Battalion Training. Divisional Fatigue.	
-do-	5th		Battalion Training. Divisional Fatigue. Preliminary orders for move to MORCOURT. Very wet cold weather. Some snow.	
-do-	6th		Battalion Training. Clearing up billeting area. Transport leave by road.	
-do-	7th		Battalion entrains for LA FLAQUE (not shown on map). Detrain at 2pm and proceed by march route to MORCOURT & occupy billets.	Ref Map. AMIENS 1/10000 Sheet 17
MORCOURT	8th		MORCOURT district divided into areas & allotted to Units to be inhabitants gathered on different dates. Battalion making Scouts reconnoitring area for having Common.	

2449 Wt. W14957/M90 750,000 1/16 J.B.C. & A. Forms/C.2118/12.

Army Form C. 2118.

WAR DIARY
or
INTELLIGENCE SUMMARY
(Erase heading not required.)

Instructions regarding War Diaries and Intelligence Summaries are contained in F. S. Regs., Part II. and the Staff Manual respectively. Title Pages will be prepared in manuscript.

Place	Date 1917	Hour	Summary of Events and Information	Remarks and references to Appendices
MORCOURT	April 9th		Battalion training on "A" area. Paying particular attention to air formation in the attack. Two companies on balloon in morning. Very wet. Greenmarking Bases for tomorrow.	
-do-	10th		On march officer recon on parade, proceeded to Hodgkin, H? Earl Eames Regt. 16 Wilton. On consolidation on new formation by a Platoon of that Regt. Two companies on bath. Remaining 9 training on "A" area. Admin arrival for move to FLAUCOURT	Ref/sgd AMIENS 17 $\frac{1}{100000}$
FLAUCOURT	11/12		Battalion proceeded by motor lorries to FLAUCOURT. On arrival FLAUCOURT via MERICOURT and CAPPY. Left MORCOURT at 9.30AM. A mass of ruins but plenty of cellar accommodation. Arrived FLAUCOURT about 3.30pm after a long trying march in full pack.	Ref/sgd AMIENS 17 $\frac{1}{100000}$
-do-	12		Battalion on training. Difficulties of communication on Brigade are 6 miles away at FRISE and all messages have to go by Orderly until a wire run out. 2/Lieut D DEAKIN Joins for duty from 3rd line	Ref/sgd AMIENS 17 $\frac{1}{100000}$
-do-	13		Battalion on training. Drawing more SAA to complete establishment.	
-do-	14		Battalion on training. Raining Battalion up to establishment in SAA today. Snow + Sleet all day.	
-do-	15		Both Training. Treatment of feet. Stamping new number on identification discs. Order issued formove to LONGAVESNES.	

WAR DIARY
or
INTELLIGENCE SUMMARY

(Erase heading not required.)

Army Form C. 2118.

Instructions regarding War Diaries and Intelligence Summaries are contained in F. S. Regs., Part II. and the Staff Manual respectively. Title Pages will be prepared in manuscript.

Place	Date 1917	Hour	Summary of Events and Information	Remarks and references to Appendices
LONGAVESNES	16th		Orderly officer & 100 O.R. proceed to PONT RÉMY on course of Musketry. Platoon proceeded to LONGAVESNES by march route via TINCHES, PÉRONNE, BUSSU & PUNCH at 8 A.M. Arrive LONGAVESNES 2.30 p.m. 2/Lieut. MEAD BDE. attached 149rd Bde.	2/Lieut G.W.S. Scott N.F. Bn ↓ 55555 AMIENS 17 ″ 5555555
LONGAVESNES	17th		Very bad billeting accommodation. A lot of the men have no blankets from the Batt: during the night. Batt: on road repairing between LONGAVESNES & BUSSU.	
LONGAVESNES	18th		C.O. & Coy commanders go up to Brigade HQrs to 143 Bde in morning. Battalion on road training all day. Some places as yesterday. Capt. G.E. Scott & Capt. F. Henderson. Lieut. H. Hampill & 2/Lieut W.A. Kelsie also the night with Battn. Boy of 18 R. Warwick for experience. Lieut F. Henderson to Hospital.	
LONGAVESNES	19th		"A" & "B" Coys on road repairs & Warwicks on the line Hythe Trent. Preliminary orders out for relief of 1/18 R [?]	
LONGAVESNES	20th		C.O. & Adjt. ride up to 18 R Warwicks HQrs. Relief of Hayton officers at 5.30 A.M. to discuss the relief. No weapons up and blown up moon roads about 9 p.m. & a splendid hit. Capt. L.S. Band RAMC (T) attached the unit & to clear at 10 p.m. (approx) no other casualties.	
LONGAVESNES	21		Transport lorry moving from Béart to SAULCOURT all morning. Funeral of Capt. L.S. Band at 12 noon first made out of LONGAVESNES at 4.30 pm. arrive SAULCOURT 7 pm & took its all transport, men, horses took via tug moved on to PÉZIÈRES 11.40 pm. Relief complete 11.40 p.m. Capt Wilson RAMC attached for temporary duty	

2449 Wt. W14957/M90 750,000 1/16 J.B.C. & A. Forms/C.2118/12.

Army Form C. 2118.

WAR DIARY
or
INTELLIGENCE SUMMARY
(Erase heading not required.)

Instructions regarding War Diaries and Intelligence Summaries are contained in F.S. Regs., Part II. and the Staff Manual respectively. Title Pages will be prepared in manuscript.

Place	Date 1917	Hour	Summary of Events and Information	Remarks and references to Appendices
P.52.I.5.R.G.	April 22nd		Battalion settles down to the new regime. "B" Coy on outpost, "A" Coy on line of Ravine, "C" Coy in support & "D" Coy in support on TURENNE LINE. Very busy patrolling the wood & front including CANAL WOOD and OBRUB WOOD. No change. [signed]	Ref Map 57c SE 1/20000
-do-	23rd		"D" Coy advance their posts 300 yds during the night but are forced to withdraw again owing to the ground for daylight. No change. [signed]	
-do-	24th		Attack by battalion on our right at 3.45AM. Logn R.P Lewin, Devon Regt, taken command of Battalion. Another attack on right by another Battalion. Our men wounded - less than 9 wounded. [signed]	
-do-	25th		Another man of D coy wounded during the night. 4 other men of D also missing. "B" coy when followed during the night intermittent shelling. Capt A.C Boord leaves to go on leave. Capt A.C Boord leaves to go on leave on HQrs of 2/5.R Devons. Staffs Regt. Improving trenches & wire. Lieut Bryans reports for duty as Medical Officer	2
-do-	26th		Very quiet night beyond intermittent shelling & batts on our right (2/6 para Regt) shelled during the night involving the lowering over of spare from them. Officer OM Harry Bone to act as Instructor at VII Corps School. Relieved by 2/6 East Lancs Regt at 8.45 pm and Battalion moves into P.52.15.R.G. [signed]	

Army Form C. 2118.

Army Form C. 2118.

WAR DIARY
or
INTELLIGENCE SUMMARY

(Erase heading not required.)

Instructions regarding War Diaries and Intelligence Summaries are contained in F. S. Regs., Part II. and the Staff Manual respectively. Title Pages will be prepared in manuscript.

Place	Date	Hour	Summary of Events and Information	Remarks and references to Appendices
PEZIERE	1917 April 27th		Battalion in most garrisoning the BROWN LINE astud in a line running in front of the village of PEZIERE, on on the Corps line of Resistance – Reserve coman of 2 bays. Bn. working on improvement & manning of BROWN LINE, hours 9 to 12 moon, 9 to 12 moon-night and 3 to 6am in morning	
PEZIERE	28th		Battalion is billeted in trenches and town to shelters as no troops are now allowed in billets in PEZIERE owing to its number of cases in village reported by M.O. Work on BROWN LINE continues. Cases of bade for men to have a rest and opp. as imposed by M.O., full breakfast as new work moved in had case. Hostile aircraft activity a fairly heavy shelling of BROWN LINE during working party. Transport lines twenty shelled at night involving the loss of 9 teams of mules & a mule.	Ref. Map. 62c NE 35 1/20000
PEZIERE	29th		Orders for relief by 48th Lancashire Regt. Work on morning on BROWN LINE as usual from 9 to 11 p.m. having drawn for anms. to VILLERS FAUCON into Reverse. Owning of Bn. to fatigues &c.; in readiness. Interrupted shelling of villa BROWN LINE & aircraft activity	Ref. Map. 62c NE 35 1/20000
VILLERS FAUCON	30		Relieve by 48th Lancashire Regt. at 3.45 am when platoon proceeded independently to VILLERS FAUCON station arriving 7.30 am. train over Bn. going on to road to SPOILCOURT to a garrison in told off to the RIDGE LINE 1 coy + 4 MBs. OC Copy (Transport Section) congratulated by C.O. for his good report on the	Ref. Map. 62c NE 35 1/20000

Army Form C. 2118.

WAR DIARY
or
INTELLIGENCE SUMMARY

(Erase heading not required.)

Instructions regarding War Diaries and Intelligence Summaries are contained in F. S. Regs., Part II. and the Staff Manual respectively. Title Pages will be prepared in manuscript.

Place	Date	Hour	Summary of Events and Information	Remarks and references to Appendices
			copy of 28 hour order transport been now submitted to a faulty heavy shelling	

R R Lewis Major.
Commanding 9 1/10th Lancashire Regiment

WAR DIARY

of

Officer Commanding, 1/10^d Manchester Regt.

Kept by

Lieut. J. C. S. ROWBOTHAM. (Adjutant)

(An Officer detailed by him for that purpose.)

From May 1st 1914   To   May 31st 1914

VOLUME 21.

Army Form C. 2118

WAR DIARY
or
INTELLIGENCE SUMMARY
(Erase heading not required.)

Instructions regarding War Diaries and Intelligence Summaries are contained in F.S. Regs., Part II. and the Staff Manual respectively. Title Pages will be prepared in manuscript.

Place	Date	Hour	Summary of Events and Information	Remarks and references to Appendices
VILLERS FAUCON	1914 May 1	—	Battalion training. Road making, fatigues, Night operations by "A" Coy	Sheet 62 c NE Edn 3A 1/20,000
	2	—	Battalion on training in the morning. In the afternoon, medical inspection and inspection of Gas Helmets. The C.O. (Major Hurst) goes on 10 days' leave to England. Major L.C. Wilde takes over command of the Battalion.	
	3	—	Day devoted to Kit inspections and general cleaning up of the men. In the evening a percentage of Officers & Signallers found to look round line held by 1/6 Lancashire Fusiliers preparatory to the Battalion taking over the line on the 4th inst.	Sheet 62 c NE Edn 3A 1/20,000
LEMPIRE	4	—	Day devoted to bathing and general clean-up preparatory to going up to the line. The Battalion marched out at 6 pm and headed LEMPIRE (62 c NE 1/20,000) at 9-30 pm and proceeded to relieve 1/6 Lancashire Fusiliers. Relief complete 10-30 pm. A, B & C Coys are in the line of resistance, the "GREEN LINE", with line platoons each an outpost in front. D Coy in reserve in east end of LEMPIRE	Sheet 62 c NE Edn 3A 1/20,000
	5	—	Very quiet day. The situation is such that we are to go "between Battn HQ and the line during the day trying to avoid having complete observation over our area. All work about switching up of trenches, wiring etc has to be done at night. Attack by Billerin on our left about 11 pm. One Company 1/5 East Lancs Regt is placed in old German trench in the GREEN LINE	

L.C. Wilde
Major Commanding 1/6 [?]

Army Form C. 2118

WAR DIARY
or
INTELLIGENCE SUMMARY
(Erase heading not required.)

Instructions regarding War Diaries and Intelligence Summaries are contained in F. S. Regs., Part II. and the Staff Manual respectively. Title Pages will be prepared in manuscript.

Place	Date	Hour	Summary of Events and Information	Remarks and references to Appendices
	1917 May 6		Very quiet day. Very little work can be done during the day owing to the enemy having accurate amounts of all our movements. At 11 pm "A" Coy took out GILLEMONT FARM from the 1/9th Manchester Rgt. D Coy present out of support into the GREEN LINE. One Company 1/5 East hand left came into LEMPIRE as Reserve Company. All four companies 1/10 Manchesters left out now in the line. Work on trench and strong points was proceeded with during the night.	
	7		At 3 pm enemy made an attack on foot at GILLEMONT FARM which was garrisoned by 2/Lt BAXTER & 14 other ranks. Enemy was driven off. 2 of our men were wounded.	
	8		At 4 AM enemy brought trench mortar fire on to the trench at GILLEMONT ⇔ 62 B NW FARM in consequence of which our forward post had to be temporarily Edition 2A evacuated. Heavy rain all day. Trenches choked with mud and it was very difficult indeed to keep the rifles & Lewis Guns in working order. Forward post re-occupied during the night. Very quiet day for B, C & D Coys. Heavy trench mortar fire on "A" Coy under Capt HARDMAN all night.	
	9		"A" Coy in GILLEMONT FARM (62 B NW Sq. 3A) was subjected to heavy bombardment all day by trench mortar and 5.9 howitzers. Our casualties "A" Coy amounted to 1 Killed and 6 wounded. Relieved at night by 1/5 East Lanc Rgt.	

L. C. Wright
Major Commanding 10th Man Rgt.

Army Form C. 2118

WAR DIARY
or
INTELLIGENCE SUMMARY
(Erase heading not required.)

Instructions regarding War Diaries and Intelligence Summaries are contained in F. S. Regs., Part I. and the Staff Manual respectively. Title Pages will be prepared in manuscript.

Place	Date 1917	Hour	Summary of Events and Information	Remarks and references to Appendices
ST EMILIE.	May 10	—	Moved wh. hts & carried on railway cutting east ST EMILIE. Day devoted to training and general clean-up. C.O. attends conference at Brigade HQ at 4-30 pm. Enemy shelled the neighbourhood with heavy guns during the night. Two companies (C & D) remained as garrison of BROWN LINE in LEMPIRE (62c NE Ed. 3A 1/20000)	62c NE Edit 3A E 24 a.9.9
	11	—	Day devoted to bathing and cleaning up the men. Enemy during the morning shelled neighbourhood of ST EMILIE with heavy howitzers. Little damage done. All companies provided working parties on the GREEN LINE at night.	
	12	—	Enemy aeroplane flew over our lines for almost an hour. One man (B Coy) wounded by splinters from our own Anti-aircraft shell. Every available man is limited out for working parties at night in the GREEN LINE. Heavy thunderstorm at night.	
	13	—	Sunday. Voluntary holy Communion at 10-30 am. Two officers of each Company go to H.Q of 1/5 East Lancs Regt at LEMPIRE (62 c NE Ed 3A) to reconnoitre dispositions preparatory to taking over from that unit tonight.	
LEMPIRE.	14	—	Major R.P. LEWIS returns from leave and re-assumes command of the Battn. Battalion marches to LEMPIRE and takes over left sub-sector of Brigade front. Relief complete by 12 PM. "B" Coy take over GILLEMONT FARM. Very quiet night. 3 companies thinly in the GREEN LINE.	62c NE Edit. 3A

R.C Webb
Major Commanding 1/18 Man. Regt

WAR DIARY
or
INTELLIGENCE SUMMARY
(Erase heading not required.)

Army Form C. 2118

Instructions regarding War Diaries and Intelligence Summaries are contained in F.S. Regs., Part II. and the Staff Manual respectively. Title Pages will be prepared in manuscript.

Place	Date	Hour	Summary of Events and Information	Remarks and references to Appendices
LEMPIRE	1917 May 15	—	Very quiet day. Work carried on vigorously especially on the completion of the "localities" D. E. & F.	
	16	—	Enemy shelled GUILLEMONT FARM with shrapnel during afternoon. No casualties occurred. At 11 a.m. a German scout approached to within 20 yards of "A" Coy's post at TOMBOIS FARM (62 c N5 Ed. 3A) and was promptly shot. All his papers were obtained and forwarded to Intelligence Dept. At 6 p.m. Sapr WISE R.E. 3rd Cavalry Brigade was killed near TOMBOIS FARM (62 c N5 Ed 3A) by a sniper while walking round front line. No casualties during the day were near Killick (D Coy). Heavy rain during the night.	62 c N5 Ed 3A
	17	—	Nothing of importance happened during day. At night the Batt" is relieved by the 3rd Hussars & one Squadron Oxfordshire Hussars. "B" Coy had 2 casualties (wounded) whilst being relieved.	
VILLERS FAUCON	18	—	Battalion marches to billets in VILLERS FAUCON arriving just before dawn. Day spent in resting and general clean-up.	
EQUANCOURT	19	—	Battalion parades at 5 a.m. and proceeds by march route to EQUANCOURT. All the limbs Guns are inspected by C.O. in the afternoon & the Batt" is inspected by 2nd in Command in the evening.	S/C S/E Edn 3A
YTRES	20	—	Parades in the morning. At 4 p.m. Battalion proceeds by march route to YTRES. Advance party sent forward into the new line at 6 p.m. to infant line held by 10th Battn K.R. Rifles. 2/Lt. Ward & Twaddle proceeds on leave to England.	S/C S/E Edn 3A

L. C. Wilde
Major
Commanding 11c "Man" Regt

Army Form C. 2118

WAR DIARY
or
INTELLIGENCE SUMMARY
(Erase heading not required.)

Place	Date	Hour	Summary of Events and Information	Remarks and references to Appendices
HAVRINCOURT WOOD	1918 May 21	—	Battalion marched out at 8-30 pm and relieved the 10 K.R. Battn. K.R. Rifles in the line. Front line extends from Q5.c.5.9 to Q11.b.central. Battn. H.Q. is in HAVRINCOURT WOOD at Q15.d.8.6. Relief complete at 2-30 am. C & D Coys in Front Line. Heavy rain during the night.	Sy c SE Feb 3A & Sy c SW Edn 3A.
	21/22	—	"A" Coy in Support and "B" Coy in Reserve in HAVRINCOURT WOOD.	Sy c SW Edn 3A
	22	—	Very quiet day. Rain made trenches very filthy but work was pushed forward very energetically and by enough stores were drawn. Heavy machine-gun fire on to fire trench during the night.	
	23	—	As though in general situation. Whole front continues to be very quiet. Work on trenches is pushed on.	
	24	—	"D" Company shelled heavily during the morning. No casualties occurred. Remainder of day passed off quietly. Again there is heavy machine-gun fire during the night. "D" Coy have 2 casualties at 9 pm through a direct hit of H.E. shell on trench.	
	25	—	"D" Coy shelled at 4-30 am and again at 10-30 am. No casualties. Remainder of day passed off quietly.	

E.C. Wicks
Major
Commanding 1/10th Manch. Regt.

WAR DIARY or INTELLIGENCE SUMMARY

Army Form C. 2118

(Erase heading not required.)

Instructions regarding War Diaries and Intelligence Summaries are contained in F. S. Regs, Part II. and the Staff Manual respectively. Title Pages will be prepared in manuscript.

Place	Date	Hour	Summary of Events and Information	Remarks and references to Appendices
	1917 May/26	—	Very quiet day. "D" Coy on again shelled slightly but no damage done. At night "D" Coy on relieved by "B" Coy and bivouac near Battalion H.Q.	
	27	—	As usual nothing of importance occurred during the day. During the night heavy machine-gun fire on to our bivouacs. Major R.P. LEWIS goes on 10 days C.O's Conference Major I.C. WILDE assumes command.	
	28	—	Again everything is very quiet. An official patrol under command of Lieut LEE & night Nicholates Clark pat in (54c SE Edit 3A 1/20000) 2/Lt E.N. WHITTAKER proceeds to Intelligence Sch, G.H.Q for instruction. 2/Lt A.W. WITHAM proceeds to ETAPLES as Instructor Q5 f.3.5. HAVRINCOURT CHATEAU (54c NE Edit 3a 1/20000) is blown up by the Germans.	
	29	—	Very quiet day. "D" Coy on shelled slightly during the morning but have no casualties. Lieut LEE again takes out Officer's patrol to Clark pat (Map ref. 54c SE Edit 3a 1/20000) Q5 L.3.5.	
	30	—	Rather more activity than usual by enemy artillery but no damage done.	
	31	—	Very quiet during day. Battalion relieved by 2/4th SHERWOOD FORESTERS Battalion then goes to Left Reserve Battalion with Head Quarters at Q.4 d.4.5.	

I.C. WILDE Major Commanding 1/5th Man Regt

WAR DIARY

of

O.C. 1/10th Manchester Regiment.

Kept by Lieut. J.C.S. Rowbotham (adjutant)

from 1st June 1914 to 30th June 1914

VOLUME 22

WAR DIARY
INTELLIGENCE SUMMARY.
(Erase heading not required.)

Army Form C. 2118.

Place	Date	Hour	Summary of Events and Information	Remarks and references to Appendices
HAVRINCOURT WOOD.	1917 June 1.	—	Day devoted to improving bivouac area and general clean-up. At night 3 Companies (A, B & C) Bdg advanced posts the trenches in front of 1/5 East Lancs Regt. Working parties heavily shelled. Our casualties were 1 Killed and 13 wounded.	
	2	—	Issue of clothing (new) to all the Battalion. At night 3 Companies (B, C & D) continued the work on new trenches. There was very machine-gun fire but only slight shelling. No casualties. 2/Lt. Q.M. HARRY Pulman to Battalion from Instructor 3rd Army Corps School.	
	3	—	At night work in front of trenches is continued. The usual sniping and machine-gun fire was maintained.	
	3 (contd.)	—	At about 11 pm the working parties sent up to the front line were shelled very heavily owing to the bright moonlight. We had 19 casualties including 1/c Killed. Our wounded were Lieut A.E. LEE & 2/Lieut E.N. WHITTAKER.	
	4	—	The usual working parties (3 Companies) were again sent out for work on the front line. Very quiet night. We had two casualties.	
YPRES.	5	—	Battalion is relieved by 1/6th Batt: Lancashire Fusiliers. Relief complete at 5.45 pm. Battalion marches into billets at YPRES. Major I.C. Wilde is awarded the D.S.O.	Sht 6 S.E. Sht. 3A 1/20,000

WAR DIARY

INTELLIGENCE SUMMARY.

(Erase heading not required.)

Army Form C. 2118.

Place	Date	Hour	Summary of Events and Information	Remarks and references to Appendices
YPRES	1917 June 6	—	Day devoted to picking out and overhauling of men's clothing. At 4 PM lecture to Cooks, Quartermaster-Sergts, on field cooking by Corps Instructor.	
	7	—	Three companies on road-making & other fatigues all day. One company Training. Lt. Col. R.P. LEWIS returns from C.O's conference and re-assumes command of the Battalion.	
	8	—	Again 3 Companies on fatigue. One company training all day.	
	9	—	Three companies on fatigue. Remaining company carried out tactical scheme under the C.O.	
	10	—	All work stopped at 3 pm so that men can attend Brigade Sports a review of the Divisional Band was in attendance & everything was a success. D Coy training Baths at	
	11	—	Two Companies in work all day. D Coy training Baths at BERTINCOURT from 2 PM to 4 PM.	
	12	—	A + D Companies working parties all day. C Coy in Training and Baths. B Coy relieved by a company of the 9th Manchesters & returning to YPRES & occupy their old billets at 8 p.m. The King approves the following Honours & Rewards:— To be 1 Companion of the Distinguished Service Order Major T.C. WILDE. Awarded the Military Cross:— The late Captain Z.B. BAIRD, RAMC. attd 1/10th Manchester Regt.	

even
WAR DIARY
INTELLIGENCE SUMMARY.
(Erase heading not required.)

Army Form C. 2118.

Place	Date	Hour	Summary of Events and Information	Remarks and references to Appendices
	1914 June 13	—	Practically the whole of the Battalion on working parties under R.E. & Town Major. Baths at BERTINCOURT. used from 2 PM to 4 PM	OR
	14	—	A Coy and 1 Platoon of B Coy on working parties under R.E. Remainder of B, C & D Coys on Training. Musketry on the range, Live Bombing & Demonstration attacks on Trenches	OR
	15	—	Battalion in Training from 9–12 noon and 2 pm to 4 pm. Busy erecting Aldershot ovens and divisional Trenches to relieve the Field Kitchens when out of line. Beautiful weather.	OR
	16	—	A Coy on fatigue. C & D Coys go to the Baths from 8 to 10 am. Training in the morning & afternoon. C & D Coys do a demonstration attack of trenches astride the road at P 19 d. All officers attend this demonstration.	OR
	17	—	C Coy on fatigue. C of E Parade Service on football ground exclusive of which the Divisional Commander presented Medal Ribbons. Battalion Ceremonial & Close Order Drill.	OR
	18	—	Still lovely weather. B Company on fatigue. Subalterns' Parade from 6.45 am to 7.45 am. NCO's parade from 10 to 11 am. Demonstration in evening (rapid) by A Coy Platoon in Trench demonstration in fire afternoon.	OR

WAR DIARY
INTELLIGENCE SUMMARY.
(Erase heading not required.)

Army Form C. 2118.

Place	Date	Hour	Summary of Events and Information	Remarks and references to Appendices
	1914 June 19.	—	Parades in morning and afternoon. Definition of Gas Helmets by Gas NCO's went by arrangements Khakiing on the range. Lecture by Lt-Col LUCKOCK, G.S.O. 1 of 4th Army, to all Officers on the "Battle of the SOMME"	
	20	—	Nearly all the Battalion on working parties. C Coy and L.G's on the range. One platoon B Coy practice attack on our platoon C Coy. Demonstrating the use of contact flares. 2/Lt. C. TWEEDALE posted to D Coy temporarily. 2/Lt. E. J. FINCH to A Coy	
	21	—	The permanent fatigue of A Coy at RUYAULCOURT withdrawn at 12 noon. Lewis Guns of A Coy firing on range. Afternoon no work. Inspections of all Coys.	
HAVRINCOURT WOOD	22	—	The Battalion relieve the 1/4th Lancs. Fusiliers in the Centre Battalion sector of the Right Brigade. Travel up in 3 trains on narrow gauge railway from YTRES to HAVRINCOURT WOOD. Entrain 9.20 p.m. — 9.30 & 9.40 p.m. detraining at P.H.C.2.1 at 10.25 p.m. 10.35 p.m. & 10.45 p.m. Order of Battle. A Coy on the Right front, B Coy Centre, C Coy left front with D Coy in Reserve. Battle D Coy Q3.d.2.4 and Rear Hd.Qrs just outside the WOOD. Hd.Qrs at Q3.d.2.4.	

WAR DIARY
INTELLIGENCE SUMMARY
(Erase heading not required.)

Army Form C. 2118.

Place	Date 1917	Hour	Summary of Events and Information	Remarks and references to Appendices
	June 23	-	Relief complete 2.45 am without casualties. Fair number of Trench Mortar shells fell on Harrison Trench and Duncan Post during the day. At 2-30 pm Sergt SUGDEN D.C.M., Pte COOKE and Pte MACNAMARA of the Scouts Section reconnoitred some ELEPHANT HUTS about 200 yards to the left front of our line and discovered a GERMAN post with a sentry astride. The sentry was attacked by Sergt SUGDEN D.C.M. (a German in pyjamas) came out and gave themselves up whole group (?) 4 in number came out to surrender and eventually the whereabouts of Sgt SUGDEN marched them back to our lines. All three were Polit awarded the MILITARY MEDAL. Later a Patrol from C Coy on Suite out and recovers the Stores left behind by the Germans viz:- 1 Small Trench Mortar rifles to new recovers. + Ammunition	
	24	-	Nothing much to report. Steady work with an Trenches. One of our Patrols encountered the enemy in superior numbers and two of our men hit. Fairly heavy shelling of HARRISON TRENCH, DUNCAN & DICK Posts with one or two direct hits.	
	25	-	A large number of Trench Mortars fired on our Front Line expected during the day. One or two of our patrols encountered the enemy when bolt Vickers suffered casualties. One of our snipers shot killed an in front after sniping line of the enemy. Was fairly quiet.	

WAR DIARY
INTELLIGENCE SUMMARY
(Erase heading not required.)

Army Form C. 2118

Instructions regarding War Diaries and Intelligence Summaries are contained in F.S. Regs., Part II. and the Staff Manual respectively. Title Pages will be prepared in manuscript.

Place	Date 1916	Hour	Summary of Events and Information	Remarks and references to Appendices
	June 26	-	Early this morning one of our patrols surprised 10 of the enemy and called upon them to surrender but 3 of them recovered themselves sufficiently to throw bombs grenades at our patrol causing (3 men) Our patrol opened fire on the enemy causing casualties. Enemy bombers our patrol back to the line, but patrol retired in order and inflicted further casualties. Our patrol sustained no casualties. Digging and improvement of the line proceeding satisfactorily.	
	27	-	An officers patrol of 1 Officer + 20 other ranks proceeded along SHROPSHIRE SPUR but was unable to advance on account of enemy fire and was within 30 yards of the enemy trenches. Patrol got to within 30 yards of the enemy before enemy opened fire so was forced to retire only to find enemy prepared to retire after a short engagement.	
	28	-	A fair amount of hostile shelling during the day. Our A Coy line extensively subjected to heavy T.M. fire several men suffering from shell-shock. Dick Post and Garrison Post heavily shelled by T.M.'s firing from K 33. d. 9. 9 and K 34. a. 1. 2. More enemy trench mortar activity. Attempt to be firing from K 28. d. 3. 8. and K 36. b. 3. 2. Patrols return safely having again gained enemy trench with the enemy. Digging progress favourably.	

1875 Wt W593/826 1,000,000 4/15 T.B.C.&A. A.D.S.S./Forms/C. 2118.

WAR DIARY
INTELLIGENCE SUMMARY
(Erase heading not required.)

Army Form C. 2118

Place	Date 1917	Hour	Summary of Events and Information	Remarks and references to Appendices
	June 29		had R.E. material being sent into the line for the first time and now adjusts. Men are now getting hot tea and stew each day. Men still attack on our life at night with considerable casualties	
	30		Patrols had nothing special to report and did not come in touch with the enemy. One patrol heard voices. Patrol of opinion Bosche a retist was taking place. 2/Lt S. HOLT and 20 men go down to Rear H.Q. to practise a raid.	
			Very wet another for the last few days and several men showing signs of "trench feet". A & B Coys changed over before dawn this morning.	

T.P. Plum Lt. Col.
Comdg 1/10 Manchester Regt

Confidential

WAR DIARY 906 176/42

of

O.C. 1/10th Manchester Regiment

~~2/Lt. F. Fletcher~~ (Captain ~~...~~)

from July 1/1914 to July 31/1914.

VOLUME 23

Army Form C. 2118.

WAR DIARY
INTELLIGENCE SUMMARY
(Erase heading not required.)

Place	Date 1917	Hour	Summary of Events and Information	Remarks and references to Appendices
HAVRINCOURT	July 1	—	Very bad weather these last few days. Through the last of 12 days of 1/5th East Lancs Regt to be relieved by the 4th East Lancs Regt who ought to have relieved us. Getting day works and hot from to the men to lie out attends the attack of the cut trenches. Getting more rare nowadays. Patrol encounters are day. Work at night. D Sgt live patrols out including a fighting patrol under 2/Lt. S. Holt to the Quarry but on entering the Quarry it was unoccupied.	Ret Rats N.E. Sty C. Fish ½ a. 7/20.000
	July 2	—	D Sgt named BURNLEY ALLEY. E Sgt named ASHTON ALLEY. Companies busy completing the wiring in front of fire trenches Patrol of 1 Officer & 8 men proceed to BURNT ROOF from A Coy lines but see nothing.	¾
	July 3	—	Work on trenches & wiring continues steadily. Plenty of hostile shelling. A little wiring done before being relieved. (two D Coy) by 1/4 East Lancs Regt. Hostile artillery active during day & night.	¾
	July 4	—	Battalion less D Coy goes into Brigade reserve. D Coy relieves 1 Coy 1/1/5 Lancs Fus. in rifle outer intermediate line. C Coy provide garrison of 2 platoons for Right sector of intermediate	¾

WAR DIARY
INTELLIGENCE SUMMARY
(Erase heading not required.)

Army Form C. 2118.

Instructions regarding War Diaries and Intelligence Summaries are contained in F. S. Regs., Part II. and the Staff Manual respectively. Title Pages will be prepared in manuscript.

Place	Date 1917	Hour	Summary of Events and Information	Remarks and references to Appendices
HAVRINCOURT WOOD	July 5		Line C.T. 2 platoons C Coy went for night work for night work 1/9 Man. Regt. on C.T. 2 platoon B Coy work for night work 1/5 East Lancs Regt. on C.T.	1/2
	July 6		Day spent in clearing up as far as possible after being in the trenches. 2 platoons of B Coy & 2 platoons of C Coy relieve D Coy in anti-Battalion Sector. A Coy provide Brigade duties.	1/2
		-	Companies use baths at METZ during day. Camp shelled about 8-30 pm. A Coy have 2 casualties.	2/2
BUS (O.16 c.59.C.118)	July 7		Baths at METZ used by C & D Coys morning. B Coy relieved on intermediate line by 2 Coys 1/5 East Lancs Regt. A Coy relieved on Right Intermediate line by 1/2 Coys 1/9 Man Regt. Battn. proceed to Camp at 0.16 by light railway. Heavy storm during journey.	1/2
	July 8		Day spent in drying & cleaning up after spell of duty in front line. Inspection by Company Commanders. CO presents M.M. ribbons to Sgt Bargain, Pte Cooke & McNamara.	3/2
BIHUCOURT C/C 51 coord. G.11.	July 9		Brigade move to BIHUCOURT by march route. March past Corps Commander first after leaving Vokaiting front. Into a man bivouac camp.	2/2

WAR DIARY
or
INTELLIGENCE SUMMARY
(Erase heading not required.)

Army Form C. 2118.

Instructions regarding War Diaries and Intelligence Summaries are contained in F.S. Regs., Part II. and the Staff Manual respectively. Title Pages will be prepared in manuscript.

Place	Date 1917	Hour	Summary of Events and Information	Remarks and references to Appendices
COURCELLES Map 57C 1/40,000 A 15 + 16	July 10	—	Morning devoted to general cleaning up of clothes, arms & accoutrements under supervision of Coy officers. Afternoon – games etc 4/1 hours close order drill.	22/1
	July 11		Bde group moves into COURCELLES and the Battalion take up billets. These billets were in a dirty state. Battalion cleaning billets and kits during afternoon.	22/1
	July 12		Commence Training programme (progressive). Most of Coys paid out during day.	22/1
	July 13		W.O.s & Sergts parade under Sergt BRYANT, Welsh Guards, from 9–10, 10–11 am other NCOs. 11 to 12 noon All subalterns. 2 to 5 pm Battalion still by Sergt BRYANT. 1 officer + 20 other ranks work on Assault Course at Brigade + 1 NCO + 20 other ranks with 428 Field Coy RE	22/1
	July 14		Musketry on Range all NCOs & 2 Platoons B Coy; Sergt BRYANT again locks all subalterns for Vinckerstein. Brigade "Turn-out" Competition, inoculated during afternoon. Future – are "Competition" 2nd in Platoons 1st in Liabees, Lewis and officers Coops. This unit	22/1
	July 15		Owing to inoculation the Battalion rests	22/1
	July 16		Platoons signalled Progressive training, carried out Musketry on range by A Coy	22/1

2449 Wt. W14957/M90 750,000 1/16 J.B.C. & A. Forms/C.2118/12.

Army Form C. 2118.

WAR DIARY
or
INTELLIGENCE SUMMARY

(Erase heading not required.)

Instructions regarding War Diaries and Intelligence Summaries are contained in F. S. Regs., Part II. and the Staff Manual respectively. Title Pages will be prepared in manuscript.

Place	Date 1917	Hour	Summary of Events and Information	Remarks and references to Appendices
	July 14	—	Training steadily carried out slip by step in all subjects. Live bombing by B Coy.	2/1
	July 18	—	Morning training according to programme. In the afternoon Sports were held and the men shewn great keenness in all events. No 5 Platoon of B Coy wins Brigade Platoon Competition. The following mentioned in Brigade Sir A. Murray's despatches for distinguished conduct in Egypt :— Major I. C. WILDE, ROMS TREVITT, Sergt SUGDEN.	2/1
	July 19	—	Programme training carried out. Musketry on range by 2 Platoons D Coy. 2 Platoons C Coy live bombing at the Spits	2/1
	July 20	—	Early morning training. Battalion scheme with contact aeroplane. Musketry on the range & live bombing. Revolver shooting was practised by all Coy officers. Lecture to 2 officers at Brigade.	3/1
	July 21	—	The Transport and the baths between 8 am & 12-30 pm during the morning afternoon half holiday.	2/1
	July 22	—	Ceremonial Drill from 9 to 9-45 am. C of E Service in the Concert Hall at 11 am. Training in wiring & bayonet fighting in the afternoon also musketry on range & live handling. Brigade Boxing Competitions are run there events.	2/1

2449 Wt. W14957/Mg0 750,000 1/16 J.B.C. & A. Forms/C.2118/12.

WAR DIARY
or
INTELLIGENCE SUMMARY
(Erase heading not required.)

Army Form C. 2118.

Place	Date 1917	Hour	Summary of Events and Information	Remarks and references to Appendices
	July 23	—	Progressive training carried out including rapid wiring fighting. Training of Coys in open musketry & live bombing. C.O. & Coy Commdrs watch field firing demonstration by 7th Division. A gas demonstration at which all ranks attended in the afternoon by Divl Gas Officer. 1 man from C Coy admitted to hospital slightly gassed.	3/1
	July 24	—	Rapid wiring. Lectures on "attack in open". Coy training. Wet morning. Musketry & bayonet fighting. Afternoon — A & B Coys have rifles inspected by Armourer Sergt. Lectures to officers at Bde HQ.	3/1
	July 25	—	C & D Coy rifles & all Lewis Guns inspected by Armourer Sergt. Progressive training during morning. Sports in afternoon including football, cross-country, etc.	3/1
	July 26	—	Battalion still — morning. Lectures — open attack. B Coy men on the range all morning & threw live bombs during afternoon.	3/1
	July 27	—	Battalion scheme in conjunction with LTMB & MG Coy. Battalion marched out down of inculcation in the afternoon. Beautiful day.	3/1

WAR DIARY or INTELLIGENCE SUMMARY

Army Form C. 2118.

Place	Date 1917	Hour	Summary of Events and Information	Remarks and references to Appendices
	July 28	—	Lieut Rowbotham - Adjutant and Lieut and S Truman Transport Officer proceeded on leave to England and their duties devolve upon 2/Lt J. Faulkner 2/Lt Yazit and 2/Lt Hawkesworth. The Transport Section was the Bath in the morning. Rest for Battalion owing to inundation.	97/1
	July 29	—	Divine Service which was brought to a sudden termination by a storm. Ceremonial Drill 11-30 a.m. to 12-30 p.m.	97
	July 30	—	Programme of progressive training carried on with. Musketry Training. 9.Divisional Sports during the afternoon. Training for men who did not attend Sports.	97
	July 31	—	Staff of 89 or 91 Training programme carried on with. Musketry on range. First impression favourable. Staff inspection by Brigadier.	97

T. P. Lewis
Lieut-Col.
Commanding 1/10 Manchester Regt

WAR DIARY.

Vol 7

of

Officer Commanding 1/10th Manchester Regiment

Kept by

2/Lieut. O. M. HARRY (Intelligence Officer)
the Officer detailed by him for that purpose

From August 1st To August 31st 1914

VOLUME XXIV.

Confidential

Army Form C. 2118.

WAR DIARY
or
INTELLIGENCE SUMMARY
(Erase heading not required.)

Instructions regarding War Diaries and Intelligence Summaries are contained in F. S. Regs., Part II. and the Staff Manual respectively. Title Pages will be prepared in manuscript.

Place	Date 1917	Hour	Summary of Events and Information	Remarks and references to Appendices
COURCELLES	Aug. 1		Owing to heavy rain the Battalion scheme was cancelled and Coys "carried on" with lectures, wiring and landscape targets. Lewis Guns "carried on" with their own work. Afternoon:– Coys in competitions at Rapid wiring. Batt. used the Baths.	Sheet 57 C. 17 N 4 1/40,000.
	2		Heavy rain all day. No parades. Lectures on various subjects. Further draft of 31 other ranks.	SMH
	3		Brigade scheme carried out from 7 a.m. to 2 p.m. No parade in afternoon.	SMH
	4		Company parades for Company training. Signallers + Scouts on the Range.	SMH
	5		Church Parade for all denominations in the morning. Ceremonial Drill 11-30 to 12-30. Football in afternoon against a Brigade XVI.	SMH
	6		Coys do their own training in the morning & in afternoon Coys do a trench attack. Scouts + Signallers firing on Range in afternoon. Nos 5 & 8 Platoons training the new draft.	SMH
	7		Morning parades Coy Commanders explain the Brigade scheme to the men. Fatigue parties collect the necessities for the scheme. Battalion Parade at 2.0 p.m. from the Brigade Scheme.	SMH
	8		Battn retires from the scheme at 6-30 a.m. No further parade in the morning. Battn have the afternoon owing the evening of the talk.	SMH

Army Form C. 2118.

WAR DIARY
or
INTELLIGENCE SUMMARY
(Erase heading not required.)

Instructions regarding War Diaries and Intelligence Summaries are contained in F.S. Regs., Part II. and the Staff Manual respectively. Title Pages will be prepared in manuscript.

Place	Date 1918	Hour	Summary of Events and Information	Remarks and references to Appendices
COURCELLES	Aug 9		Parade for Battalion Scheme at LOGEAST WOOD. Afternoon Coy training which followed the latest drafts.	Sheet Sept 2 1918
	10		Batt. Parade for Scheme. Trench to Trench fighting. Parties met the talks during the afternoon.	1/40.000
	11		Batt: paraded in the morning for Scheme on A area of Brigade Training Ground. Paraded for football in afternoon. Voluntary sports.	
	12		Church Parade for all denominations. Large Bugles & Drums Parade Mr Tanners and Cooks were presented with the Military Medal by Major General Mitford at the end of C & D service of D Coy in front of HAVRINCOURT WOOD.	
	13		Progressive training carried out. Musketry on the Range under 2/Lt T. Faulkner. Ranking by 2 Platoons of D Coy.	
	14		Battalion Training. Trench to Trench attack on the Brigade Area. Lecture to all officers at Brigade Hdqrs.	
	15		Battalion Scheme with contact aeroplane on training in "A" area. Afternoon sports.	
	16		Battalion training and musketry on the Range. Going to the Afternoon being Short lectures were given by the Company officers.	

Army Form C. 2118.

WAR DIARY
or
INTELLIGENCE SUMMARY
(Erase heading not required.)

Place	Date 1917	Hour	Summary of Events and Information	Remarks and references to Appendices
COURCELLES	Aug 17	-	Battalion training. Trench to Trench attack on the Brigade Trenches. Afternoon :- Bayonet fighting and Musketry.	Sheet 57H Sy C 9M11 1/40000 9M11
	18		Beginning training by Companies on Battalion training ground. Musketry shoots & paper done in afternoon.	9M11
	19		Church Parade & Ceremonial Drill carried out. New draft came out to trench to trench demonstration.	9M11
	20		Battalion training. Trench to Trench attack. Lewis Gun Practice on the range. Afternoon :- Battalion prepare to leave COURCELLES.	9M11
FORCEVILLE	21		Battalion leave COURCELLES by Route march for FORCEVILLE where they arrive the same day & stay the night in billets.	Sheet 57H Sy D
PROVEN & WATOU	22		Battalion leave FORCEVILLE at 9 P.M by route march for BEAUCOURT-SUR-ANCRE & entrain for PROVEN. Detrained & marched to WATOU. Battalion under canvas and in billets.	1/40000 Sheet 57H (Belgium & France)
WATOU	23		No parade for training. Inspection of Kit & Billets.	28 9M11 1/40000
	24		Battalion parade as usual for Route march. In the afternoon the Battalion parades for training in the Brigade training ground and in accordance with Memo. G.S.9. to be carried out.	9M11
	25		Battalion practice a Trench to Trench attack. No parade in the afternoon.	9M11

Army Form C. 2118.

WAR DIARY
or
INTELLIGENCE SUMMARY
(Erase heading not required.)

Instructions regarding War Diaries and Intelligence Summaries are contained in F. S. Regs., Part II. and the Staff Manual respectively. Title Pages will be prepared in manuscript.

Place	Date 1917	Hour	Summary of Events and Information	Remarks and references to Appendices
WATOU.	Aug 26		Church parade at 8-45 a.m. Ceremonial drill in Church parade dress in afternoon.	
	27		Battalion paraded for Route March. The Corps Commander inspected the Battalion on the march as they passed Brigade H-Qrs. Company training in the afternoon.	
	28		Battalion paraded at 9 a.m. to march to Brigade training Ground "attack" to practice "attacks" on strong posts." Battalion during the afternoon.	
	29		The Battalion proceeded to Training area & practising the "Attacks" on Strong Posts. Afternoon :- Nil.	
	30		Battalion proceeded by Route March to POPERINGHE where they entrained for YPRES and took over the camp of the 1/6 Lancashire Fusiliers going into the line this Battalion in Brigade Support.	
	31		Companies training & round the line preparatory to taking over food round the "Attack" on Strong Posts". The C.O.	

R.P. Lewis Lieut-Col.
Commanding 1/10 Manchester Regt.

1/10th Manchester Regiment. Operation Order No 17.

By

Lieut Colonel R.P. Lewis Commandg.   August 20/17.

Copy No

Ref Map 57 D. 1/40.000.

1. The Brigade Group will move by March Route to the Area Mailly Maillet - BERTRANCOURT, FORCEVILLE tomorrow the 21st inst:

2. The starting point will be on the COURCELLES-ABLAINZEVILLE Road opposite Brigade Headquarters.

   The route will be via BUCQUOY-PUISEUX-AU-MONT.

3. The 1/10t Manchester Regiment will pass the starting point at 7-43 A.M.   Hour of March 7-20 A.M.

Order of March:- Band, Headquarters, "D","C","B","A" Companies.

The Battalion will parade on Battalion Parade ground in Full Marching Order with packs and greatcoats at 7 A.M.

4. The Battalion will march with their 1st line transport closed up with an interval of 400 yards between units.

5. Units will halt from 10 minutes until the clock hour and for 5 minutes from the half hour until the half hour.

During the 5 minutes halt equipment will not be removed.

All Officers will dismount at the halts and the removal of the loads of Pack Animals will be arranged for at all the 10 minute halts.

6. The Battalion will have a rear party to ensure that billets are left in a sanitary condition.   The party will be composed as under:-   "A" Coy 1 N.C.O. 2 men.
                "B" "   "   2 "
                "C" "   "   2 "
                "D" "   "   3 "

This party will march in rear of the 430th Coy A.S.C, under an Officer to be detailed by the O.C. 1/4th East Lancs Regt.

The 430th A.S.C. pass the starting point at 9 A.M

7. Parade states will be rendered to the Adjutant by 6 am

8. Cookers will be marched in rear of the Battalion and the Transport Officer is responsible that:-
   a) No one is allowed to hang on to or ride on any vehicle.
   b) Not more than one man follows each vehicle as brakesman.
   c) No rifle or equipment is carried on any pack animal.
   d) Wire stays are properly fitted to the chimney of cookers when they are vertical.

9. No man will be allowed to straggle.

No man will be allowed to fall out without written permission.

O.C. "A" Coy will detail one Officer and one Sergt to march behind the 450th Coy A.S.C. (who have the starting point at 8A.) and they will collect any men who have been allowed to fall out and march them in formed bodies with the halts necessary to enable them to proceed. This applies to all men who are not admitted to Ambulance Wagons by the Medical Officer.

10. Platoon Commanders will march in rear of their platoons so that they can exercise the necessary supervision.

No compliments will be paid on the march except that all officers will salute General Officers.

11. Returns will be sent to Battalion Headquarters as soon as possible after arrival in camp showing by ranks:-
    1) Numbers carried in Ambulance Wagons.
    2) " dealt with as in para 8.

12. The Isolation Party of 14 men, under the guard will march in rear of the 450th Coy A.S.C.

13. ACKNOWLEDGE.

AUGUST 20th, 1917.   Lieut & Adjt.
                             1/10th Manchester Regiment.

Issued by Orderly at ....

Copy No 1. Commanding Officer.
" " 2. Major A.C. Wilde D.S.O.
" " 3. O.C. "A" Coy.
" " 4. " " " "
" " 5. " " " "
" " 6. " " " "
" " 7. " "C" "
" " 8. " "C" "
" " 9. " "D" "
" " 10. " "D" "
" " 11. QUARTERMASTER.
" " 12. 5443-9945- TRANSPORT OFFICER.
" " 13. R.S.M.
" " 14. Intelligence Officer.
" " 15. Signalling Officer.
" " 16. WAR DIARY.
" " 17. WAR DIARY.
" " 18. FILE.

ADMINISTRATIVE INSTRUCTIONS ISSUED WITH OPERATION ORDER NO17.

1. SUPPLIES.

Orders as to the change of refilling point will be issued later.

2. TRANSPORT.

The 2nd Line Transport (Baggage Wagons) will report at Quartermasters Store at 6-30 A.M. tomorrow. Guides will be sent to report at 430th Coy A.S.C. at 6 A.M.

Two Motor Lorries will report to this unit at 8 A.M. on the 20th inst and will be loaded and returned to Brigade Headquarters by 9-30A.M.

A Baggage Party of 1 N.C.O. and 4 men per lorry will travel with the lorries and will take three days rations.

These stores will be taken direct to Railhead at BEAUCOURT-SUR-ANCRE, where they will be dumped to await entraining on the 22nd inst:

The parties detailed to accompany these lorries will remain responsible until entrained by units on the 22nd inst:

Suitable loading parties will be detailed when the time is notified on the 22nd.

3. ADVANCE PARTIES.

An advance party composed as under will meet CAPT W.H.Lillie at Brigade Headquarters at 9A.M. on the 20th inst to proceed to BERTRANCOURT Area by lorry.

2/Lieut T. Faulkorner and 3 other ranks.

This party will arrange to meet the Battalion near the Factory K.32d0-0.

A further Advance party of 1 Officer & 3 O.R. composed as under will rendezvous at the Brigade Transport Officers Lines at 1-30 p.m. on 20th inst: and proceed in charge of senior officer to ACHIET-LE-GRAND Station meeting the Staff Captain at R.T.O's Office at 3 p.m. The railway journey will last over 12 hours and all ranks must take three days rations, a G.S. Limbered Wagon to be detailed by the B.T.O. will convey the men's packs and Officer's Kits to the Station.

    2/Lieut B.E.H.Hughes.
    L/Cpl Lang, & 2 other ranks of "C" Coy.

2 Bicycles will be taken with this party. The Officer in charge of this party will take Map 11 LENS Sheet 1/100000 and if possible Sheet 1/40000 57.D.

Para 4. MOBILE RESERVE.

The Battalion will march with its full Mobile Equipment of S.A.A., Bombs, Flares etc., Any Flares, etc, surplus to above will be returned to Corps Grenade School, BIHUCOURT.

5. FIRST LINE TRANSPORT.

All 1st Line Transport has to be loaded with its recognised Stores & Equipment in accordance with Mob: Store Table 1098, in addition the following articles will be carried Surplus pack saddles on the rear animal of limbered vehicles, all YUKON Packs and any spare ropes issued for the pack saddles to be taken.

6. TENTAGE.

Pending further instructions all Tents and bivouac shelters will be left standing. No tents or bivouac shelters will be taken from this area. A receipt will be obtained from Town Major, Obtained from Town Major. COURCELLES.

7. BAGGAGE.

The following stores will be stacked at the Quartermasters Dump at the undermentioned times:-

Company Stores..................6 A.M.
Officers Kits..................6-15 A.M.
Mess Furniture..................6-30 A.M.
Lewis Guns..................6 P.M. to-night.

A loading party of 2 N.C.O's & 30 men to be detailed by the R.S.M. will report to Quartermaster at 6-30A.M.

Field Kitchens will be cleaned and replenished with water etc, by 8-45 A.M. ready to move off.

Water bottles will be filled by 8-30A.M.

8. REVEILLE.

REVEILLE will be at 5 A.M.
BREAKFAST " " " 5-30 A.M.

9. Watches will be synchronised at Battalion Headquarters at 6-30A.M.

10. ACKNOWLEDGE.

Selwyn Rowbotham
Lieut & Adjutant,
1/10th Manchester Regiment.

SECRET.

1/10th Manchester Regiment OPERATION ORDER No 20.

Ref: 27 & 28 1/10000.
"Trench Map".
August 29th, 1917.

1. The 42nd Division will move in to the 15th Division Area, in order to take over the Right Sector of the 19th Corps Front, on 29th, 30th and 31st of August.
   On completion of the relief 125th Infantry Brigade will be in the front line, 126th Infantry Brigade in the Support and 127th Infantry Brigade in Reserve.

2. On the Right of the Division is the 17th Division and on the Left is the 61st Division.

3. All Transport of the Brigade Group will proceed by march route to H.16.d.9.4. under the command of Captain ARIS, A.S.C.
   Route:- Road in L.9.a, and b. SWICH Road North of POPERINGHE-MAIN YPRES Road.

6. A gap of 200 yards will be left between the transport of Units and gap of 20 yards between each group of 6 vehicles.

7. A detachment of 1/3rd East Lancs Field Ambulance will march with the column as far as the Main POPERINGHE Road, when it will leave the column and proceed to POPERINGHE.

8. Transport of units will pass the starting point Cross Roads L.7.d,7.3. at the following times:-
   Detachment of 1/3rd E.L. Field Amb: .... 2 p.m.
   126th Brigade Headquarters .... 2-7 p.m.
   126th Machine Gun Company .... 2-12 p.m.
   1/10th Manchester Regiment .... 2-17 p.m.
   1/4th East Lancs Regiment .... 2-22 p.m.
   1/5th East Lancs Regiment .... 2-22 p.m.
   1/9th Manchester Regiment .... 2-27 p.m.
   126th Field Company R.E. .... 2-32 p.m.
   430th Coy A.S.C. .... 2-36 p.m.

9. The normal hourly halts will be observed throughout the march.

10. The Officers and other ranks laid down in S.S.135. Section XXX. and "The Organisation of an Infantry Battalion" Appendix 11, will, until further notice, remain behind in their transport lines when the Brigade goes into the line.

11. Completion of all moves will be notified to Brigade Headquarters.

12. Brigade Headquarters will close at LES TRAPPISTES to-morrow at 3-0 p.m. and will open at YPRES South on arrival.

13. BREAKFAST will be at 7-30 A.M.
    MID-DAY. Meal will be at 11 A.M.

August 29th, 1917.
Lieut & Adjt,
1/10th Manchester Regiment.

Copy No 1. FILE.   Copy No 7. O.C. "C" Coy.
        2. WAR DIARY.   8.   "D" "
        3. C.O.   9. Quartermaster.
        4. 2nd in Command.   10. Transport Officer.
        5. O.C. "A" Coy,   11. Headquarters Officers & R.S.M.
        6.   "B" "

SECRET & URGENT.   1/10th Manchester Regiment.

PRELIMINARY ADMINISTRATIVE INSTRUCTIONS TO OPERATION ORDER NO 20.

August 29th 1917.

Ref: Map Sheets 27. & 28.

1. **RAILHEAD.** From the 30th inst: Railhead will be at EDSWAAR SHOEK (G.a.b5-3.)

2. **SANITATION.** A rear party composed as under will remain behind to give the necessary billeting certificates to the Area Commandant and to ensure that vacated camps are clean.
1/10th Manchester Regiment:- 2/Lieut E.J.Finch and 1 N.C.O.and 6 men to be detailed by O.C."A" Coy.
This rear party will rendezvous at the present Brigade Headquarters at 4 p.m. and proceed by Motor Lorry to YPRES ASYLUM in charge of Captain F.Hardman (the Brigade Field Officer of the Day) who will collect the following rear parties:-

Each Infantry Battalion	1 Off:	7. O.R.
Machine Gun Company	1 "	4. "
Light Trench M. Bty	1 "	3. "
Brigade Headquarters	-----	3. "
428th Fld Coy R.E.	1. "	4. "
TOTAL.	7.	42.

Units will send guides to meet these rear parties at the ASYLUM YPRES, on arrival.
The Motor Lorries will <u>not</u> be sent round to distribute the party in detail.

3. **TRANSPORT.** (a) **BAGGAGE WAGONS.** Baggage wagons will report to units at 10 A.M. on the 30th inst: and will be returned to 430th Coy A.S.C. fully loaded by noon.
(b) **MOTOR TRANSPORT.** Motor lorries as follows will be at Brigade Headquarters on the 30th at a time to be notified later to convey authorised extra baggage to New Area.

Each Infantry Battalion .... 1 Lorry.

After loading lorries will rendezvous at the Cross Roads K.17.b.5.7. and proceed to YPRES ASYLUM as one convoy where they will be met by Units guides.
After unloading the lorries allotted to the Machine Gun Coy and the Light T.M.Bty will return to present Brigade Headquarters to convey Rear Party.

4. **ADVANCE PARTY.** An advance party composed as under will proceed by Motor Lorry from Brigade Headquarters this morning at 8-30 A.M. to YPRES SOUTH AREA, with two days rations.
2/Lieut B.E.H.Hughes and 6 other ranks.
This party will ascertain location of billets from Camp Commandant erect bivouac sheets and etc: as required.
They will also arrange guides to meet the Battalion on arrival.

5. **MOBILE RESERVE OF S.A.A. ETC:** The Battalion will carry full mobile reserve of S.A.A.,Grenades and Flares on the 1st Line Transport This Reserve will be kept on the Transport Lines and will not be taken into the line.

CONTINUED:-

6. TRENCH STORES.

All trench stores, Tents, Bivouac Sheets, S.A.A., Grenades and Flares will be taken over from the 15th Division. A complete list to be handed in by 4 p.m, on the 31st inst: to Battalion Orderly Room.

7. SUPPLIES.

When in the Line supplies will be drawn on the Supply Wagons from H.8.Central, and when out of the line on 1st Line Transport from G.15.Central.
On going into the line every man will carry 2 Days rations plus the iron ration, When out of the line Transport for Rations will be provided under Regimental Arrangements.
Further Instructions will be issued as to the Transport of Rations when in the line.

8. D.A.D.O.S.

D.A.D.O.S., will be located at H.7d. 4.9.

9. WATER.

Horses will water at the Horse Troughs H.18.c.4.9.
DRinking Water may be drawn at the Tanks H.16;c. or G.18.a.5.8

August 29th, 1917.

Lieut & Adjt,
1/10th Manchester Regiment.

Copy No 1. FILE.
2. WAR DIARY
3. COMMANDING OFFICER.
4. O.C."A" Coy.
5. "B" "
6. "C" "
7. "D" "
8. 2nd in Command.
9. Quartermaster.
10. Transport Officer.
11. Headquarters Officers & R.S.M.

SECRET.   ADDENDUM NO 1.TO ADMINISTRATIVE INSTRUCTIONS ISSUED IN
             CONJUNCTION WITH OPERATION ORDER NO89.   August 29th/17.

1. The Battalion will entrain at POPERINGHE Station at 4-15p.m.
   to-morrow.   The train will depart at 5 P.M.

2. The hour of march and order of march from WATOU to POPERINGHE
   will be notified later.

3. Major S.H.P.SIMON will act as entraining Officer and Major L.C.
   WILDE, D.S.O.,will proceed on the first train and will act as
   detraining officerfor the whole Brigade.

4. No Baggage,stores and etc: will be sent by train.

5. The station of detrainment is the Railway Crossing at the
   ASYLUM. YPRES. (Sheet 28.H.12.d.

6. The undermentioned stores etc: will be stacked at the Guard
   Tent at 10 A.M. to-morrow.
      S.A.A., Grenades, Flares, Iael., Lewis Drums W.A.A.

   The Leading Party(1M.G.O.& 20,men will be detailed by O.C.
   "D" Coy.
   The undermentioned Stores etc: will be stacked on the
   Quartermasters Dump by 10 A.M.
   Officers Kits, Quartermasters Stores, Signalling Equipment and
   Company Stores.
   The Officers Mess Panniers will be sent to Quartermasters
   Store not later than 12 noon.

                                         Selwyn Rowbotham
August 29th,1917.   Lieut & Adjt,
                                        1/10th Manchester Regiment.

Copies issued to all recipients
of Operation Order No89.

ADDM. **ADDENDUM No 1. OPERATION ORDER No 30.** August 29th, 1917.

1. Reference para 2. The rear party will rendezvous at Brigade Headquarters at 3-30 p.m. and not at 4 p.m.

2. Reference para 5. Guides for baggage wagons will be sent by this office to report to 450th Coy A.S.C. at 7-30 A.M. to-morrow. After loading these wagons will march with the Battalion 1st Line transport.
A guide will also be sent from this office to conduct the Motor Lorry from Brigade Headquarters, reporting at Brigade Headquarters at 9 A.M. to-morrow.

3. Para 7. is cancelled and the following substituted "Rations will be drawn from refilling point at P.16.b.4.6. and will be delivered by Supply Wagons to the Battalion Transport Lines.

4. The following special arrangements apply to the 30th inst:
The Quartermaster and the Quartermaster Sergt (mounted) will report to 450th Coy A.S.C. at their present camp at 7-30 A.M. and proceed to the Transport Lines at P.16.d. with the Battalion Supply Wagons.
Immediately on arrival these wagons will be unloaded and returned to refilling point at P.16.b.

5. A guide found by the Brigade Transport Officer will conduct these party to the site of the Transport Lines.

6. The 2nd days issue of rations will probably be made in the evening. O.C. 450th Coy A.S.C. will notify this Battalions Representative direct.

7. The baggage wagons which accompany the 1st line Transport will be returned to the 450th Coy A.S.C. with the wagons which bring the second days rations in the evening.

August 29th.1917.   Lieut & Adjt,
                                              1/10th Manchester Regiment.

Copies to all recipients of
Operation Order No 30.

Ref Loading party of 1 NCO + 20 men from
D Coy, this party will report to the Quartermaster
at his Stores at 8.30 AM

SECRET.   ADDENDUM NO 1. TO ADMINISTRATIVE INSTRUCTIONS ISSUED IN

CONJUNCTION WITH OPERATION ORDER NO 20.   August 29th/17.

1. The Battalion will entrain at POPERINGHE Station at 4-15p.m. to-morrow. The train will depart at 5 P.M.

2. The hour of march and order of march from WATOU to POPERINGHE will be notified later.

3. Major H.S.P. SIMON will act as entraining Officer and Major L.C. WILDE. D.S.O., will proceed on the first train and will act as detraining officer for the whole Brigade.

4. No Baggage, stores and etc: will be sent by train.

5. The station of detrainment is the Railway Crossing at the ASYLUM. YPRES. (Sheet 28.H.12.d.

6. The undermentioned stores etc: will be stacked at the Guard Tent at 10 A.M. to-morrow.
   S.A.A., Grenades, Flares, Tools, Lewis Guns and S.A.A.

   The Loading Party (1 N.C.O. & 20 men will be detailed by O.C. "D" Coy.
   The undermentioned Stores etc: will be stacked on the Quartermasters Dump by 10 A.M.
   Officers Kits, Quartermasters Stores, Signalling Equipment and Company Stores.
   The Officers Mess Panniers will be sent to Quartermasters Store not later than 12 noon.

August 29th, 1917.   Lieut & Adjt,
                                           1/10th Manchester Regiment.

Copies issued to all recipients
of Operation Order No 20.

Confidential

WD 8 116/42

WAR DIARY
of the
1/10 MANCHESTER REGIMENT
Kept by
2/Lieut O. M. HARRY
the Officer detailed by the
Commanding Officer

Vol XXV

Army Form C. 2118.

WAR DIARY
or
INTELLIGENCE SUMMARY
(Erase heading not required.)

Instructions regarding War Diaries and Intelligence Summaries are contained in F. S. Regs., Part II. and the Staff Manual respectively. Title Pages will be prepared in manuscript.

Place	Date	Hour	Summary of Events and Information	Remarks and references to Appendices
YPRES	1-9-17		Companies practice taking Strong Posts. During the afternoon the Commanding Officer had a demonstration of Lewis Gun in conjunction with Conct in Camouflage.	BELGIUM Sheet 28 N.W. 1/20000 MH
—do—	2-9-17		Voluntary Holy Communion. Kit Inspection by Coy Officers.	MH
—do—	3-9-17		Company training in Attack on Strong Posts. Afternoon preparing for going into Brigade Support. 1/4th Battalion paraded to relieve 1/4th East Lancs Regiments in Dug-out at RAILWAY WOOD (Brigade Support) Ref Map. 28 N.W. 1/20000 I.11.B.6.4.5. Route taken KRUISSTRAAT. WARRINGTON ROAD. HELL FIRE CORNER. MENIN RD. BIRR CROSS TR̂ES to RAILWAY WOOD. Relief complete 11.45 p.m. very successfull.	MH
—do—	4-9-17		Battalion on Fatigue & Guards ie Carrying Ammunition for 126 Machine Guns Co. to firing line Rations Water Fatigues. Commanding Officer went to firing line during the morning to inspect before out taking over.	MH
—do—	5-9-17		"A" & "B" Coys during fatigue ammunition & water fatigues during the morning & commenced preparations for relieving the 1/4 & 8th East Lancs Regt. This relief was very successfully carried out and completed at 10.30p.m. "A" & "B" relieving the "A" & "B" Coys of the 1/4 East Lancs Regt and this was completed by 12.15 on Sept 6th only 3 casualties during the move.	MH

2449 Wt. W14957/Mgo 750,000 1/16 J.B.C. & A. Forms/C.2118/12.

Army Form C. 2118.

WAR DIARY
or
INTELLIGENCE SUMMARY

(Erase heading not required.)

Instructions regarding War Diaries and Intelligence Summaries are contained in F. S. Regs., Part II. and the Staff Manual respectively. Title Pages will be prepared in manuscript.

Place	Date	Hour	Summary of Events and Information	Remarks and references to Appendices
YPRES	6.9.17		Early morning fairly quiet. Our Artillery sent out quite a number of Gas shells. At 7.45 AM there was a general barrage on the enemies line, an attack was delivered by our left. About 11.0 AM the enemy delivered a counter attack, preceded by heavy barrage. Heavy firing continued until 1.30 PM. At 3.0 PM. Enemy Aircraft flew very low over our lines for 1/2 of an hour. Day very bright and warm. 4.0 PM. Kit and Kat Battalion H.Qrs heavily shelled for 1/2 an hour. 9-30 PM heavy barrage again put down by both sides followed by attack. At 10-30 PM another barrage was put out. No information yet as to the result of the attack this morning.	BELGIUM Sheet 28 N.W. 1/20000. OMH
—do—	7.9.17		The Commanding Officer got badly hit in the head this morning at about 1.10 PM — died at 3.25 PM. Heavy shelling of Kit Kat at different periods. "A" Coy sent out patrols around "SANS SOUCI FARM" but came across a strong fighting patrol & were forced to retire. 2/Lieut Williams utilising Battalion were relieved by the "6th" East Lancs Reg.t. Relief being complete at 1-30 AM on the 8.t	——— OMH
	8.9.17		Battalion marched down as they were relieved proceeded by WARRINGTON ROAD to YPRES. were they bivouaced. Battalion rest and clean up. Commanding Officers funeral at 3.3 PM	——— OMH

Army Form C. 2118.

WAR DIARY
or
INTELLIGENCE SUMMARY
(Erase heading not required.)

Place	Date	Hour	Summary of Events and Information	Remarks and references to Appendices
YPRES	9-9-17		Kit inspection by Company Commanders & Voluntary Holy Communion. Battalion moved up to Cambridge Road and took over from the 1/7th Manchester Regiment. Had 3 Casualties.	B#OWM SHEET 28. N.W. 1/20000 TMH
—	10-9-17		Usual heavy firing A & B in the firing line 'C' in support 'D' in Reserve. Heavy Gas shelling all night	— " — TMH
—	11-9-17		Heavy firing all day to Casualties	— " — TMH
—	12-9-17		Heavy barrages at different times of the day	— " — TMH
—	13-9-17		Battalion relieved by the 1/7th Manchester Regiment and marched by YPRES to same camping ground as formerly held	— " — TMH
—	14-9-17		Rest in Camp & cleaning up and Rifle Inspection	— " — TMH
—	15-9-17		New Commanding Officer Major W.R. PEEL taken over. Day training in morning. Battalion parade for fatigue in Kit Kat. 'C' Company of this Battalion relieved one Company of the 1/5 East Lancs in YPRES	— " — TMH

Army Form C. 2118.

WAR DIARY
INTELLIGENCE SUMMARY

(Erase heading not required.)

Instructions regarding War Diaries and Intelligence Summaries are contained in F.S. Regs., Part II. and the Staff Manual respectively. Title Pages will be prepared in manuscript.

Place	Date	Hour	Summary of Events and Information	Remarks and references to Appendices
YPRES	16/9/17		Inspection of Battalion by Commanding Officer in the morning. Two hours Saluting drill and platoon Drill. Battalion paraded by parties in fatigue to Kit and Kit. First party leave camp at 9.15 p.m., last party 10.5 p.m. 'C' Company did not leave their billets in YPRES until 10.30 p.m. owing to the difference in the distance there were no casualties.	BELGIUM Sheet 28 N.W. 1/20000. MH
—	17/9/17		Inspection, Physical Training & Bayonet fighting. The 9/0 Manchester Regiment was relieved by 9/ Seaforth Rifles in the YPRES South area. Relief commencing at 8 p.m. ne relief the Battn proceeded by Route March to DERBY CAMP. H.10.80. 1 ne Coy of 9/ Scottish Rifles relieved 'C' Company of the Battalion in YPRES	BELGIUM FRANCE Sheet 28 (word) MH
	18/9/17		Rested in Camp. Kit Inspection	MH
	19/9/17		Parades from 9. A.M. to 12.30 Companies cleaning up Equipment	MH
	20/9/17		Battalion paraded at 11 a.m. and proceeded by Route March to WINNEZEELE VIA the POPERINGHE ROAD, WATOU and DROGLANDT	MH
WINNEZEELE	21/9/17		Battalion parade from 9 a.m. - 12.30 Kit Inspection in afternoon + Lecture to N.C.O.s	MH BELGIUM FRANCE Sheet 27 MH

Army Form C. 2118.

WAR DIARY
INTELLIGENCE SUMMARY.
(Erase heading not required.)

Instructions regarding War Diaries and Intelligence Summaries are contained in F.S. Regs., Part II and the Staff Manual respectively. Title pages will be prepared in manuscript.

Hour, Date, Place	Summary of Events and Information	Remarks and references to Appendices
WINNEZEELE 22/9/17	Battalion paraded for Route march from WINNEZEELE - WORMHOUDT. Rest in afternoon.	BELGIUM & FRANCE SHEET 27 1/40,000 DMH
23/9/17	Brigade 'B' Group proceed by Route march from WORMHOUDT to TETEGHEM. Route taken via WILDER GAIGHOEK. Rested in billets for rest of day	BELGIUM & FRANCE SHEET 27 1/40,000 DMH
24/9/17	Battalion marched off at 6.30 PM from TETEGHEM via UXEM ADDINSKIRKE to LA PANNE. Just infiltration in Camp Rested remainder of day	BELGIUM SHEET 27 1/40,000 DMH
LA PANNE. 25/9/17	Battalion now took up Coast Guard duties at LA PANNE. Battalion in Billets	BELGIUM SHEET 11 1/40,000 DMH
26/9/17	Two Companies on Coast Guard duty. The remaining 2 Companies. Company drill	" " DMH

Army Form C. 2118.

WAR DIARY
or
INTELLIGENCE SUMMARY
(Erase heading not required.)

Instructions regarding War Diaries and Intelligence Summaries are contained in F. S. Regs., Part II. and the Staff Manual respectively. Title Pages will be prepared in manuscript.

Place	Date	Hour	Summary of Events and Information	Remarks and references to Appendices
LA PANNE	27/9/17		2 Companies attached to the R.E.s, one hour Physical Training and Drill. The remaining 2 Coys training from 3-4.30 p.m. At night Rapid wiring.	OMA
—	28/9/17		One hours drill for the 2 Coys attached to R.E. Coy. Physical Training & Bayonet fighting for the remaining 2 Coys.	OMA
—	29/9/17		1 hour physical training and drill for A & B Coys attached to the R.E. Coy. "C" & "D" Company platoon training from 9 a.m. to 12.30 p.m. 2-0 p.m. to 4.0 p.m. Wiring	OMA
—	30/9/17		Voluntary Holy Communion & Services. Afternoon "C" & "D" Coy platoon training Wiring	OMA

v. R. Peel
Lieut-Col
Commanding
1/10 Manchester Regiment

SECRET.

ADDENDUM TO OPERATION ORDER NO 21.

September 5/1917.

1. Reference para 2. "C" Coy will remain in camp YPRES, Southern Area and be prepared to move at 10 minutes notice.
"D" Coy will remain in YPRES, and be prepared to move at 10 minutes notice.

2. O.C. "A" & "D" Coys will send forward an Officer and Sergt to Railway Wood. They will start from here at 4 p.m. punctual. 2/Lieut Harry will act as guide.
The above party will make themselves familiar with the dug-outs allotted to their units.

3. Guides from 1/4th East Lancs Regt will meet the Battalion at BIRR CROSS ROADS at 10 p.m.

4. Reference para 5. Hour of march 7-45 p.m.

5. The Quartermaster will be prepared to send up 2 days rations on the night of the 5/6th.
They will proceed by MENIN GATE-HELL FIRE CORNER-BIRR CROSS ROADS, and up CAMBRIDGE ROAD.
A guide will meet them at BIRR CROSS ROADS at 10 p.m.
All available YUKON PACKS will be sent up with this convoy.

6. Reference para 6 men will carry their mess tins in their packs.

Lieut & Adjt,
1/10th Manchester Regiment.

Distribution as for
Operation Order No 21.

Hoffma

Storm a Drang

OPERATION ORDER NO 25.
by
Major J.H.ALLAN. COMMANDING 1/10th Manchester Regiment.

Ref: Map Sheet 28.N.W.1/20000.   Sept 9th,1917.

1. The 1/10th Manchester Regiment will relieve the 1/7th Manchester
   Regiment to-night the 9/10th inst: in the support line of the
   Right Sector of the Left Brigade.

2. Approximate map reference of Companies are as follows:-
   "A" Coy.........I.6.a.6.2. to Rly at I.6.d.1.6.
   "B" " ....I.6.a.6.2. to I.6.a.3.8.
   "C" " ....I.6.c.2.2. to I.6.c.1.9. (Ice Trench)
   "D" " ....I.5.d. Central.

3. One guide per Company and one for Battalion Headquarters will be at
   the MENIN GATE at 8 p.m. from 1/7th Manchester Regt.

4. Companies will march in the following order:-
   "A","B","C","D" Coys and Headquarters, the head of "A" Coy
   will pass the MENIN GATE at 8 p.m.

5. Companies will relieve corresponding Companies of the 1/7th
   Manchester Regiment.

6. Battalion Headquarters will be situated at I.11.b.2.8.

7. Companies will report completion of relief to Battalion Headquarters
   the code word "IMPSHY" being used.

8. Company Commanders will at once take steps after completion of relief
   to acquaint themselves of the nearest route to any part of the front
   line, as they may be called upon to reinforce any portion of the line
   at short notice.

9. Coys will march by Half Platoons at a 100 yards interval and in single
   file going through 6943½-YPRES. care must be taken that connecting
   files keep touch throughout the march.   The leading Company("A")
   will march out of camp at 7-15 p.m.

10. Companies will march in fighting kit as before and will take with
    them the following:-
       1 L.G. Magazine per man (carried in the pack)
       2 Days rations in the pack.
       170 rounds of S.A.A. in the pouches and bandoliers.
       15. Petrol Tins of Water per Coy.
    The water taken up will be sufficient for one day and will then be
    replenished from a water cart at Battn Headquarters.
    Companies must exercise the greatest care with Petrol Tins and all
    taken up to the line must be brought back as they are exceedingly
    difficult to replace.   All water Bottles must be filled prior to
    leaving and Company Commanders will satisfy themselves that this has
    been done prior to marching out.

11. A parade state will be handed in to this office by 4 p.m. to-day
    shewing strength in the line by Officers and other ranks.

12. The party proceeding on leave on the 11th inst: will remain behind
    and report to the Asst Adjt on the departure of the Battalion when
    they will receive instructions as to their disposal.

13. ACKNOWLEDGE.

                                                    Captain,
                                                    Adjutant.

Copy No 1. O.C."A" Coy.   Copy No 7. Hdqtrs Officers & R.S.M.
        2.   "B" "   8. Major L.C.Wilde. D.S.O.
        3.   "C" "   9. 2&4 WAR DIARY.
        4.   "D" "   10. WAR DIARY.
        5. Qmr & T.O.   11. Asst Adjt.
        6. C.O.

1/ature Manchester Regiment.

Battalion Operation Order No.57 by Major R.B.Fitchett D.S.O. Commanding.

1. Reference 125th Brigade Operation Order No. 68.

2. "C" Company, 1/19th Manchester Regiment, will arrange to relieve the Company of 1/5th East Lancs Regt. in AVOCA by 4 p.m. Monday, 19th inst, under arrangements to be made by Company Commanders concerned.

3. All Stores, S.A.A., etc, will be handed over and receipts obtained.

4. Completion of relief will be notified to this office by special runner.

5. Acknowledge.

                                                    [signature]
                                                    for Captain,
                                                    Adjutant,
14/9/17.   1/19th Manchester Regiment.

    Distribution:-
    Copy No. 1.   O/C. "A" Coy.
           2.   " " "B" "
           3.   " " "C" "
           4.   " " "D" "
           5.   Scouting Officer.
           6.   Major L.Trifitt D.S.O.
           7.   Quartermaster & Transport Officer.
           8.   Ex-Area Officers & Staff.
           9.   "A" Staff.
          10.   "Q" "
          11.   File.

WARNING ORDER.
by
Major W.R.PEEL D.S.O. COMMANDING 1/10th Manchester Regiment.

Ref: Map 28 N.W.1/20000.   September 16th, 1917.

1. The 1/10th Manchester Regiment will be prepared to move to-night at
   8 p.m. by MARCH ROUTE into the BRANDHOEK AREA.

Copies to all recipients of   Captain,
Operation Order No 28.   Adjutant,
                                                 1/10th Manchester Regiment.

OPERATION ORDER No 22.
by
Major W.R.PEEL. D.S.O. Commanding 1/10th Manchester Regiment.   Sep:16/1917.

Ref: Map 28. A.W.1/20000.   Copy No 10

1. The 126th Infantry Brigade will be relieved by the 27th Infantry B'de on the night of 16/17th inst: On relief the 126th Infantry Brigade will move to BRANDHOEK AREA.

2. The Command of the Brigade will pass at 6 A.M. on the 17th inst: The Brigade H.Q. will open at RIDGE CAMP at G.11.a.4.5. on arrival.

3. The 1/10th Manchester Regiment will be relieved on the night of the 18th inst: by the 9th Scottish Rifles in the YPRES,SOUTH AREA.relieving troops will commence to arrive at 8 p.m. on the 18th inst: On relief the 1/10th Manchester Regiment will proceed by march route to DERBY Camp (H.1.a.8.0.)

4. The Battalion will march in the following order:-
Headquarters, "A", "B" and "D" Coys by Platoons at 200 yards intervals The Assistant Adjutant will proceed in advance to the new camp and arrange platoon guides to meet platoons at the cross roads at H.2.a.4.8. who will lead them to their positions.

5. "C" Company at present stationed in YPRES will send 5 guides (1 for Coy H.Q. and 1 for each platoon) to report to the Adjutant at the present camp to guide relieving Company of the 9th Scottish Rifles to "C" Coy H.Q., in YPRES. not later than 7pm

6. On relief "C" Coy will march independently to the new camp in the formation laid down in para 4 above reporting their arrival to the Adjutant.

7. The Battalion Details stationed at BURNS Camp will rejoin the Batt'n on arrival at DERBY Camp. These details will move under arrangements to be made by Major Kerr D.S.O.,M.C.

8. During the 19th inst: the party from this unit attached to the 428th Field Coy R.E. will rejoin under arrangements to be made by the O.C's concerned.

9. O.C.Companies and Intelligence Officer will return to Orderly Room forthwith all Trench Maps Aeroplane Photographs and Sketches, these should be returned at the latest by 2 p.m. Linen backed maps should only be retained.

10. Administrative instructions will be issued separately.

11. ACKNOWLEDGE.

                                              CAPTAIN.
                                              ADJUTANT.
                                              1/10th Manchester Regiment.

DISTRIBUTION :-
         NORMAL.

ADDENDUM No. 1 TO
ADMINISTRATIVE INSTRUCTIONS ISSUED IN ACCORDANCE WITH
BATTALION OPERATION ORDER No. 28.

September 18th 1917
Reference Map, Sheet No. 27 N.E. Copy No. 10

1. **BAGGAGE.**
   Reference para 1.
   1 Motor lorry will be available to-morrow, the 19th inst, to convey surplus stores and heavy baggage and the remaining packs of N.C.O's & men of this Unit.
   The R.S.M. will detail No. 275866 L/Cpl BIRCHALL xxxxxxxxxx to proceed to the 126th Brigade Hd-Qrs to - morrow morning arriving there at 8-45 a.m. He will proceed from there on the motor lorry allotted to the 1/9th Manchester Regiment to the new billeting area and after same has been unloaded he will guide this lorry back to the Camp occupied by this Unit (DERBY CAMP).
   On arrival at this Camp the lorry, at once, will be loaded by the rear party.

2. **REAR PARTY.**
   A rear party consisting of 1 Officer, 1 N.C.O, and 6 men will be left behind to clear up the Camp and load the lorry.
   This party will be carried on the lorry and will be detailed later.

3. **BILLETS.**
   The approximate location of billets in the new area for this Unit will be :- J 11. a 8. 1.   and   J 5. c 5. 7.

4. **ADVANCE PARTY.**
   Company Commanders will each detail 1 N.C.O. to parade outside Battalion Orderly Room to-day at 6-15 p.m.
   No.275807 L/Cpl LANG will parade at the same time.
   This party will proceed in advance to the new billeting area under the Asst. Adjutant and will meet their Companies at the road junctions at BROUKANDT, J 12. b 8. 7. and guide them to their billets.

5. Officers' kits, mess-stores & paniers, surplus stores, etc., will be dumped outside the Guard-tent at a time to be notified later.

6. Further orders will be issued later.

7. ACKNOWLEDGE.

                                              Captain & Adjutant,
18/9/17   1/10th Manchester Regiment.

        Distribution:-   As for Operation Order No. 28.

ADMINISTRATIVE INSTRUCTIONS
in accordance with Operation Order No. 22

September 16th 1917
Copy No 10

1. **TRANSPORT.**
   Baggage wagons will be sent to Units to-day at times to be arranged direct by O.C. Units with O.C. 450th Coy A.S.C.
   No motor transport is available for the move on the night
2. of the 16/17th insts., and if necessary 1st Line Transport & Baggage wagons must do two journeys to the new Area.

2. **AMMUNITION.**
   All Units will move complete with their establishment of S.A.A., Bombs, Grenades, Flares, etc., on wheels.

3. **TRENCH STORES.**
   All trench and Area stores will be handed over to the 27th Brigade, including Hot Food Containers, latrine buckets, Gum boots (thigh), petrol tins, etc.,
   All ammunition, flares, grenades, R.E. stores etc., in known trench dumps will be handed over to the relieving Unit.
   All trench stores must be collected and arranged in convenient dumps, and every effort made to salve any other stores scattered about the Area, as possible, even though they may not have been definitely handed to Units on arrival.
   Receipts will be obtained for all stores handed over, and two copies of these receipts must be sent Battalion Orderly Room immediately on arrival in the new Camp.
   2/Lieut Bouskill will hand over the Camp to the incoming Unit, obtaining receipts for bivouacs, tents, etc., and certificate of cleanliness of the Camp.

4. **ACCOMODATION.**
   The following is the new Camp allotted to this Unit:-
   DERBY CAMP,   H 1. a 8. 6.

5. **D.A.D.O.S.**
   Will remain in his present location pending further orders.

6. **BAGGAGE.**
   Officers valises, and surplus mess-stores will be stacked at the Guard-tent by 2 p.m.
   Only such mess-stores and kit as will be required for dinner will be kept back.

7. Dinners will be at 4 p.m. to-day.

8. Cookers and water-carts of A, B, & D Coys will move at 5 p.m. and of "C" Coy at 4-30 p.m.
   Two limbers for Lewis Guns of A, B, & D Coys will be at the Camp, together with the mess-cart, at 7-30 p.m.
   One limber for Lewis Guns etc., will report to O.C. "C" Coy at 5 p.m.

9. Kit inspection ordered for this afternoon will be postponed till arrival in the new Camp.
   Companies will spend the afternoon in clearing up their areas.

10. A C K N O W L E D G E.

16/9/17

Captain & Adjutant.

Distribution
as O.O. No 26

OPERATION ORDER NO 22.
By
Major C.R.PYE D. S. O. Commanding 1/10th Manchester Regiment. Sept.18/1917.
Oilman Sheet 28.N.E. 1/20000.

1. The 126th Infy Brigade Group will move from the STAMHOPE Area to
   DICKEBUSCH Area on L, on the 19th inst;
   Route will be via CHIPPS ROAD-North of POPERINGHE-Road JUNCTION L.4.b.8.2
   RENINGHELST.

2. Starting Point will be Cross Roads G.5.c.5.2.

3. The 1/10th Manchester Regiment will pass the starting point at 7-30 a.m.
   Falling in at ... on ground immediately N.E. of the present camp at each Coy
   Group, ready to move off.
   Order of March:- HQ, Headquarters, A, B, C, D Companies.
   Dress:-   Fighting Kit, Steel Helmets, Box Respirators slung.

4. Halts will be as follows:- 10 minutes in the short hour until the clock
   hour and 5 minutes from the half hour until the half hour.

5. 200 yards distance will be maintained between Coys head of Coys to Coys.
   At the first half hourly halt after passing the Cross Roads L.4.b.8.2
   the head of the Battalion will wait for sufficient to enable the Coys
   in rear to close up.
   A distance of not less than 200 yards will be maintained between this
   Battalion and the 1/4th East Lancs Regt immediately preceding.
   "D" Coy will detail 1 Officer and 6 N.C.O. to remain behind upon
   reaching the starting point.
   They will act as Rear Party and will march in rear of the 2/2nd (E.L.)
   Field Ambulance.   Minute to pass the starting point:-7-10 a.m.
   It will be their duty to march all men of this Unit who are given leave
   to fall out (but not given a ticket by Medical Officer for admittance
   to an Ambulance Wagon) in a formed body to their destination.

6. All transport of the 126th Infy Brigade Group will march under the orders
   of the Brigade Transport Officer.
   The 1/10th Manchester Regiment Transport will pass the starting point
   at 8-30 a.m.

7. A gap of 200 yards will be left between the Transport of Units and a gap
   of 50 yards between each group of 4 Vehicles.

8. Transport will not observe the hour and half hourly halts until the halt
   at 9-30 a.m.

9. N.C.Oys and Transport Officer will pay strict attention to march dis-
   cipline in accordance with the memorandum issued recently from this office
   and Transport Officer will ensure that not more than one man marches in
   rear of each vehicle.
   All Spare Transport personnel, Cooks and Batmen will march with their
   Coys.
   One Cook per Cooker will prepare Tea on the line of March for Issue on
   arrival.

                                              [signature] Robotham
                                                        CAPTAIN.
                                                        ADJUTANT.
                                              1/10th Manchester Regiment.

DISTRIBUTION:- NORMAL.

ADMINISTRATIVE INSTRUCTIONS
TO BATTALION OPERATION ORDER NUMBER 29
Reference Map, Sheet 27 N.E. 1/20000

September 18/9/17
Copy No.

1. Reveille will be at 4 a.m.
   Breakfast will be at 4-30 a.m.

2. **REAR PARTY.**
   A rear party composed as under will remain behind and clean up the Camp, and the Officer in charge will obtain a certificate of cleanliness from the Area Commandant before leaving. This certificate to be handed in to this office on his arrival in the new area. They will also load baggage in accordance with para 3 and unload on arrival in new area.
   2/Lieut S. HOLT
   Corpl DYSON & 3 other ranks (to be detailed by O.C. Companies in accordance with a list sent out from this office)

3. **BAGGAGE.**
   One motor lorry will be available to-morrow, the 19th inst, to convey surplus stores & heavy baggage, and the remaining packs of N.C.O's and men of this Unit.
   The R.S.M. will detail 375406 L/Cpl BIRCHALL TO PROCEED TO THE 126th Brigade Hd-Qrs to-morrow morning arriving there at 6-40 a.m. He will proceed from there on the motor lorry allotted to the 1/9th Manchester Regiment to the new billeting area and after the same has been unloaded he will guide this lorry back to this present Camp (DENBY CAMP). On arrival at this Camp the lorry will at once be unloaded by the rear party who will proceed in to the new area in charge of the lorry.

4. **ADVANCE PARTY.**
   Company Commanders will detail 1 N.C.O. to parade outside Battn. Orderly Room at 6-15 p.m. This party will proceed in advance to the new billeting area in charge of the Asst. Adjt. and after being shewn their billets will meet their Companies at the road junctions at DROGLANDT, J 12. b 8. 7. and guide them to their billets. (1 days rations will be taken)
   375867 L/Cpl LANG will also proceed with this party and will represent Battalion Hd Qrs.

5. Officers kits , mess-stores & paniers, and all surplus stores will be dumped outside the Guard-tent not later than 5-30 a.m. As much extra stores as possible should be stacked to-night. All Lewis Guns, L.G. ammunition, S.A.A., Bombs, tools, etc., will be loaded on the limbers to-night and the R.S.M. will detail the necessary fatigues under arrangements to be made by the Transport Officer. The two Lewis Guns at present mounted, anti-craft, will remain in position until 4-30 a.m. to -morrow and will then be dismounted and loaded on the limbers

6. **BILLETS.**
   The approximate location of billets in the new area of this Unit will be :-   J 11. a 8. 1. and J 5, c 3. 7.

7. Leave party will march in rear of the Battalion and fall out on arrival in POPERINGHE and will be marched under the senior man to the R.T.O. POPERINGHE.

8. These Administrative Instructions cancel No.1 Addendum to Administrative Instructions to Operation Order No. 29.

9. ACKNOWLEDGE.

Captain and Adjutant

OPERATION ORDER No.22.

by
Major H.P.FOX D.S.O. Commanding 1/19th Manchester Regiment.
Ref: Map of B.E.1/40000.   Sept 29th,1917.

1. The 127th Infy Brigade Group will move from the BISSEZEELE area by route march to the WINNEZEELE area to-morrow the 31st inst.
   Route will be via Cross Roads J.21.b.6.7. to WINNEZEELE.

2. The Starting Point will be at Road Junction J.10.D.8.8.

3. The 1/19th Manchester Regiment will pass the starting point at 10-1 a.m.

4. The Battalion will parade at 9-30 a.m. in column of route on the road leading from "D" Camp having its Whizzbangs South,in the following order.
   Band,Headquarters,"C","D","B" and "A" Coys.
   The Head of the column will rest on the first road junction from the camp at approximately J.11.c.8.3.

5. The Battalion will march closed up with an interval of 200 yards between Units.
   O.C."A" Coy will detail 1 Officer and 1 N.C.O. to remain behind as rearguard, the starting point. They will act as Rear Party and will march in rear of the 1/2nd East Lancs Field Ambulance - Timed to pass the starting point at 10-40 a.m. It will be their duty to march all men of this unit who are given leave to fall out (but not given a chit by the Medical Officer to a Field Ambulance) in a formed body to their destination.

6. The usual halts will be observed .

7. The Dress for Parade will be Full Marching Order with packs and haversacks slung.

8. All Transport will march under the Brigade Transport Officer and the 1/19th Manchester Regiment Transport will pass the starting point at
   9-1 a.m.   A gap of 200yards will be left between the Transport of units and a gap of 10 yards between each group of 4 vehicles.

9. Watches will be synchronized at Battalion Orderly Room at 7-30 a.m.

10. ACKNOWLEDGE.

                                                    [signature]
Copies to all recipients of   CAPTAIN.
BATTLE ORDER.   ADJUTANT.
                                                    1/19th Manchester Regiment.

ADMINISTRATIVE ARRANGEMENTS ISSUED WITH OPERATION ORDER NO.9.

Ref: War Off. S.S.1/27773.   Sept. 28th, 1917.

1. Reveille .... 5 a.m.
   Breakfasts .... 5-30 a.m.

2. **REAR PARTY.**
   A rear party composed as under will remain behind and clear up the Camp, and the Officer i/c will obtain a certificate of cleanliness from the Area Commandant before leaving, such certificate to be handed in to this office on arrival in the new area.
   They will also load baggage in accordance with para. 6. and unload on arrival in new area.
        Lieut. C.S.COOPER, 1 N.C.O.& 2 other ranks.
        Each Company 1 N.C.O. & 3 other ranks to be selected from light duty men by the Medical Officer by 7 a.m. and as 2 other ranks to be detailed by the Q.Mr.

3. **BAGGAGE.**
   A motor lorry will be available for this Battalion to convey surplus stores and heavy baggage sixths of this Unit to the new area.
   This motor can do 2 journeys if required but a guide must accompany the lorry on the first trip, to show theway.
   The Quarter-master will arrange to meet the motor lorry and bring it to the Camp at the road junction, J 17 b 2.2. at 6 a.m. to-morrow.

4. **AMMUNITION.**
   The Battalion will move with complete mobile reserve S.A.A., grenades etc., on wheels.

5. **ADVANCE PARTY.**
   Company Commanders will detail 1 N.C.O. and 2 other ranks per Coy and the M.G.O. will detail 1 N.C.O. & 2 other ranks to represent Batta. Hd-qrs, one of which will be a Scout N.C.O.
   This party will rendezvous at Batta. Orderly Room at 6 a.m. prompt and proceed to the new area in charge of Lieut R.H.W.HUGHES.
   After taking over accommodation they will meet the Battalion at the entrance to the village & guide Companies & Batta. Hd-qrs to their respective billets.   All men forming the Advance Party should be able to ride cycles.

6. **KITS AND STORES.**
   Officers kits , mess-stores & panniers and all surplus baggage will be stacked at the undermentioned places at the following times:-
       (a) "A" Camp...... Batta. Orderly Room........ 7-30 a.m.
       (b) "B" Camp...... Guard Tent..................... 7-45 a.m.
   The R.S.M. will detail loading parties to load these stores at the abovementioned times.
   The Q.Mr will arrange to load all LEWIS GUNS, L.G. ammunition, S.A.A. bombs, flares, and tools at "B" Camp and the Transport Officer will send the G.S. limbered wagons to "B" Camp to-night ready to load first thing to-morrow morning.   The R.S.M. will detail the required loading parties.

7. **BAGGAGE WAGONS.**
   Baggage wagons will report to Unit Camps at 6-30 a.m. and will be returned to the 42th Coy A.S.C. representative at the Cross-Roads, J 11 c 2. 1. at 9-25 a.m.

8. **SICK PARADE.**
   Sick parade will be at 6-30 a.m.

9. **ACKNOWLEDGE.**

                                                    [signature]
                                               Captain & Adjutant,
                                               1/10th Manchester Regiment.

1/10th Manchester Regiment.

WARNING ORDER.

1. The Brigade Group, less 1/2nd E.L. Fld Ambulance will be prepared to move by 7-0 a.m. tomorrow, 24th inst.

2. No Unit will have to march more than 3 miles.

3. ACKNOWLEDGE.

Captain & Adjutant,
1/10th Manchester Regiment.

23/9/17

Copy No. 1 O.C. "A" Coy
     2 "   " "B" "
     3 "   " "C" "
     4 "   " "D" "
     5   Q-Mr & T.O.
     6   R.S.M.

Copy No. 7 H-Qrs Officers
     8   Commanding Officer
     9   Major L.C.Wilde D.SO
     10   War Diary
     11   "   "
     12   File.

OPERATION ORDER No 31.

by

Major W.R.PEEL D.S.O., Commanding 1/10 th Manchester Regiment.

Ref: Map DUNKIRK. 3A. 1/100000.   September 21st, 1917.

1. The 126th Infy B"de Group will march to-morrow the 22nd inst: to
   TE ROHEM.

2. The starting point will be at road junction C.11 b.6.7.(Sheet 27)

3. The 1/10th Manchester Regiment(less will pass the starting point as
   follows and in the order named:-
   Band H.Q. "B" & "A" Coys ----------9-36 a.m.
   First Line Transport & Baggage wagons 9-40 a.m. (Starting point Road Junction
   "C" & "D" Coys   10-14 a.m. (at T 19 c. 4 4)
   Estimated time required to march from square WORMHOUDT to starting
   point 20 minutes.

4. The Battalion will march with first line Transport closed up with
   distances of 200 yards, the supply wagons will march with the 430th
   Coy A.S.C. passing the starting point at 10-3 a.m.

5. The usual hourly halts will be observed in addition there will be a
   halt of one and half hours from 12 noon to 1-30 p.m. for the mid-day
   meal.
   Cookers will not be brought up from the rear in such a manner as to
   block the road.   Horses will be fed and watered, the petrol tins
   carried in the limbers being employed for that purpose
   O.C. Coys and QMr will ensure that cookers and petrol tins are filled
   up before marching out.
   All spare cooks will march at the head of the Transport under the
   Master Cook

6. The route will be via WILDER-LES-CINQ-CHEMINS, cross roads C.17 d.10-25
   GALGHOEK.

7. Major KERR D.S.O., M.C., 1/5th East Lancs Regt will marshall the
   Transport of all units and will be responsible for their taking their
   correct place in the column as units are marching to the starting
   point.

7. 3 Horse ambulances of 1/2nd East Lancs Fld Amb: and 1/3rd East Lancs
   Fld Amb: will march in rear of their respective groups .

8. REVEILLE will be at   6-a.m.
   BREAKFAST "   " "   6-30 a.m.
   Sick parade " "   6-45 a.m.

10. ACKNOWLEDGE.

Copies to all recipients of
WARNING ORDER.

                                                        CAPTAIN,
                                                        ADJUTANT.

OPERATION ORDER No 21 (ADMINISTRATIVE INSTRUCTIONS)
by
MAJOR .W.R.PEEL., D.S.O. Commanding 1/10th Manchester Regiment.

Copy No.....

1. **SUPPLIES.**
   Supplies for the 22nd inst: have been drawn to-day, and supplies for the 23rd inst: will be drawn at TETESNEY.

2. (a) **Baggage wagons.**
   These will report to Battalion Headquarters at 6-30 a.m. and the Quartermaster will send a guide to take them to his stores from Battalion Headquarters. These wagons will be retained and will march with the Battalion.
   (b) One motor lorry is expected to be available, and the Qmr will send a guide to Brigade Headquarters to draw this lorry at 8 a.m. to-morrow. If this lorry is used to make a second trip a guide will be sent on the first trip and return with it.

3. **AMMUNITION.**
   Complete mobile reserve S.A.A., Grenades etc: will be carried on wheels.

4. **ADVANCE PARTY.**
   Lieut A.T.G.Hughes (A/Adjt) and the 4 Coy Qmr Sgts and Cpl Hall (representing Battn H.Q.) will rendezvous at Battalion Ord: Room at 6-15 a.m. and will precede the Battalion to TETESNEY and take over billets there.
   This party will meet the Staff Captain at the Area Commandant's Office, FORNHOUDT at 8 a.m. This party must be able to ride cycles, and be in possession of exact numbers of their Companies etc: required to be billeted.

5. **SANITATION.**
   Lieut C.B.Cooper will be i/c charge of a rear party composed as for to-days march. Party to rendezvous at Battalion Headquarters at 9 a.m. under Lieut Cooper when they will proceed to inspect the vacated billets and clean up any which are found to be unsatisfactory. A certificate of cleanliness to be obtained from the Area Commandant. This party will then proceed to the Quartermaster's stores and assist in loading the motor lorry and proceed on the same on the last trip, Lieut Cooper to report to the Adjt immediately on arrival.

6. **KITS & SURPLUS BAGGAGE.**
   All Officers Kits, Mess stores etc: will be stacked at each Company and Battalion Headquarters by 7-30 a.m. and will be collected by the T.O. at that same hour.

7. **ACKNOWLEDGE.**

[signature]
CAPTAIN,
ADJUTANT.
1/10th Manchester Regiment,

Copies to all recipients
of O.O.No 21.

OPERATION ORDER No 22.
by
Major W.R.PEEL. D.S.O. Commanding 1/10th Manchester Regiment.
Ref: Map FURNES 1/20000.   Sept 23rd, 1917.

1. The 125th Infy Brigade will relieve the 198th Inf: B'de in the
   COXYDE-BAINS COAST DEFENCE SECTOR on the 24/9/17, all reliefs to be
   completed by 11 a.m.

2. The 1/10th Manchester Regiment will relieve the 2/10th Manchester Regt
   at present located in billets and defensive works, with Headquaters in
   VILLE DES MOERES.

3. The relief will be as follows:-
   "D" Coy 1/10th Manch: Regt will relieve "D" Coy 2/10th Manchester Regt
   in posts 1 to 6 inclusive.
   "C" Coy 1/10th Manch: Regt will relieve "A" Coy 2/10th Manchester Regt
   in posts 7 to 9 inclusive.
   "B" Coy will relieve "B" Coy in billets.
   "A" " "   "   "   "C" "   "   "

4. O.C. "C" & "D" Coys and 1 N.C.O. (per Coy) for each post will report to
   2/10 th Battalion H.Q. at 7 a.m. to-morrow and will arrange details of
   relief with the O.C. Coys they are relieving.
   "C" & "D" Coys will march off at 7-20 a.m. and will arrive at 2/10th
   H.Q. at 8 a.m. where they will meet guides who will conduct them to
   their respective Sectors.
   "A" & "B" Coys and Battalion H.Q. will march off at 8-20 a.m. and will
   march straight to their billets.
   The Signalling Officer & 7 Signallers will report at 2/10th Batt'n
   H.Q. at 7 a.m.
   LEWIS GUN LIMBERS will accompany the Companies.

5. Distances of 200 yards between Coys and columns of Train upest of
   equivalent length will be maintained during the march.

6. The A/Adjt will arrange for Batt'n H.Q. and Companies to be met at the
   entrance to the village and to be guided to their respective billets.
   Completion of reliefs to be at once notified to Batt'n H.Q. on taking
   over.

7. All Defence Schemes, Trench and Area Stores, Secret Maps, Aeroplane P
   Photographs etc: will be taken over and receipts given.
   Such receipts to be sent to Battalion Orderly Room.

8. ACKNOWLEDGE.

Copies to all recipients   (Signed)
of WARNING ORDER.   J.C.S.ROWBOTHAM,   CAPTAIN.
                                                        ADJUTANT.

ADMINISTRATIVE Instructions ISSUED TO ACCOMPANY OPERATION
ORDER No 55. Dated 22/6/17.

1. **TRANSPORT.**
The Transport will march under the orders of Transport Officer arriving at their destination on the first trip not earlier than 9 a.m. Baggage wagons will report Batt'n H.Q. at 8 a.m. to-morrow morning and will march with the Regtl Transport, after loading.
After unloading they will return to the ROCK A.S.C.
No motor lorries are available for this unit.
The Quartermaster will arrange to guard any stores which cannot be taken on the first trip and these will be returned for by 1st & 2nd line Transport immediately after unloading on the 1st trip.

2. The Quartermaster will notify the Transport Officer on the Battalion marching out what transport he requires to remove remaining stores. The R.S.M. will detail a loading party to report to the Quartermaster under arrangements to be made by Qmr.

3. Officer's Kits, Mess Paniers etc; will be stacked at Coy and Batt'n H.Q. by 7-00 a.m. and the Transport Officer will arrange to collect the same, and deliver.

4. **Rear Party.**
Lieut C.H.Cooper,(18.C.G. per Coy(to be detailed by O.C. Coys) and 2 Light Duty men per Coy will act as rear party and remain behind to clean up the camp and assist in loading baggage.
Lieut Cooper will obtain the usual certificates of Cleanliness from the Area Commandant.
This party will rendezvous at Battalion Orderly Room at 8-30 a.m.

5. **AMMUNITION.**
While in the line the mobile Reserve of S.A.A. & Grenades etc; will remain on wheels at the transport lines, and all S.A.A. & Grenades etc; will be taken over.
Copies of receipts to be sent to Batt'n H.Q.

6. **GUARDS & DUTIES.**
O.C.Coys will arrange to relieve any small guards, police duties etc: previously found by the Coy they relieve.

7. REVEILLE. will be at 5-30 a.m.
BREAKFAST " " " 6-15 a.m.
SICK PARADE. will be at a time to be notified later, on arrival in the new area.

8. The water Cpl will report to the Adjutant on arrival in La PASSE to be pointed out positions of all water points.
On receipt of this information he will arrange to fill the water cart immediately.

(Signed) A.C.P.HIGGOTHAM. CAPTAIN.
ADJUTANT.

1/10 Manchester
Vol 9

On His Majesty's Service.

D. A. G.
3rd Echelon
Rouen.

WAR DIARY

of

1/10th MANCHESTER REGIMENT.

Kept by Lieut F. Howarth. (Intelligence Officer) the Officer detailed by the O.C. for that purpose.

From October 1st to 31st. 1914.

Vol XXV

Army Form C. 2118.

WAR DIARY
or
INTELLIGENCE SUMMARY.
(Erase heading not required.)

Instructions regarding War Diaries and Intelligence Summaries are contained in F. S. Regs., Part II. and the Staff Manual respectively. Title pages will be prepared in manuscript.

Place	Date 1917 October	Hour	Summary of Events and Information	Remarks and references to Appendices
LA PANNE	1st		2 Companies on Coast Defence. Training from 9am to 12.30pm Physical Drill for A & B Coy attached to R.E.s	Map Sheet 11 OOST DUNKERKE
-do-	2nd		2 Coys on Coast Defence usual training	-do-
-do-	3rd		2 Coys on Coast Defence usual training	-do-
-do-	4th		} 2 Coys on Coast Defence	-do-
-do-	5th		}	-do-
-do-	6th		Coys on Coast Defence. Advance party left for NIEUPORT to take over from the 2nd Batt. R. Leicester Regiment. Battalion do usual drill	-do-
COXYDE	7th	10AM	Battalion moved from LA PANNE to Australia Camp COXYDE arriving for Lunch. Men proceeded to NIEUPORT B Coy on right, D Coy left, B Coy in support & A in reserve. Voluntary church service.	-do-
NIEUPORT	8th		Front more or less Quiet. Usual work done, cleaning of trenches etc No casualties	Sheet 12.SWD BELGIUM 1/20000
-do-	9th		Very Quiet. Cleared up Gap thro general work on trenches. Weather improving wind in East.	-do-
-do-	10th		Fairly Quiet. NIEUPORT about Batt HQ was heavily shelled during the afternoon Work on cleaning trenches & digging sump holes	-do-
-do-	11th		Quiet day. Battalion relieved by 1/5th East Lancs Regt. & proceeded to OOST DUNKERKE when they went into billets.	Map Sheet 11 OOST DUNKERKE
OOST DUNKERKE	12.		Day spent in cleaning up & resting	-do-

Haworth Knott
Lt. Col. 1/10th Batt. Manchester Regt.

Army Form C. 2118.

WAR DIARY
or
~~INTELLIGENCE SUMMARY~~
(Erase heading not required.)

Instructions regarding War Diaries and Intelligence Summaries are contained in F.S. Regs., Part II. and the Staff Manual respectively. Title pages will be prepared in manuscript.

Place	Date Oct	Hour	Summary of Events and Information	Remarks and references to Appendices
OOST DUNKERKE	13th		Battalion hard at work of Generally cleaning 9 up.	Sheet 11 OOST DUNKERKE
-do-	14th		Boys parade for bathing in the morning & baths in the afternoon.	-do-
-do-	15th		Voluntary Holy Communion Church service. Afternoon paraded to relieve 1/5th East Lancs Regt in NIEUPORT. Relief safely carried out, Coys taking over turn out.	-do-
NIEUPORT	16th		Enemy Quiet but usual shelling of NIEUPORT ie HF & gas shells	Sheet 12 S.W. BELGIUM 1/20000
-do-	17th		Quiet Day nothing out of the ordinary occurring.	-do-
-do-	18th		Day was very Quiet but towards evening enemy put a fair number of Gas shells over. Was relieved by 1/5th East Lancs Regt. relief was complete by about midnight & companies marched down to WULPEN	Sheet 11 OOST DUNKERKE
WULPEN.	19th 20th 21st		Battalion in billets at WULPEN. Companies Spent the day in cleaning up & bathing. Working parties go up to NIEUPORT each evening by barge for work on the line	-do-
-do-	22nd		Battalion relieved 1/5th East Lancs Regt in the NIEUPORT line. Relief completed about 11.30 pm	Sheet 12 S.W. BELGIUM 1/20000
NIEUPORT	23.		Battalion in the line, nothing to report. Capt C.E. HIGHAM from 1/7th Lancashire Regt. joined for duty on HQrs vice Major L.C.WILDE, D.S.O. to ENGLAND.	-do-
-do-	24 25		Battalion in the line, Very Quiet. Work on trenches	-do-

Howarth Lieut
O./1/10th Batt Manchester R.

Apr 21. Wt. w1251g/M1297. 750,000. 1/17. D.D & L., Ltd. Forms/C2118/14.

Army Form C. 2118.

WAR DIARY
or
INTELLIGENCE SUMMARY.
(Erase heading not required.)

Instructions regarding War Diaries and Intelligence Summaries are contained in F. S. Regs., Part II. and the Staff Manual respectively. Title pages will be prepared in manuscript.

1917

Place	Date Oct.	Hour	Summary of Events and Information	Remarks and references to Appendices
NIEUPORT	26		Battalion relieved by the 1/5th East Lancs Regt. & Platoon marched down to billets in OOST DUNKERKE.	Sheet 11 OOST DUNKERKE —do—
OOST DUNKERKE	27 28 29		Battalion stood their time in bathing, cleaning up & physical training	
NIEUPORT	30		The Battalion relieved the 1/5th Batt. East Lancs Regt. & took over the same line as previously. Relief complete.	Sheet 12 SW BELGIUM 1/20000
—do—	31	9.45pm	Quiet day; nothing to report.	

1/11/14

Chateau Major
Commandg 9/4th Lancashire Regiment

OPERATION ORDER NO 24.
by
Lt. Colonel W.A.Smith.D.S.O. Commanding 1/10th Manchester Regiment.
October 5th, 1917.
Ref: Map Sheet 11, WEST DUNKIRKE. 1/20000.

1. The 126th Infy Brigade will be relieved on the 6th inst: in the NORTH BAINS COAST DEFENCE SECTOR by the 124th Infy Brigade.
   Reliefs will be completed by 12 noon.

2. On completion of relief the 1/10th Manchester Regt will be in Divisn'l Reserve to 32nd Division.

3. On the night of the 6/7th inst: the 126th Infy Brigade (less 126th M.G. Coy) will relieve the 14th Infy Brigade in the Right Section of the NIEUPORT SECTOR.

4. All details of relief will be arranged by the O.C's concerned.

5. The 1/10th Manchester Regt will be relieved by the 21st K.R.R.C. in the Left Sector. Times and order of relief as follows:-
   "C" Coy 21st K.R.R.C. will relieve "C" 1/10th Manchester Regt in left Sect
   "A"   "   "   "   "   "   "D"   "   "   "   "   " right "
   "B & D" " "   "   "   "   "A & B" "   "   "   "   " Billets
                                              vacated by them.

6. On relief companies will en-bus for COXYDE DUNKIRKE.
   Buses will be at Battalion Headquarters at 10-30 a.m.
   Each bus will accommodate 30 other ranks.
   2/Lieut F.Eggitt will superintend the bussing of the Battalion.

7. The following guides will be found to guide relieving posts.
   8 guides by "C" Coy at Coy Post at 8-45 a.m.
   8   "   " "D" "   "   "   " 8-50 a.m.
   Batt'n H.Q.& 2 Coys in billets will each have a guide at Batt'n H.Q. at
   9-15 a.m.

8. The working party ("A" & "B" Coys) found by this unit will be relieved at 4 p.m. to-day by a similar party from the 31st. Division.
   On relief these companies will proceed by march route to billets in LA PANNE.

9. An advanced party composed as under will proceed to the H.Q. of the 2nd. Manchester Regt. arriving by 10 p.m. to-day where they will pick up instructions regarding the Coys, to be relieved by the companies of this unit.
   The latter information will be left by the commanding Officer this morning.
   This party will rendezvous as follows:-
   Batt'n H.Q. & "D" Coys. at Batt'n H.Q. 5 p.m.
   "A" & "B" Coys.   " MONT BLANC SECTION at 5 p.m.
   These parties should be equipped for the line.
      Batt'n H.Q.   2/Lt.Garvy R.H. and Scout Cpl.
      "A" Coy.   "   Salt S.   " 1 N.C.O. per Platoon.
      "B" "   "   Pearce H.J. "   "   "   "
      "C" "   "   Morris S.G. "   "   "   "
      "D" "   "   Howarth T. "   "   "   "

10. All trench stores will be taken over and receipts(in triplicate) will be obtained, such receipts will be forwarded to Batt'n H.Q. immediately for transmission to Brigade Headquarters.
    No maps are to be handed over on relief except those containing special information desired.

11. Completion of reliefs will be notified at once to Batt'n H.Q. the word "BUCK" being used.

12. Marching out states will be rendered to Company H.Q. before moving off.

13. ACKNOWLEDGE.

                                                    Captain.
                                                    Adjutant.
October 5th, 1917.
Issued as confirmation of WARNING ORDER.

1/10th. Manchester Regiment.
Addendum No1. to Administrative Instructions.   October 5th. 1917.

1. 2/Lt. Drewitan F.L. and 4.C.Q.M.S. will rendezvous Batt'n H.Q. at 9 a.m. to-morrow to proceed to AUSTRALIA CAMP, where they will meet the Buses on arrival and allot Coy's Areas.
Care will be taken to keep the road clear of men and Buses opposite the camp.

1st.Line Transport will leave by road at 9 a.m. with all S.A.A., Grenades Tools etc.

"A" & "B" Coys. will arrange to load the 4 Guns & 2 Guns respectively at the Transport Lines to-night without fail and 1 Lewis Gun per Section will accompany these Guns to unload at the other end.

The Maltese Cart will proceed as soon as loaded.

Blankets of "A" & "B" Coys properly rolled in bundles of 10 will be dumped at the Gazino by 8-30 a.m.

All "C" companies Stores will be stacked at Batt'n H.Q. by 8-30 a.m.

All anti-aircraft Sights and Mountings for Lewis Guns will accompany these Guns and will not be handed over.

[signature]
Captain.
Adjutant.

1/10th. Manchester Regiment,

Addendum No.2. to Operation Order No.34.

October 5th, 1917.

1. 30 Motor Lorries for the Transport of this Unit to AUSTRALIA CAMP will arrive at the cross roads W.20.b.88. at 10 a.m. to-morrow the 6th.inst.

   2nd/Lt.Eggott and 6 O.R. to be detailed by the R.S.M. will rendezvous at Batt'n H.Q.at 9-15 a.m, and proceed to the above mentioned cross roads to guide the lorries to these Headquarter One guide will be detailed to every 6 Lorries and 1 guide left to with the traffic man at this corner to direct all Lorries. These Lorries will be lead to these H.Q. via the road passing through W.14.d. 0.3. - W.14.b. 4.2. and should be halted in groups of 6, each six lorries to occupy a space of 80 yards to allow of Transport passing. Two lorries may be used to convey surplus Baggage from Q.Mr Stores to new site, but these must be unloaded at once and returned to Corps Park. *The Qmr will inform Lt Haslewood if he requires these lorries.*
   Lieut.W.A.Haslewood will act as embussing Officer in accordance with separate instructions issued herewith.

2. Refilling Point will be at W.17.d. 6.3.

3. Salvage Dumps are established at:-

Divnl.H.Q.	W.6.c.2.7.
Canada Camp	W.18.b.9.6.
Coxyde	X 14.a.3.5.
Coat Dunkerke	X 4. c.4.4.
Zouave Road	S.3.a.4.7.
Wulpen Road.	S.9.a.1.8.

   J Selwyn Rowbotham
   Captain
   Adjutant
   1/10th. Manchester Regiment.

1/10th. Manchester Regiment,

Addendum No. 2. to Operation Order No. 34.

October 5th, 1917.

1. 30 Motor Lorries for the Transport of this Unit to AUSTRALIA CAMP will arrive at the cross roads W.20.b.88. at 10 a.m. to-morrow the 6th.inst.

2nd/Lt. Eggett and 6 O.R. to be detailed by the R.S.M. will rendezvous at Batt'n H.Q. at 9-15 a.m, and proceed to the above mentioned cross roads to guide the lorries to these Headquarters. One guide will be detailed to every 6 Lorries and 1 guide left to with the traffic man at this corner to direct all Lorries. These Lorries will be lead to these H.Q. via the road passing through W.14.d. 0.3. - W.14.b. 4.2. and should be sited in groups of 6, each six lorries to occupy a space of 80 yards to allow of Transport passing. Two lorries may be used to convey surplus Baggage from Q.Mr Stores to new site, but these must be unloaded at once and returned to Corps Park. The QM will inform Lieut Haslewood if he requires these lorries Lieut. W.A. Haslewood will act as embussing Officer in accordance with seperate instructions issued herewith.

2. Refilling Point will be at W.17.d. 6.3.

3. Salvage Dumps are established at:-

    Divnl. H.Q.   W.6.c.2.7.
    Canada Camp   W.18.b.2.6.
    Coxyde   X 14.a.3.5.
    Oost Dunkerke   X 4. c.4.4.
    Zonave Road   C.3.a.4.7.
    Wulpen Road.   H.9.a.1.8.

                 J C Selwyn Rowbotham
                   Captain
                   Adjutant
               1/10th. Manchester Regiment.

Administrative Orders In Accordance with Operation Orders No.34.

October 5th.1917.

1. **BAGGAGE.**
    Officers kits and Mess Stores will be stacked outside the Officers mess in Rue des Ancres by 10 a.m. Canteen Stores will be stacked outside the Canteen at the same time.

2. **LEWIS GUNS AND S.A.A.**
    All Lewis Guns and spare parts will be dumped outside the officers mess by 9-30 a.m. and will be carried on the Busses.
    Lewis Gun Magazines S.A.A. etc. Orderly Room boxes will be loaded on Transport at Orderly Room at 10 a.m.

3. **CLEANLINESS:Certificates of;**
    Company Commanders will obtain from the relieving companies Certificates(in duplicate) of cleanliness of all Huts,Dug-outs,Billets and Trenches handed over. The certificates to be handed in to Batt'n Orderly Room before embussing. Lieut,Hasleweed will obtain certificate of cleanliness from(in duplicate) for Officers Mess.

4. **R.E.MATERIAL**
    R.S.M. will obtain receipts in triplicate for all material handed over to the relieving unit.

Captain
Adjutant.
1/10th.Manchester Regiment.

Copies to all recipients of
Operation Orders No.34.

BATTALION ORDERS No. 78.by

Lieut.Colonel W.G.Peel D.S.O. Commanding 1/10 Manchester Regiment.

October 8th.1917.

1. The Battalion will relieve the 2nd.Manchester Regt, in the St.Georges sector on night of 8/9th.October.

2. A.Coy.will relieve A Coy. 2nd.Manchester Regt.
   B.Coy. "   "   B   "   "   "   "
   C.Coy.will relieve C   "   "   "   "
   D.Coy will relieve D   "   "   "   "

3. O.C."A" Coy will arrange to relieve the 2 Machine Guns of the 51st Machine Gun Company of the 51st. at N.35.a.8.7. with two of his Lewis Guns.

4. Companies must be ready to march off from AUSTRALIA CAMP at 5 p.m. on the 8th.inst. Companies will march off in the following order;
   H.Q.R.A.P., Sgts. R.E.Stretcher Bearers, 200yds.interval will be maintained between Platoons.
   Dress.---- Full marching order, Greatcoats in sacks.
   Head of column will not pass WULPEN BRIDGE before 5 p.m.
   Route.

5. Guides 1 per Platoon and R.Hrs. will meet the Battalion at Bawge Bridge.

6. LEWIS GUNS.
   Lewis Guns will be carried in limbers to TRIPAN DUMP.
   The limbers will march at the head of the leading platoon of each Company.
   Companies must ensure that there is no delay at unloading these limbers AT TRIPAN DUMP. In view of the rain these Limbers may precede the Limbers and not accompany it.

7. Officers Mess Stores will come up with Rations to TRIPAN DUMP. Ration Limbers will follow the Battalion to TRIPAN DUMP. The meat Ration will be taken in the Cookhouses. The dry ration and breakfast ration will be issued before leaving camp/DR and will be carried on the men. This does not apply to A Coy & L.Gns. Their rations will be drawn from the dump.
   O.C."A"Coy.will detail sufficient men to carry up water to C.& D.Coy as soon as they arrive and Tea for Breakfast and the Midday meal in sufficient time to deliver it before dawn.
   O.C's B.C.D.Coys will send guides to O.C."A" Coy for these parties.
   Headquarters will arrange to draw their own rations from the Dump.

8. The following will be issued to Companies at AUSTRALIA CAMP.

   S.Cartridges.

9. O.C.Companies will forward as soon as possible duplicate Receipts of all Trench Stores taken over.

10. Each Coy will send one runner to H.Q. who can guide H.Q's runners to their respective Companies.

11. Companies will ensure that every man fills his water bottle at AUSTRALIA CAMP before marching off.

12. Dinners at AUSTRALIA CAMP will be at 4-30 p.m.

13. Completion of relief to be reported to Battalion Hqrs. by Code words PARADE.

14. Casualties will be evacuated from Regimental Aid Post to the Advanced Dressing Station at N.34.a.8.0.

15. All dead will be evacuated for burial under Battalion arrangements, and will be buried at GODWIN Military Cemetery. Battalion Hqrs.must be notified at once when any such require burial,when transport will be arranged.

J.Selwyn Rowbotham
Captain & Adjutant.

1/10th.Battalion Manchester Regiment.

October 7th.1917.

REPORT.

To O.C. 1/9th.Manchester Regiment.

A patrol will proceed from the trench at M 30.d.6.6. at 9-45 P.M. to-night the 7th.inst. and proceed along the track in 25.W. in a Northerly direction with a view to ascertaining if this track is still passable and how far patrols can proceed toward the enemy wire. ~~somewhere~~
Patrols will return the same way, approximate time of return cannot definately be stated.
Please warn all concerned.

[signature]
for Lieut Col.Commanding 1/10th,
Captain & Adjutant,
Manchester Regiment.

7/10/17.

"Copy"

1/10th. Manchester Regiment.

October 7th, 1917.

To Quartermaster:-

1. The Commanding Officer wishes you to make every endeavour to obtain clean socks as often as possible, for at any rate B.C.& D.Coys; in view of the bad weather, the Brigade or the Divn'l Laundry may be able to supply you, or failing them Ordnance.

2. Please send up 1 doz stout pint bottles to issue whale oil to the front Platoons.

3. Also indent for 6 Latrine Seats and send up as soon as possible.

4. The Doctor is arranging to send down all empty tins from the cook-house on the empty ration limbers, to be incinerated.

5. Could a further supply of Whale Oil be obtained.

6. Also arrange to draw the 25 tins of Solidified Alcohol daily from Brigade.

Captain.
Adjutant.
1/10th. Manchester Regiment.

SECRET.   COPY.

B.M.50/135.

o.c.1/10th Manchester Regt.

1. 1/4th E.Lancs Regt will arrange for a party of 200 men (minimum working strength) to report to Lieut NUNLIN R.E. at TRIGAR DUMP at 8-30 p.m. to-night for work on front line defences in the Left Batt'n Sector. The officers who took part in the reconnaissance this morning in the company of Major RIDDICK 428th Fld Coy R.E. should be in charge of this party.

2. Battalions in the line will concentrate on wiring of their line wherever this is necessary. In the case of the Left Batt's particular importance is given to the wiring of the front between the PAASSCHENDAELE CANAL and HIGH POST.

(SIGNED) E.SANDERSON, Captain,
B'de Major.
126th Infy Brigade.

October 8th,1917.

---2---

To:T.4. " " Coy.

For information.

Captain,
Adjutant.

1/10th MANCHESTER REGIMENT.

WARNING ORDER.

October 9th 1917.

1. The Battalion will be relieved by the 1/5th Batt. East Lancs. Regiment on the night of 9th/10th October 1917.

2. Advance Party will proceed to DOMT CURREQUE and take over the Camp & Billets occupied by the relieving Battalion. O.C.P.C's will meet Lieut R.E.T.HUFFER at the 1/5th Batt. East Lancs Hd-Qrs at 11 a.m. to-morrow.

3. Dinners will be carried up at 5-30 p.m.
O.C. "A" Company will arrange to collect all petrol tins and containers at the Cookhouse directly dinners are issued.

4. Lewis Gun limbers will be at VMIGAR DUMP at 10 p.m. Companies will leave 4 Lewis Gunners to load the same.

Captain & Adjutant
1/10th Manchester Regiment.

Reference Operation Order No, 36. by
Lieut-Col. W.R. PEEL. Commanding 1/10th Battalion Manchester Regiment.

Para 2 should read as follows:- October 20th 19

"A" Company will be relived by "B" Coy 1/5th. East Lancs Regt.
"B"   "   "   "   "   " "D" "   "   "   "   "   "
"C"   "   "   "   "   " "C" "   "   "   "   "   "
"D"   "   "   "   "   " "A" "   "   "   "   "   "

J Chelwyn Rowbotham
Captain & Adjutant.
1/10th. Manchester Regiment.

October 10th. 1917.

OPERATION ORDER No. P.59

By Lieut Col R.J. PARR. D.S.O. commanding 1/10th Manchester Regiment.

Ref: Map YPRES Sheet Areas 1/20000.   October 10th, 1917.

1. The Battalion will be relieved by the 8th East Lancs Regt on night of 10/11th October.

2. "A" Coy will be relieved by "D" Coy 1/8th East Lancs Regt.
   "B" "   " "   "   " "A" "   "   "   "   "
   "C" "   " "   "   " "C" "   "   "   "   "
   "D" "   " "   "   " "B" "   "   "   "   "

3. Each Coy will arrange for a guide to conduct the two Lewis Gun Teams of the relieving Coy to the position L.G.A.A./S an Officer should go with this party.

4. "A" Coys will each detail:-
        1 guide per platoon.
        1   "   " Coy Headquarters.
   to report at Battalion H.Q. at 7 p.m.

5. Companies on completion of relief will proceed by EAST POPERINGHE via RAILWAY SIDING and WIPPER Bridge where R.S.M. & Gpts will meet Companies. 200 yards will be maintained between Platoons.

6. The Lewis Gun Teams in POTSDAM & BORRY FARM Posts and right post of "A" Coy will be relieved by three Lewis Gun Teams of "D" Coy 1/8th E.L. Regt at dawn, these teams will be conducted to "D" Coy's B.H.Q. by Batt'n R.S.M. guides.
   Lieut A.GIBB and 2/Lieut R.J.WALKER will arrange to meet these teams and conduct them to their respective posts. Lieut GIBB will leave at A.M.A. with each team at POTSDAM and BORRY POINTS LEWIS till dawn.
   Lieut GIBB will also remain in the line until the evening of 11th October. The teams relieved will at once proceed to "D" Coy's B.H.Qrs where they will have their dinners. They will proceed with R.S.M. Coy to EAST POPERINGHE Lieut GIBB will have guides at "D" Coy's B.G.'s conduct the relieving unit Rifle and Bombing Sections to BORRY POINTS FARM and POLESE Farm.

7. Lewis Gun Limbers will be outside the Cookhouses at 10 p.m. Companies will leave their guns at this point with 2 gunners per Company who will load the guns and proceed to EAST POPERINGHE with the Limbers.

8. O.C. "A" Coy will arrange to relieve 2 anti-aircraft guns of the 8th East Lancs in RED DOT. A guide will conduct O.C. "A" Coy to these guns in the evening of the 10th inst. Relief will be completed by dawn. The 2 relieved Lewis Gun Teams of the 8th East Lancs Regt will be conducted to "D" Coy's B.H.Q. where they will be met by Lieut GIBB and 2/Lieut FOSTER. 2 days rations for the 2 teams of "A" Coy will be brought up on night of the 10th inst.

9. O.C.Coys will ensure that all schemes for engt. defences and patrol reports are carefully explained to the incoming unit.

10. Duplicate receipts for Trench Stores etc; will be forwarded to Orderly Room as soon as possible.

11. Officers Trench Kits, Mess Stores, Patrol Kits, Pixies, and Scoland Stoves will be dumped by the Cookhouses as soon after dark as possible. O.C."A" Coy will arrange to load these stores on limbers.

                                                J C Lemoyn Rowbotham
                                                    Captain & Adjutant.

October 10th, 1917.

Copies to all recipients of warning order
and extra copy to:-
    O.C.1/8th East Lancs Regt.
    Lieut A.GIBB.
    2/Lieut R.J.WALKER.

WAR DIARY

SECRET.   OPERATION ORDER No. 58.
by Lieut-Colonel W.R. PEEL, D.S.O. Commanding 1/10th. Manchester Regiment.
                                                    October 17th, 1917.
Ref. Maps 4 & 8 1/10000.

1. The Battalion will be relieved by the 5th.E.L.Regt. on the night of 18/19th. October 1917.

2. Companies will be relieved as follows:-

   "D" Company by "B" Company 5th.E.L.Regt.
   "C"   "   " "D"   "   "   "   "
   "B"   "   " "C"   "   "   "   "
   "A"   "   " "A"   "   "   "   "

3. O.C.Companies will send guides 1 per Coy Hqrs & 1 per Platoon to meet the relieving unit as follows:-

   (1) 4 Guides from "D" Coy to meet "B"Coy 5th.E.L.Regt. close to WHITE HOUSE at 7-30 p.m. Guides to be at this point at 7 p.m.

   (2) 8   "   "   "C" "   "   " 2 Platoons of "D"Coy 5th.E.L.Regt. going to PARIS ALLEY AVENUE & OLD ALLEY at WHITE HOUSE at 7-30 p.m. Guides to be at this point at 7 p.m.

   (3) 8   "   "   "B" "   "   " Hqrs & 1 platoon "C"Coy 5th.E.L.Regt. going to BRICKSTACKS & GUN AVENUE at ELIZABETH BRIDGE at 8 p.m. Guides to be at this point at 7-30 p.m.

   (4) 4   "   "   "B" "   "   " "D"Coy & 1 L.Gun team "A"Coy 5th.E.L. Regt. to go to GUN AVENUE at ELIZABETH BRIDGE at 8 p.m. Guides to be at this point at 7-30 p.m.

   (5) 4   "   "   "A" "   "   " "A"Coy 5th.E.L.Regt. as for (4).

4. On completion of relief Companies will march independently to WULPEN by platoons at 200 yards interval.
   ROUTE:- ELIZABETH BRIDGE.   PELICAN BRIDGE.

5. The following party will relieve a similar party of the 5th.E.L.Regt. at TRIGAR DUMP.
        1 Officer.   30 O.R.   "A" Company.
   O.C."A"Company will arrange to take over the Dug-outs from the 5th.E.L. Regt. and all work etc. Rations for the above party will be delivered at TRIGAR DUMP at 6 p.m.
   O.C."A"Coy will keep two cooks & 1 Sanitary man & 2 Stretcher Bearers and the necessary dixies.

6. L.M.G. limbers will be at TRIGAR DUMP at 11 p.m.
   O.C.Companies will each arrange to have 4 men to load these guns.
   Sergt. Bradshaw will superintend the loading, and will accompany the party and limbers to WULPEN.
   The Transport Officer will detail sufficient limbers to take back the dixies, petrol tins, etc. except those mentioned in para. 5 above.
   These limbers will be at TRIGAR DUMP at 6 p.m.
   The Mess cart & Maltese cart will report at Battn. Hqrs at 6 p.m.

7. An advanced party composed of the 4 C.Q.M.S. under Lieut. Hughes will report to the Hqrs. of 5th.E.L.Regt. at 2 p.m. 18th.Oct. to take over billets. Lieut. Hughes will arrange for guides to meet the Battn. at the entrance of WULPEN VILLAGE. He will ascertain what fatigues, guards, Anti aircraft positions and full particulars of all working parties to be found.

8. The Quartermaster will arrange for the Battn. to have baths commencing at 9 a.m. on Oct.19th. He will if necessary use the Drummers to work these baths. He will arrange to draw clean clothing on the 18th.inst.
                            continued.

"2"

8.(continued)

All officers kits and blankets will be taken to WULPEN before the arrival of the Battalion.

9. The Quartermaster will arrange to have hot tea or soup for the Battn., less the party mentioned in para., 5 on arrival in billets.

10.
Trench stores will be handed over, and receipts obtained. Copies will be forwarded to Battn.,Hqrs., by noon on the 18th.Inst., also certificates as regards cleanliness etc.

11.
O.C."A"Coy will arrange to hand over 28 Food containers & 96 Petrol Tins to O.C."A"Coy 5th.E.L.Regt.

12.
Gum Boots will be stacked at Company Hqrs., with the exception of those at HOOGE REDOUBT & FIRBIT FARMS. These will be handed over at the Farms. O.C.Companies will ensure that the gum boots are properly tied in pairs and placed in a convenient position at their Hqrs., for the incoming unit.

13.
Completion of relief will be reported by wire to Battn.,Hqrs.,by code words RATIONS ISSUED,and by runner on arrival in Billets.

October 17th.,1917.

Captain & Adjutant,
1/10th.Battalion Manchester Regiment.

Operation Order No 57? Lt-Col V.R.PERL D.S.O.
Commanding 1/10th.Battalion Manchester Regiment.
October 12th.1917

Map Sheet No 44B. 1/10000.

1. The Battalion will relieve the 1/5th.Batt.East Lancs.Regiment in the left sub sector of the ST. QUENTIN sector on the night 14/15th.October.

2. Firing Line:-
    "W" Coy will relieve "A" Coy 5th.East Lancs. Regt.
    "X" "   "   "   "B" "   "   "   "   "
   Support Line:-
    "Y" "   "   "   "C" "   "   "   "   "
   Reserve:-
    "Z" "   "   "   "D" "   "   "   "   "

   Companies will move in the following order:-
    "W" Company & M.G. & Personnel.
    "X" Company.
    "Y" Company less 1 Platoon.
    "Z" Company less 2 Platoons.
    Headquarters.

   "W" Company will start at 5-30 p.m. 200 yard intervals will be maintained between platoons.
   Route:-
        WOLFED BRIDGE, PELICAN BRIDGE, ELIZABETH BRIDGE.

3. GUIDES.
        1 guide per platoon and 1 guide per company Headquarters will meet the Battalion at ELIZABETH BRIDGE.

4. The 2 Lewis Gun teams of "A" Company, the 1 Section of Bombers & 1 Section of Rifle Grenadiers to take over the posts at WOODS FRONT FARM and GOLDEN FANTAIL REDOUT at 5th.East Lancs. Headquarters at 7 p.m., where they will be met by a guide who will conduct them to the Posts. An officer should be in charge of this party.

5. The three A.A.Guns of "A" Company will report at Battn.Hqrs., 5th.East Lancs.Regt. at 7-15 p.m. 2 Guns will be met here by a guide who will conduct them to the position in HUN AVENUE at 8.30.a.C.V. The remaining team will go to Reserve Coys Head Quarters and await the arrival of "A" Company.

6. The Lewis Gun limbers will rendezvous at the Main Cross Roads COSY CORNER ROUX at 5-30 p.m. and proceed under Lieut.Howarth to TRIVAN DUMP where they will unload. 4 Lewis Gunners per company will accompany the guns of each Company. Lieut.Howarth will arrange that the guns are properly stacked by the wayside so that there will be no delay when companys arrive.

7. The positions of A.A. guns in the neighbourhood of COSY CORNER will be handed over to the representatives of the incoming unit (4th.East Lancashire Regt.) These guns will be withdrawn at 4-30 p.m.

8. The Mess cart,Maltese Cart and 1 Limber will report at Battalion Headquarters at 5 p.m. These together with the Ration Limbers & Limbers carrying Hooker Minies & Patrol Kits,will follow last platoon.

9. Dress for the trenches will be full marching order less haversacks. The following articles will be carried in the packs:-
        Greatcoat, cardigan, towel, 1 pair of socks, ground sheet, holdall, soap, iron ration and dry ration for the following day.
   Surplus kit to the above will be packed in the haversack.

10. Blankets rolled in bundles of 10 securely tied and labelled,& haversacks clearly marked with owners name will be stacked outside Company Orderly Rooms by 3 p.m. The Q.M. will make arrangements to collect and carry these to the Q.M.Stores.

11. All trench stores will be taken over and receipts given. O.C. "A" Company will be responsible for taking over petrol tins and SAA boxes containers at the dockhouse near INDIAN DUMP. Copies of receipts will be forwarded to Battn. Hqrs. by noon on the 18th inst.

12. O.C. Companies will forward the exact dispositions of their companies by 12 noon 18th inst.

13. The Battalion Signallers, 4 scouts & 2 Batt'n. Runners will proceed under Lieut. Harry to report at Battn. Hqrs. 20th East Lancs. Regt. at 5.30 p.m.
Lieut. Harry will take over all Battn. Stores.
O.C. Companies will each detail 1 N.C.O. to proceed with Lieut Harry to the day Headquarters they are relieving, to check Trench Stores being handed over &c.

14. Completion of relief will be wired to Battalion Headquarters by one word "RATIONS".

J. Chelwyn Rowbotham

October 12th, 1917.

Captain & Adjutant.
1/10th. Battalion Manchester Regiment.

File

1/10th. Battalion Manchester Regiment.
                                                October 21st.1917.
To:- O.C. Companies,   )
     " 1/5th East Lancs   )
     Lieut Bohlin 428th R.E.) for information.

Carrying parties and working parties required for to-night are as
follows:-
1st Party. "C" Coy 2.Officers & 50 o.r. & 2 S.Bearers with Stretcher

This party will parade at Battalion Orderly Room at 7-15 p.m. to proceed
under the Senior Officer by march route to Tricar Dump reporting to
Headquarters 1/5th East Lancs Regt at the CAPRICORNE SUPPORT en
route. This party will carry rations and material for this Batt'n.

2nd. Party.
              1 Officer & 50 other ranks of "B" Coy,and 2 S.Bearers
                                                   with stretcher.
Parade at Battalion Orderly Room at 8-15 p.m. and proceed by march
route under the charge of the officer to TRICAR DUMP reporting to Lieut
BOHLIN R.E. on arrival for work under this officer.
DRESS:- Fighting kit,less packs.

3rd Party.
              1 Officer & 25 O.R. "D" Coy.
              1   "   " 25 O.R. "A" "   & 2 S.Bearers with Stretcher.

This party will parade at Battalion Orderly Room at 7-15 p.m. and
proceed i/c Senior Officer by march route to TRICAR DUMP reporting to
Lieut BOHLIN R.E. for work under this officer.
The Officer in charge of each party will report to the Adjutant before
moving off.
DRESS:- Fighting Kit, less packs.

O.C.Companies will arrange to have hot tea for these parties on their
return to WULPEN.

                                            J C Selwyn Rowbotham
                                                        Captain,
21-10-17.   Adjutant,
                                            1/10th Manchester Regiment.

1/10th. Battalion Manchester Regt.
October 19th. 1917

To O.C. Companies.
" 1/5th. E.L. Regt.)
Lieut. Echlin 428 R.E.) For information.

Carrying and working parties required for to-night are as follows;
1st. Party. "C" Company   1. off & 40 O.R.
            "D"   "   40 O.R.

            Total   1. off & 80 O.R. & 2 S. Bearers with Stretcher.
This party will parade at Battn. Orderly Room at 7-45 p.m. to proceed under an officer to be detailed by O.C. "C" Coy. This party will proceed by Barge to PELICAN BRIDGE and thence by march route to TRICAR DUMP., reporting to Hqrs. 1/5th. E.L. Regt. at the SARDINERIE NIEUPORT en route.
        This party will carry rations and R.E. material for this Battn.

2nd. Party. 1 Officer & 58 O.R. "B" Company & 2 S. Bearers with stretcher. Parade at Battn. Orderly Room 7-45 p.m. to proceed under the officer to be detailed by O.C. "B" Coy, by the same means and to the same destination as 1st. Party reporting on arrival to Lieut. Echlin 428 Coy. R.E., for work under this officer. The officer in charge of each party will report to the Adjutant before moving off.
Dress:- Fighting kit, less packs.
O.C. Companies will arrange to have hot tea for these parties on their return to WULPEN.

                                        J Chlwyn Rowbotham
19-10-17.   Captain & Adjutant.
                                        1/10th. Manchester Regiment.

OPERATION ORDER No.39. by Lieut-Colonel W.R.PEEL, D.S.O. Commanding
1/10th. Battalion Manchester Regiment.

October 21st.1917.

SECRET.
Ref. Sheets 4 & 5 1/10,000.

1. The Battalion will relieve the 1/5th. East Lancs. Regt. on night of 22/23rd. Oct. 1917.

2. Companies will relieve as follows:-
   (a) "A" Coy. relieve.......... "B" Coy. 1/5th. E.L. Regt. with exception of posts mentioned in (b).(c)
       "C" Coy. in ROODE POORTE & POLDER FARMS.
       (1 L.G. Section & 1 Section in each farm)

   (b) "C" " " .... "D" Coy. 1/5th. E.L. Regt.

   (c) "B" " " .... "C" Coy. (except garrison of ROODE POORT & POLDER FARMS)
       "B" Coy the L.G. Post & Rifle Post near
       junction NICE WALK & NICE AVENUE.

   (d) "D" " " .... "A" Coy.

3. During the hour of duty in the trenches 1.L.G.Section of "D" Coy. is attached to "A" Company.

4. Guide will meet the Battalion as follows.
   (a) 2 Guides will meet "A" Coy at White House at 6-45 p.m.
   (b) 3 " " " "C" " " ELIZABETH BRIDGE at 6-45 p.m.
   (c) 3. " " " "B" " " " " at 6-45 p.m.
   (d) 3. " " " "D" " " " " at 6-45 p.m.

5. Battalion will march off from the present billets in the following order:-
   "A" Coy. "C" Coy. "B" Coy. "D" Coy. Hqrs. 1st.Line Transport.
   200 yards will be maintained between platoons, the leading platoon will march off at 5-30 p.m.
   Route for "A" Coy......... RAMSCAPPELLE ROAD
                              TRACK
                              MAIN ROAD
                              WHITE HOUSE.
   Route for remainder...... PELICAN BRIDGE.
                             ELIZABETH BRIDGE.

6. Lewis Gun Limbers will be loaded at 4-45 p.m. and will leave at 5-15 p.m. They will unload as follows:-
   "A" & "B" Coys. near WHITE HOUSE. "C" & "D" Coys. TRICAR DUMP.
   Each company will send 4 Gunners to accompany their guns, Sgt. Bradshaw will be in charge of the convoy.

7. Relief of garrisons for ROODE POORTE and POLDER FARM will march by small parties to TRICAR DUMP where they will arrive at 4-30 p.m. They will have dinner at TRICAR DUMP. They will meet guide at WHITE HOUSE at 5-30 p.m.

8. Advance party of 1 Officer per "C" & "B" Coys & 1 N.C.O. "A" Coy will report at Battn., Hqrs., 5th. E.L. Regt. at 3-0 p.m. They will arrange to take over all Trench Stores.
   Hqrs. Signallers not on duty; Scouts, Gas N.C.O. will proceed under Lieut. Howarth reporting to Battn. Hqrs. 5th. E.L. Regt. at 3-30 p.m.
   Lieut. Howarth will take over all Hqrs. Stores etc.
   O.C. "D" Coy., will detail Lieut. Stamford at present at TRICAR DUMP, to take over stores A.A. positions from the Reserve Company.

9. The transport taking up rations will as soon as unloaded load up with stores, dixies etc, belonging to the 1/5th. E.L. Regt., and convey these to OOST DUNKERKE. The T.O. will there receive instructions from Qmr. 5th. E.L. Regt., as to where to dump these.

"2"

10. Blankets rolled in bundles of ten and labelled, officers valises, surplus mess stores will be dumped outside Company Orderly Room by 12 noon. These the T.O. will arrange to convey to the Qmr. Stores.

11. All trench stores will be taken over and receipts given. Copies to be forwarded to the Orderly Room by 11 a.m. 23rd. inst.

12. Dispositions of companies will be forwarded to reach the Orderly Room by 11 a.m. 23rd. inst.

13. Completion of relief to be wired to Battn. Hqrs. by code word "RUM".

J Celwyn Rawshothaw

21-10-17.

Captain & Adjutant,
1/10th. Manchester Regiment.

Copies to:- O.C.Coys.   M.O.
           T.O.& Qmr. O.C.5th.E.L.Regt.
           R.S.M.   File
           L.G.Officer. War Diary
                        War Diary.

OPERATION ORDER No.40 by Lieut-Colonel W.R.PEEL, D.S.O.

Commanding 1/10th.Battalion Manchester Regiment.

October 25th.1917.

Map Ref. S. 1/10,000.

1. The Battalion will be relieved by the 5th.E.L.Regt., on the night 26th./27th.inst.

2. Companies will be relieved as follows:-

   "A" Coy. will be relieved by "C" Coy. 5th.E.L.Regt.
   "B" "   "   "   " "B" "   "   "
   "C" "   "   "   " "A" "   "   "
   "D" "   "   "   " "D" "   "   "

3. Guides will be provided as follows:-

   1. Guide at Battn.H.Q. at 6-15 p.m. for POLDER & ROODE POORTE FARMS.L.G. 2
                                         Sections, "C"Coy 5th.E.L.Rgt.   4

   2. Guides "A" Coy to be at WHITE HOUSE 6-45 P.M.
   3.   "   "C" " for "A" Coy at ELIZABETH BRIDGE at 6-45 p.m.
   3.   "   "B" " for "B" " at   "   at 6-45 p.m.
   3.   "   "D" " for "D" " at   "   at 6-45 p.m.

4. ADVANCE PARTY 5th.E.L.Regt.
        1 Officer & 1 N.C.O. per Coy of 5th.E.L.Regt will report at the respective Coy.Hqrs., at 3-30 p.m.

5. GUM BOOTS.
        Gum Boots at the POLDER & ROODE POORTE FARMS will be handed over at the posts.
   Remainder will be collected and stored at Coy.Hqrs., under cover. Special care must be taken that the Boots are kept dry and the flaps not turned down.

6. Lewis Gun Limbers will be at TRICAR DUMP at 11 p.m. O.C.Coys will each leave 4 L.Gunners to load these. The L.G. Limbers with the gunners will proceed under Sgt.Bradshaw to OOST DUNKERKE. *A+B.Whitehorse C+D. wear (one only)*

7. On completion of relief Companies will march independently to OOST DUNKERKE,100 yards will be maintained between platoons.

8. "D" Coy will take over the 5 Anti Aircraft L.Guns in the NIEUPORT area at present held by the 1/5th.E.L.Regt.
   O.C."D" Coy will send an Officer during the day to visit these positions. The L.G.teams at these positions will take 1 days rations with them.

9. The 1/5th.E.L.Regt. 1st.Line Transport will bring up rations etc.
   2 Limbers will,as soon as unloaded,be loaded up at TRICAR DUMP with the cooker dixies,petrol tins etc., not handed over,and will proceed to OOST DUNKERKE to the Qmr.Stores. The company cooks will accompany these limbers.
   O.C."D" Coy will detail an Officer to supervise this loading.
       Similarly the Mess cart & Maltese Cart of the 5th.E.L.Regt., will be loaded at Battn.Hqrs.

10. O.C."D"Coy will hand over all food containers and 26 Petrol Tins.

11. An advance party composed of the Company Quartermaster Sgts.,under the Qmr.,will arrange to take over the billets of the 1/5th.E.L.Regt.
        The signalling Officer will report at Battn.Hqrs.,5th.E.L.Regt. at 2-30 p.m.,and take over all Defence Schemes etc.,and anti-aircraft gun positions in the OOST DUNKERKE area.
   C.Q.M.S.,will meet their Companies at the entrance to the village.

Continued.

Addendum No.1. to Operation Order No.39. 1/10th.Manchester Regiment.

October 22nd.1917.

Paras. 2. (a) & (c) are amended as follows:-

    (a) "A" Coy. relieves "B" Coy.1/5th.E.L.Regt. in NICE TRENCH,NICE AVENUE(from junction NICE AVENUE & NICE WALK),and in ROODE POORTE & POLDER FARMS. (1.L.Gun section in each Farm.)

    (c) "B" " " "C" Coy 1/5th.E.L.Regt. in NICE ALLEY,NICE AVENUE ~~& NICE WALK~~ (up to junction NICE AVENUE & NICE WALK). and NICE WALK

Para. 3. is cancelled.

22-10-17.

[signature]
Captain & Adjutant.
1/10th.Manchester Regiment.

Copies to all recipients of
    Operation Order No.39.

'2'

12. The Qmr. will have all blankets, haversacks and officers valises distributed to the various billets previous to the arrival of the Battalion.

13. The Qmr. will arrange for hot tea or soup to be issued to the troops on arrival in billets.

14. The Qmr. will draw clean clothing and arrange for the bathing of the Troops commencing at 9-30 a.m. on the 27th.inst.

15. Receipts will be obtained for all trench stores, maps etc,, handed over. Copies will be forwarded to Battn. Hqrs., by 11 a.m. on the 27th.Inst.

16. Completion of relief will be wired to Battn., Hqrs., by code word 'RUM'. Arrival in billets will be reported to Battn.Hqrs by runner.

```
Copies to:- O.C.Coys.            R.S.M.
            C.O.                 O.C.1/5th.E.L.Regt.
            2nd.in Command.      2nd.in Command.
            Qmr.& T.O.           War Diary
                                 War Diary
                                 File.
```

(signed) J.C.L. Rowbotham
Captain & Adjutant
1/10th. Manchester Regiment.

25-10-17.

Confidential

Vol 10

WAR DIARY
OF
1/10 MANCHESTER REGT.
Kept by
Lieut O. M. HARRY
the Officer detailed to do so by the
Commanding Officer

Vol: XXVI

Army Form C. 2118.

WAR DIARY
or
INTELLIGENCE SUMMARY.

(Erase heading not required.)

Instructions regarding War Diaries and Intelligence Summaries are contained in F. S. Regs., Part II. and the Staff Manual respectively. Title pages will be prepared in manuscript.

Place	Date	Hour	Summary of Events and Information	Remarks and references to Appendices

Army Form C. 2118.

WAR DIARY
or
INTELLIGENCE SUMMARY.
(Erase heading not required.)

Instructions regarding War Diaries and Intelligence Summaries are contained in F. S. Regs., Part II. and the Staff Manual respectively. Title pages will be prepared in manuscript.

Place	Date	Hour	Summary of Events and Information	Remarks and references to Appendices
Nov 1st			The Battalion move into the line nothing out of the ordinary to report	WPP
	2/11/17		Quiet day, usual additional work. The parapet in True Trench was rebuilt the Stop' river on 3 sides. Patrol was sent out to report on enemy wire	WPP
	3/11/17		1/10 Manchester Regt was relieved by 1/7th East Lancs Regt relief very successful.	WPP
	4/11/17 5/11/17		Companies cleaning up and bathing & Physical Drill.	WPP
	6/11/17		Voluntary Church Services & Holy Communion	WPP
	7/11/17		1/10 Manchester Regt relieved 1/5 East Lanc' Regt on the same front as formerly. Relief successfully carried out. Usual activities nil to report	WPP
	8/11/17		Very Quiet. During the night work was done on front line & True Trench	WPP
	9/11/17		Fairly Quiet, enemy shelling. General repairs done on front line Trench.	WPP

Army Form C. 2118.

WAR DIARY
or
INTELLIGENCE SUMMARY.
(Erase heading not required.)

Instructions regarding War Diaries and Intelligence Summaries are contained in F. S. Regs., Part II. and the Staff Manual respectively. Title pages will be prepared in manuscript.

Place	Date	Hour	Summary of Events and Information	Remarks and references to Appendices
	10/4/17		Heavy Enemy Shelling. Several improvement of Trenches	WRP
	11/4/17		Fairly quiet. Patrol succeeded in crossing the PLOEGSTEERT Canal to Boyle front, but were unable to report anything.	WRP
	12/4/17		Battalion relieved by 1/5 East Lancs Regt. Relief uneventful. Billets in OOST DUNKERQUE.	WRP
	13/4/17 14/4/17		Companies cleaning up clothes and Saluting Drill	WRP
	15/4/17		Battalion moves to BRISBANE Camp	WRP
	16/4/17		Voluntary Holy Communion & Church Parades. B.O. WR PEEK resumes command of the Battalion.	WRP
	17/4/17		Voluntary R.C. in the Nissen Hut. C.O's Inspection of Details	WRP
	18/4/17		Battalion except "B" Coy moved to SYNTHE by Motor Buses	WRP

Army Form C. 2118.

WAR DIARY
or
INTELLIGENCE SUMMARY.
(Erase heading not required.)

Instructions regarding War Diaries and Intelligence Summaries are contained in F.S. Regs., Part II. and the Staff Manual respectively. Title pages will be prepared in manuscript.

Place	Date	Hour	Summary of Events and Information	Remarks and references to Appendices
	19/11/17		Battalion moved by route march to WORMHOUDT area Route: DUNKERQUE, BERGUES. Battalion left billets at LA BELLE VUE and proceeded to billets at ESQUELBECQ.	WRP
	20/11/17		Battalion proceed by route march to L'ANGE	WRP
	21/11/17		Battalion proceed from L'ANGE to billets in STAPLES.	WRP
	22/11/17		Battalion proceed to billets in RINGS.	WRP
	23/11/17 to 24/11/17		Companies cleaning up Baths + Drill "B" Coy. rejoined Battalion from NIEUPORT.	WRP
	26/11/17		Battalion proceeded by route march to ROBECQ. Route: AIRE. ISBERGUES. GUARBECQUES. BUSNES. ROBECQ.	WRP
	27/11/17		Battalion moved by route march from ROBECQ to BUSNVRY. Route: OBLINGHEM. BETHUNE. BEUVRY.	WRP
	28 to 30/11/17		Cleaning up Bath + Company Training	WRP

W R Pyl Lt Col
Commg 1/10 Manchester Regt.

OPERATION ORDER NO ??

by Major C.?.?????, Commanding 1/10th Battalion Manchester Regiment.

Ref., Map 28 S.?.Belgium 1/20,000.   November 8th, 1917.

1. The battalion will relieve the 1/8th.?.L.Regt. on night of 7/8th. Nov.

2. Companies will relieve as follows:-
    "A" Company relieve "D" Coy. 1/8th.?.L.Regt. on the Right & in cha???.
    "B"   "   " "B" "   "   "   "   " "   " left.
    "C"   "   " "A" "   "   "   "   " "   " in support.
    "D"   "   " "C" "   "   "   "   " "   " Reserve.
   Dispositions will be taken over as formerly held by companies of this
   unit irrespective of how held by 1/8th, ?.L.Regt.

3. An advanced party composed as under will report to Battn. H.Q. & the
   Coys. they are relieving respectively at ? p.m. and will take over all
   trench stores & duties beforehand.

   Battn. H.Q.   Lieut. O.?.Harry with a proportion of
                            Sigs., & Scouts.
   "A" Coy.   1 Officer & 1 N.C.O.
   "B" "   2   "   & 1 "
   "C" "   1 N.C.O.
   "D" "   1 Officer & 1 N.C.O.
   O.C.Companies will give their advanced parties written instructions &
   they will proceed independently to their respective Coy.Hqrs., etc.

4. Two L.?.Sections of "A" Coy will proceed in small parties to 1/8th.,
   ?.L.Regt. to arrive there at 4-15 p.m., where they will have dinners.
   1 Cook from "A" Coy with one man from the above teams and 1 scout will
   proceed with a pack cob loaded with 1 dixie and the dinner ration for
   the above party, to PELICAN BRIDGE. The pack cob will be unloaded here,
   and the rations carried by the 2 men to Battn°.Hqrs.,1/8th.?.L.Regt.,
   where dinners will be cooked. This party will leave WULPEN at 12-30 p.m.
       The two teams will start at 2-15 p.m. under Lt.Howarth with 2 pack co?
   cobs,carrying the L.Gun? Ammunition. This will be unloaded at PELICAN
   BRIDGE and carried from there to the Battn. Hqrs.,1/8th.?.L.Regt. A
   guide will meet the party at 1/8th.?.L.Regt H.Q. & guide them to the
   ?????.

5. Lewis Gun limbers will be loaded by 4-45 p.m. & will proceed to
   ??????.DUMP where they will unload. O.C.Coys will each detail 4 men
   to accompany these guns under Sergt. Bradshaw.

6. ? Guides will meet "A" Coy at WHITE HOUSE at 5-45 p.m.
      "   "   "   "B" " " ??????? ????? " 6-45 p.m.
      "   "   "   "C" " "   "   "   " 5-45 p.m.
      "   "   "   "D" " "   "   "   " 6-45 p.m.

7. Order of march:-
              "A" Coy, "D" Coy, "B" Coy, "C" Coy , Hqrs.
   200 yards will be maintained between platoons. The leading platoon will
   march off at 5-10 p.m. Route:- PELICAN BRIDGE.

8. Dinners will be at 4-15 p.m.

9. Cooker dixies etc.,will be loaded up immediately after dinner. The
   Waltoss & Mess Cart will report at Battn. H.Q. at ? ?.?.

10. The transport will bring back the Cooker,dixies,kit etc.,of the 1/8th
    ?.L.Regt. to CAMP DURANTON using route infantry track from WULPEN.

11. Single?'s packs,officers valises,leather jerkins etc.,will be stacked
    in the archway immediately adjoining Battn.Orderly Room by 12 noon.

'2'

11. (continued)
The QMR. will arrange to collect there.

12. All trench stores etc., will be taken over & receipts given, copies of which (in duplicate) will be forwarded to Battn. HqRs. by 10 a.m. on the 8th.inst.

13. O.C.Coys. will forward the dispositions of their Coy accompanied by a rough sketch by 10 a.m. on the 8th.inst.

14. Completion of relief will be wired to Battn.H.Q. by code word "NUTS".

15. The usual list of returns to be rendered will remain in use.

16. ACKNOWLEDGE.

Issued by Orderly at:-

Copy No.1 O.C."A" Coy.
     2   " "B" "
     3   " "C" "
     4   " "D" "
     5. O.C.1/8th.K.L.Regt.
     6. C.O.
     7. QMR & T.O.
     8. R.S.M.
     9. H.Q.Officers(Lt.Harry to return.)
    10. File.
    11. War Diary
    12.   "

                                    Captain & Adjutant
                            1/10th.Manchester Regiment.

6-11-17.

OPERATION ORDERS No 42.
by
Major C.E.HIGHAM.Commanding 1/10th Manchester Regiment.   2/11/17.

Ref: Map 4 & 5 1/10000.

1. The Battalion will be relieved by the 1/5th East Lancs Regt in the Left Sub-sector of the St Georges Sector on the night of the 3/4th Nov:1917.

2. Companies will be relieved as under :-
   FIRING LINE. "D" Coy will be relieved by "D" Coy 1/5th East Lancs Regt.
   --do--   "C" " "   "   "   "B" "   "   "   "   "
   SUPPORT.   "A" " "   "   "   "A" "   "   "   "   "
   RESERVE.   "B" " "   "   "   "C" "   "   "   "   "

3. On relief Companies (less the party mentioned in para 5) will move into billets in WULPEN via PELICAN BRIDGE. C.Q.M.Sgts to meet their Coys at entrance of WULPEN village.
   200 yards will be maintained between platoons.

4. The two Lewis Guns Sections of the 1/5th East Lancs Regt for relief of ROODE POORTE and POLDER Farms will arrive at Batt'n H.Q. at 4-15 p.m, where they will have dinner before proceeding.
   Guides will be provided by Companies as follows:-

COMPANY.	NO OF GUIDES.	REPORT AT.	TIME.
"D"	1 guide for L.G.Sects	Batt'n H.Q.	4-15 p.m.
"D"	2 guides.	WHITE HOUSE.	6-45 p.m.
"C"	3 "	ELIZABETH BRIDGE.	6-45 p.m.
"A"	3 "	--do--	6-45 p.m.
"B"	3 "	--do--	6-45 p.m.

5. The following party will remain behind and take over accommodation vacated by the 1/5th East Lancs Regt near TRICAR Dump and relieve the working parties of that Battalion.
   Lieut A.HIRD and 60 other ranks of "B" Coy.
   O.C."B" Coy will arrange details of relief with the officer of the 1/5th East Lancs Regt.
   Rations for this party will be delivered at TRICAR DUMP at 8 p.m.
   O.C."B" Coy will keep two cooks ,1 sanitary man and 2 stretcher bearers and the necessary cooking utensils.

6. An advanced party of 1 officer per Battalion H.Q. and "D" & "B" Coys and 1 N.C.O. for "A" & "C" Coys of the 1/5th East Lancs Regt will rpeort to Batt'n H.Q. and the Coys to be relieved at 3-30 p.m. and take over in advance.
   Lieut Hughes and the 4 C.Q.M.Sgts of this unit will report to H.Q. 1/5th East Lancs Regt at 3 p.m. on the 3rd of Nov: and take over billets in WULPEN and all duties etc:

7. Gum boots will be collected and stored at Coy H.Q. under cover and handed over. Those at the farms will be handed over there.

8. Lewis Gun Limbers will be at Tricar dump at 9 p.m.
   O.C.Coys will each leave 4 Lewis Gunners to load and accompany the limbers. Sergt BRADSHAW will be in charge of these guns and will supervise the loading. When loaded they will proceed direct to WULPEN.

9. The first line transport of the 1/5th East Lancs Regt as soon as unloaded will be loaded up at TRICAR DUMP with the buckets,dixies,petrol tins and etc: not handed over and proceed to WULPEN.
   Coy Cooks will accompany these limbers.
   O.C."B" Coy will detail an officer to superintend this loading.

CONTINUED:-

--2--

Mess Cart and Maltese Cart of the 1/8th East Lancs Regt will similarily be loaded at Batt'n H.Q.,
O.C. "B" Coy will hand over all food containers and SO petrol tins.

10. Officers Kits and blankets (two per man) will be taken to WOLPEN before the arrival of the Battalion, also the greatcoats of "A" & "C" Coys. These Coys will arrange to stock their leather jerkins at Coy H.Q., immediately after drawing their greatcoats.

11. The Quartermaster will arrange to have hot tea or soup for the Battalion (less the party mentioned in para 5) on arrival in billets. The Asst Adjt will arrange for baths for the Battalion for the following day.

12. Completion of relief to be wired to Batt'n H.Q. by code word "HAPPY" and by runner on arrival in billet.

13. A C K N O W L E D G E.

2/11/17.

J.C.Rowbotham
Captain,
Adjutant,
1/10th Manchester Regiment.

Issued by Orderly at ......

Copy No1. O.C. "A" Coy
     2.   "B" "
     3.   "C" "
     4.   "D" "
     5.   S.O.
     6.   O.C. 1/8th East Lancs Regt.
     7.   Qmr & T.O.
     8.   Sig. Off:
     9.   M.O.
    10.   A/Adjt.
    11.   WAR DIARY.
    12.   --do--
    13.   FILE.
    14.   R.S.M.

ary 91"

WAR DIARY

of

Officer Commanding
1/12 1/10 Manchester Regiment

Kept by

Lieut. O. M. HARRY (Intelligence Officer)
(the Officer detailed by him
for that purpose)

From :- December 1st 1914.

To :- December 31st 1914.

Army Form C. 2118.

WAR DIARY
or
INTELLIGENCE SUMMARY

(Erase heading not required.)

Instructions regarding War Diaries and Intelligence Summaries are contained in F. S. Regs., Part II. and the Staff Manual respectively. Title Pages will be prepared in manuscript.

Place	Date 1917	Hour	Summary of Events and Information	Remarks and references to Appendices
BEUVRY	Dec 1 to Dec 9		Battalion in Billets in BEUVRY. Training and gas through. The whole Company	D.M.H.
GUINCHY	Dec 10		Battalion relieved the 1/5th Lancashire Fusiliers on the GUINCHY front. Relief completed by 10.30 am. Daylight relief. During the night the enemy projected gas on this Battalion front. It is the first occasion that gas has been projected by the enemy on the British front. Our men behaved splendidly and beat off the attempted raid with ease. But casualties fairly heavy. 40 men were awarded the M.M. and several Congratulatory cards received (2 by Officers)	D.M.H.
	Dec 11 to Dec 15		Nothing to report. Front fairly quiet.	D.M.H.
LE PREOL	Dec 16		Battalion was relieved by 1/5th Batt. East Lancs. Regt. Battalion moved into billets at LE PREOL (Brigade Reserve).	D.M.H.
	Dec 17 to Dec 21		Battalion in billets. Company drill. Companies spent the time cleaning up working parties on the Corps Defence Line.	D.M.H.

Army Form C. 2118.

WAR DIARY
or
INTELLIGENCE SUMMARY

(Erase heading not required.)

Instructions regarding War Diaries and Intelligence Summaries are contained in F. S. Regs., Part II. and the Staff Manual respectively. Title Pages will be prepared in manuscript.

Place	Date 1914	Hour	Summary of Events and Information	Remarks and references to Appendices
QUINCHY	Dec 22		Battalion relieves the 1/5th East Lancs Regt on the same front. Relief complete by 10 a.m.	J.M.H.
	Dec 23		Quiet.	J.M.H.
	Dec 24		During the night we projected two gas cylinders and over 1500 Stokes mortar shells on the enemy. We sustained a few casualties.	J.M.H.
	Dec 25 to Dec 27		Front very quiet.	J.M.H.
	Dec 28		Battalion relieved by 1/5th East Lancs Regt and went into support in the Village Line.	J.M.H.
	Dec 29 to Dec 31		Battalion working on the Defences in the Village Line (Kuipes xv)	J.M.H.

h. R. Rull
Lieut-Col.
Commanding 1/10 Manchester Regt.

2449 Wt. W14957/M90 750,000 1/16 J.B.C. & A. Forms/C.2118/12.

OPERATION ORDERS. No. 60. Copy No......

SECRET.

by

Lieut: Col: W.R.PEEL. D.S.O. Commanding 1/10th.Manchester Regiment.
_____

December 27th 1917.

(1) The Battalion will be relieved to-morrow morning, the 28th inst, in the Left sub Sector, by the 1/5th. East Lancashire Regiment, as follows :-

"A" Coy. will be relieved by "B" Coy. 1/5th. East Lancs. Regt.
"B" "   "   "   "   " "D" "   "   "   "   "
"C" "   "   "   "   " "C" "   "   "   "   "
"D" "   "   "   "   " "A" "   "   "   "   "

"C" Coy. 1/5th. East Lancs Regt. will take over No. 42 & 43 posts.

(2) All Trench stores will be handed over and receipts obtained. Copies of which will be forwarded to Battalion H.Qrs. by 4 p.m. on the 28th.inst.

(3) Completion of relief will be reported to Battalion H.Qrs. by code word "RATIONS" (by wire).

(4) After relief Companies will move into the area of the Support Battalion, as follows, and will take over the trenches and Keeps, vacated by the 1/4th. East Lancs. Regt. :-
"A" Coy. will take over ORCHARD & SPOIL BANK KEEPS from "A" Coy. 1/4th. East Lancs.Regt.
"B" Coy. Half Coy. in ESPERANTO ST. and half Coy. in GUNNER SIDING vacated by "D" Coy. 1/4th. East Lancs. Regt.
"C" Coy. will take over MARYLEBONE ST from "A" Coy. 1/4th. E.L.Regt
"D" Coy. will take over BRADNEL CASTLE & MOUNTAIN KEEP, from "B" Coy. 1/4th. East Lancs. Regt.

(5) An advance party of 1 officer per Coy. and 1 N.C.O. per Platoon will report at the respective Coy. H.Qrs. 1/4th. East Lancs.Regt. at 8 a.m. to take over Trench Stores, etc.
Lieut: Schofield and the R.S.M. will report at the same time to Battalion H.Qrs. 1/4th. East Lancs.Regt. and take over all Trench Stores, Defense schemes, etc.

(6) "B" Coy. will be in immediate Support to the Left Battalion. O.C. "B" Coy. will arrange that all approaches to the Battalion Front are thoroughly reconnoitred.
"C" Coy. will be in immediate Support to the Right Battalion, and O.C. "C" Coy. will arrange to reconnoitre all approaches, etc.
O.C's "B" & "C" Coys. will, when their Coys. are in position report personally to the respective Battalion Commanders.

(7) Lists of Trench Stores, etc, taken over, will be sent to Battalion H.Qrs. by 4 p.m.

(8) Companies will notify Battalion H.Qrs. when they are in position, by code word "BLIGHTY" (by wire).

(9) ACKNOWLEDGE.

Distribution:- No.1. O.C. A.Coy.
" 2.   "   B "
" 3.   "   C "
" 4.   "   D "
" 5.   " 1/5th.E.L.Regt.
" 6. C.O.
" 7. L.M.&T.O.
" 8. M.O
" 9. R.S.M.
"10. H.Qrs.Coy.
"11.12.& 13. War Diary.
and File.
"14. 2nd in Command.

Captain.
Adjutant.

PRELIMINARY ORDER.   SECRET.

by

Lieut: Col: W.A.PEEL. D.S.O. Commanding 1/10th. Manchester Regiment.

December 26th 1917.

On relief the Battalion will go into Brigade Support.
Companies will be disposed as follows:-

"A" Coy. relieves   { Coy. Headquarters A.21.b.1.3.
"B" Coy. E.L.Regt. { Company in MARYLEBONE ROAD.
                    { Close Support to Right Battalion.

"B" Coy. relieves   { Coy. Headquarters A.15.c.4.5.
"C" Coy. E.L.Regt. { Half Company ESPERANTO TERRACE.
                    { Half Company GUNNER SIDING.
                    { Close Support to Left Battalion.

"C" Coy. relieves   { Coy. Headquarters A.15.c.5.8.
"A" Coy. E.L.Regt. { Half Company. SPOIL BANK KEEP.
                    { Half Company. ORCHARD KEEP.

"D" Coy. relieves   { Coy. Headquarters A.20.b.9.5.
"D" Coy. E.L.Regt. { Half Company. BRASSEL CASTLE.
                    { Half Company. MOUNTAIN KEEP.

O.C. Companies will send 1 Officer per Coy. to-morrow, 27/12/17, to look over the respective sectors that their Companies will take over. The following points should be ascertained:-
(1) Location of Company Cookhouses.
(2) Location of water.
(3) Where rations are brought to.
(4) If blankets are allowed.
(5) If men may take boots off at night.
(6) What is the action of the Company in case of attack.
(7) What working parties are found.
(8) Accomodation.
(9) Whether gum boots are necessary.

O.C. Coys. will report in writing on the above points by 4 p.m. to-morrow.

H.Fearne
2/Lt.
for Captain.
Adjutant.

SECRET.

OPERATION ORDER No. 57.

by

Lieut: Col. W. K. PEEL. D.S.O. Commanding 1/10th. Manchester Regiment.

Copy No. 11.

December 21st/17.

1. The 1/10th. Manchester Regiment will relieve the 1/5th East Lancs. Regt. in the Left sub-Sector on the morning of the 22nd. inst.

2. Companies will relieve as follows:—
   Right Company "A" Coy. 1/10th Manchester Regt. relieves "C" Coy. 1/5th East Lancs
   Centre Company "B" "   "   "   "   "   "   "B" "   "   "   "
   Left Company "D"   "   "   "   "   "   "   "D" "   "   "   "
   Support Company "C" "   "   "   "   "   "   "A" "   "   "   "

3. Companies will march independently to the trenches in the following order:
   "A" "B" "D" "C" Coys. Battalion H.Q.
   Distances of 200 yards to be maintained between Platoons throughout the march.
   "A" Coy. will march out of billets at 8-30 a.m.

4. Dress for the line will be fighting order, great coats rolled and carried slung round the Haversack, ground sheets under the flap of Haversack. Jerkins slung on the belt at the back.
   Packs containing spare kits and caps, blankets properly rolled in bundles of 10 and labelled will be stacked at Coy. H.Qrs. by 7-30 a.m.
   Officers valises and surplus mess stores etc will be stacked at Coy H.Qrs by 8-0 a.m. Any Mess stores, trench kits etc for use in the line will be sent to-night, a limber will call at Coy. Messes at 8-30 p.m.
   O.C. "C" Coy. will arrange to send an N.C.O. with the limbers to-night to take charge of the dump at HARLEY STREET School, and he will form a guard from the Coy. storemen, and stay until the dump is cleared to-morrow, when he will rejoin his Coy. in Support.
   Dixies, Petrol tins etc required for cooking mid-day meal will be sent with these limbers. The Coy. cooks will proceed in advance to-morrow morning to prepare this meal.

5. The T.O. will detail a limber to be at Battalion Orderly Room at 9 p.m. to-night to carry Orderly Room boxes, Headquarters Mess stores and trench kits to the Harley Street dump, and collect from Coy. Messes.
   2 Lewis Gun limbers will report to Lieut: Howarth at Bridge near Battalion Headquarters at 7-15 a.m. to convey Lewis Guns to WESTMINSTER BRIDGE where they will be drawn by Coys. as they pass.

6. ROUTINE.   Reveille........6-30 a.m.
              Sick parade.....7-0 a.m.
              Breakfast.......7-30 a.m.
              March out.......8-30 a.m.

7. Lieut. W.A. H.SLEWOOD will hand over billets to incoming unit and obtain the necessary certificates of cleanliness, etc.

8. An advance party of 1 N.C.O. per Platoon and 1 Officer per Coy. will leave present billets at 7-30 a.m. to-morrow morning.
   Receipts for trench stores (in duplicate) and rough sketch showing dispositions will be forwarded to Battalion H.Qrs by 4 p.m. on the 22nd. inst.

9. Completion of relief will be wired to Battalion H.Qrs by code word "YORK".

10. ACKNOWLEDGE.

Distribution:—   No. 6. C.O.
No. 1. O.C. A.Coy.   " 7. Q. & T.O.
 " 2. "   B "   " 8. I.O.
 " 3. "   C "   " 9. R.S.
 " 4. "   D "   "10. H.QRS.Coy.
 " 5. 1/5th E.Lancs.   "11.&12. War Diary.
                             "13. FILE.

Captain.
Adjutant.

OPERATION ORDERS. No. 58.

SECRET.

by

Copy No 7

Lieut: Col: W.R.PEEL. D.S.O. Commanding 1/10th.Manchester Regiment.

December 22/17.

1. The following reliefs will take place tomorrow, the 23rd inst.
   (a) C Coy.will relieve B Coy. in posts 38 and 39.
   (b) C Coy.will relieve D Coy. in posts 40 41(day only) and 42.

2. After relief B Coy.will have one Platoon plus one Lewis Gun in DEATH OR GLORY Sap, and ARTILLERY ROW. One Platoon plus one Lewis Gun in BAYSWATER, finding the Lewis Gun post in BAYSWATER, at present found by C Coy.
   C Coy. will have 1 Platoon plus 1 Lewis Gun in the front line between ORCHARD ROAD & FINCHLEY ROAD, both inclusive.i.e. posts 38 39 40 41 (day only) and 42.
   1 Platoon plus 1 Lewis Gun in the North end of BAYSWATER & OXFORD TERRACE,finding the A.A. Lewis Gun post in OXFORD TERRACE.
   D Coy. will have 1 Platoon plus 1 Lewis Gun , plus 1 section with Lewis Gun in the Front line from FINCHLEY ROAD.exclusive, to the left of the Battalion Sector. i.e. posts 44 45 47.
   1 Platoon in CAMBRIDGE TERRACE, finding post at North end of CAMBRIDGE TERRACE and necessary gas guards.

3. Respective Coy.H.Qrs. will remain as at present.

4. B C & D Coys. will in future provide carrying parties for rations and R.E. material, from the Support Platoons.
   H.Qrs. Coy will carry rations and R.E.material for "A" Coy.

5. B Coy. will find the Right post between DEATH OR GLORY Sap & ORCHARD ROAD, and patrol to C Coy.
   C Coy. will patrol up ORCHARD ROAD round 38 39 40 & 42 posts, and down FINCHLEY ROAD. D Coy. will patrol round its own posts.

6. Completion of reliefs to be reported to Battalion Headquarters.

7. ACKNOWLEDGE.

Distribution :- Copy No. 1. A. Coy.
                  "   "   2. B   "
                  "   "   3. C   "
                  "   "   4. D   "
                  "   "   5. H.Q. "
                  "   "   6. 2nd in Command.
                  "   "   7. 126th Infy Bde.
                  "   "   8. File.
                  "   "   9. War Diary.
                  "   "   10.
                  "   "   11. T.O.
                  "   "   12. Q.M.

22/12/17.

F. Howarth Lieut
for Captain.
Adjutant.

SECRET.

1/10th. Manchester Regiment.

OPERATION ORDER. No. 88.

by

Lieut: Col: W. R. PEEL. D.S.O. Commanding 1/10th. Manchester Regiment.

December 15th 1917.

1. The 1/10th. Manchester Regiment, less C Coy will be relieved in the Left Sector of the Right Brigade Front on the morning of the 19th. inst. by the 1/8th Battalion East Lancs. Regiment.

2. C Coy. 1/10th. Manchester Regiment in Battalion Support will not be relieved until after 8 p.m. on the 18th inst.

3. On relief the 1/10th. Manchester Regiment will proceed to LE PREOL to Brigade Reserve.

4. All Trench Stores, maps, etc. will be handed over on relief and receipts obtained.

5. Certificates will be obtained to the effect that the trenches, dug-outs, cookhouses, etc. have been left in a clean and sanitary condition.

6. The Transport Officer will detail 2 limbers to be at the HAMLEY ST. ration dump at 8-30 p.m. to-night, the 15th inst. to convey all surplus kits, mess stores and Orderly Room boxes to LE PREOL.

7. The Lewis Gun limbers, less C Coy. will be at WESTMINSTER BRIDGE at 12 noon to collect Lewis Guns, spare parts, ammunition, etc. C.D. Coys. will leave sufficient Lewis gunners to load these limbers.
Sergt. Bradshaw will be in charge of this dump and report to the Adjutant on arrival at LE PREOL when it is cleared.
C. Coy. Lewis Gun limber will be at POST SIX at 9 p.m.

8. All cooking utensils will be stacked at the HAMLEY ST. ration dump by the Support Coy. on relief, (except A Coy. who will be responsible that their own are carried there,) and 1 man per Coy. will be left with these and accompany a limber to be detailed by the Transport Officer to collect these at 4 p.m. and convey to LE PREOL.

9. The Quartermaster will detail a billeting party to take over billets from the 1/8th. East Lancs. Regt. and allot to Coys.

10. Distances of 200 yards will be maintained between Platoons on the march to LE PREOL.

11. Relief complete will be wired to Battalion H.Q. by code word - "PARIS" and arrival in billets will be notified to Battalion H.Q. by runner.

12. ACKNOWLEDGE.

15/12/17.   Distribution as under :-

No. 1. O.C. A. Coy.   No. 10. Headquarters Coy.
 " 2. "   B. "   " 11. War Diary.
 " 3. "   C. "   " 12. File.
 " 4. "   D. "
 " 5. " 1/8th. East Lancs.Regt.
 " 6. C.O.
 " 7. Q.M. & T.O.
 " 8. I.O.
 " 9. R.S.M.

Captain.
Adjutant.

OPERATION ORDER. NO. 54.

by

Lieut: Col: R. H. Peel, D.S.O. Commanding 1/10th. Manchester Regiment.

1. The following reliefs will take place to-day, the 12th. inst.

2. "A" Coy. will relieve "D" A.Coy in the Left Sector.
   " B "   will relieve "E" Coy. in the Centre Sector.
   "D" "   will proceed to PERNE for the days rest.

3. The men of "C" Coy. at present in the Support Line will relieve a part of "B" Coy. who will in turn relieve the remainder of "D" Coy. in the front line. The remainder of "B" Coy. when relieved will relieve "D" Coy. in the front line.

4. Men of "A" Coy. returning from R.E. will relieve the 2 sections of "D" Coy. at present attached to "A" Coy. These will rejoin "D" Coy. after being relieved.

5. The men of "D" Coy. returning from R.E. or leave will be attached to "B" Coy.

6. O.C. "B" Coy. will arrange to reconnoitre "A" & "B" Coys. line, and O.C. "A" Coy. "B" Coys. line.

7. O.C. "D" Coy. will leave an officer with O.C. "B" Coy.
   O.C. "C" "   will leave Lieut: Harrison, for the night with "A" Coy.

8. "D" Coy. will not proceed to PERNE until the men attached to the R.E. have rejoined.

9. One Company of the 4th. East Lancs. Regt. will remain in Support.

10. Completion of relief will be reported by code word "RUM"

11. All trench stores will be handed and taken over and copies sent to Battalion Headquarters.

12/12/17.

W. Schofield Lieut
for Captain.
Adjutant.

Distribution :- O.C. A Coy.
                "   B "
                "   C "
                "   D "
                "   4th. East Lancs. Regt.
                "   M.Gun.Coy.
                Q.M. & T.O.
                C.O.
                R.S.M.
                War Diary. 2.
                File.

SECRET. 1/10th. Manchester Regiment.

SECRET. **OPERATION ORDER. No. 55.**

by

Lieut: Col: W. R. PEEL. D.S.O. Commanding 1/10th. Manchester Regiment.

December 14th. 1917.

1. C Coy. 1/10th. Manchester Regiment, at present at LE PREOL will relieve B Coy. 1/4th. East Lancs. Regt. at present acting as support Coy. to this unit on the morning of the 15th. inst.

2. C Coy. this unit will march out of billets at LE PREOL at 8-30 a.m. on the 15th inst.

3. O.C. C. Coy. will send an Officer in advance to take over and make all necessary arrangements with O.C. B. Coy. 1/4th. East Lancs. The Coy. cooks will accompany this Officer.

4. The Quartermaster and Transport Officer will make arrangements to transport the surplus kits of this Coy. to the Quartermasters stores and Transport Officer will arrange for transport required for the line.

5. Code word for relief complete will be "ARSENAL"

6. Copies of Trench stores and dispositions (in duplicate) to be forwarded to this office by 12 noon on the 15th. inst. together with certificate that billets vacated at LE PREOL were left in a clean and sanitary condition.

7. O.C. C. Coy. will render a state showing exact strength of this Coy. to this office as soon after receipt of these orders as possible.

8. On relief B Coy. 1/4th. East Lancs. Regt. will proceed to LE PREOL and rejoin their Battalion.

9. The Commanding Officer desires to place on record the excellent work done by B Coy. 1/4th. East Lancs. Regt. under very trying circumstances, and thanks all ranks on behalf of the 1/10th. Battalion Manchester Regiment.

10. ACKNOWLEDGE.

14/12/17.

Distribution as under:-

NO. 1. O.C. A. Coy.
" 2. "   B "
" 3. "   C "
" 4. "   D "
" 5. "   1/4th. East Lancs. Regt.
" 6. "   B "   "   "   "
" 7. C.O.
" 8. Q.M. & T.O.
" 9. I.O.
" 10. R.S.M.
" 11. O.C. Headquarters Coy.
" 12. War Diary.
" 13. "   "
" 14. FILE.

Captain.
Adjutant.

1/10th. Manchester Regiment.

PRELIMINARY ORDER.
XXXXXXXXXXXXXX

1. The Battalion will relieve the 6th Lancashire Fusiliers on the morning of the 10th. inst. in the left Battalion sector.

2. "A" Coy. will relieve "A" Coy. of the 6th. L.Fs.
   "B" " will relieve "B" " of the 6th. L.Fs.
   "C" " will relieve "C" " of the 6th. L.Fs.
   "D" " will relieve "D" " of the 6th. L.Fs.

3. An advance party of 1 Officer per Coy. and 1 N.C.O. per platoon will proceed to the trenches on December 9th. remaining with the respective Coys. until the Battalion arrives.
   Lieut: Harry and Signalling Sergeant will go to Battalion H.Q. of the 6th. L.Fs. and take over all Maps, Defence Schemes, etc.
   This advance party will meet guides at F.10.b.2.2. at 10 a.m. on December 9th.   They will parade at Battalion Orderly Room under Lieut: Harry at 9 a.m.   24 Hour Rations will be taken.

4. The Battalion will march to the trenches in the following order:-
   "A" "B" "C" "D" Coy, and H.Q.
   Guides will meet the Battalion at F.10.b.2.1. at 9-30 a.m.

5. Lieut: Schofield will visit the Battalion Headquarters of the 6th. Lancashire Fusiliers to-morrow the 9th inst. to arrange communications.   He will take 4 Battalion runners with him for this purpose.

8/12/17.

Captain.
Adjutant.

ADDENDUM TO PARA. 8.

Mid-day meals for A B & D Coys. will be served at LE PAROL.
C Coy. will arrange to have their mid-day and evening meal
before relief.

1/10th Manchester Regiment.

Reference Operation Order No. 59.

SECRET

This will take place tonight 24/25th inst.

See Section 3. para A.

The actual sentries will not wear Box Respirators but will be ready to put them on in a moment, and must be specially warned to watch for short rounds.

Special attention is drawn to Section 3 para (b)

O.C. Coys. will ensure that all gas curtains are put down.

24/12/17.

[signature]

Captain.
Adjutant.

File. Copies Sent to all Companies.

SECRET.   1/10th. Manchester Regiment.

Operation Order No. 59.
Ref. Map 1/10,000
Trench Map LA BASSEE.   December 23rd 1917.

1.   On a night to be notified later, a gas attack, accompanied
by shrapnel and machine gun fire will be made :-
(a) On the enemy trench system within the following limits:-
Southern limit - A.16.c.25.25. - A.16.c.95.25.
Northern limit - A.10.b.30.00. - A.10.b.85.00.
(b) On the enemy trench system in the vicinity of A.10.a.90.
(c) On the Headquarters at A.23.a.55.05. - A.22.b.70.42.
   A.17.b.72.30. - and A.11.c.90.45.
(d) On the T.M's within area (a) and at A.16.d.50.05.

2.   The first attack will commence at Zero hour and will continue
until Zero, plus 5, the attack will be repeated at Zero plus
1 hour 40' and Zero plus 4 hours 10'. Between these attacks,
and for 1 hour after the third attack, the Headquarters in
(c) will be subjected to a slow H.E. and gas bombardment by heavy
artillery and 4.5" Howitzers, and the machine guns will fire
bursts of fire at irregular intervals on the Front system
in (a) and (b).

3. Special precautions.
(a) In the area East of the line A.16.c.2.0. A.15.d.3.6. A.15.b.9.2.
all sentries will be warned to be on the look out for any rounds
that may fall short: all other personnel will wear their Box
Respirators and gas curtains will be closed from Zero till Zero
plus 10, Zero plus 1 hour 40' to Zero plus 1 hour 50' and Zero
plus 4 hours 10' to Zero plus 4 hours 20'
(b) In the areas A.15.b. and A.9.c.(Eastern half) and d., all gas
curtains will be closed and all personnel will wear box
respirators from Zero - 5 until the message "all clear" is
received, except that sentries in the Saps may take off their
respirators at Zero plus 10'

4.   Watches will be synchronised by the Signalling Officer at
Battalion Headquarters at 1-30 p.m. on the day of the attack.
All Coys. will send representatives to attend.

5. CODES.   Operation will take place as ordered - BON.
Operation put off for 3 hours, and will take
place commencing at Zero plus - 3 hours   - MAL.
First Gas attack completed.............NOBODY.
Second Gas attack completed............SOMEBODY.
Third Gas attack completed.............EVERYBODY.
Operation postponed for the night......MALISH.

6.   Every precaution will be taken to prepare against enemy gas
shelling in retaliation, especially at Coy.H.Qrs.

7. ACKNOWLEDGE.

Copy No.1. O.C. "A" Coy.
 "   " 2.   " "B" "
 "   " 3.   " "C" "
 "   " 4.   " "D" "
 "   " 5.   " "H.Q." Coy.

                                                Captain.
                                                Adjutant.

WAR DIARY

of

Officer Commanding
1/10th Battn. Manchester Regt.

From January 1st 1918 To January 31st 1918

Army Form C. 2118.

WAR DIARY
or
INTELLIGENCE SUMMARY.
(Erase heading not required.)

Instructions regarding War Diaries and Intelligence Summaries are contained in F.S. Regs., Part II. and the Staff Manual respectively. Title pages will be prepared in manuscript.

Hour, Date, Place	Summary of Events and Information	Remarks and references to Appendices
1918		
Jany 1st. CUINCHY	Battalion in Supports in Right Brigade Sector (CANAL SECTOR). Work on Keeps. ORCHARD KEEP shelled during the day.	WRP
Jany 2nd	ORCHARD KEEP and SPOIL BANK KEEP shelled at night with gas shells. Work as above.	WRP
Jany 3rd. HINGETTE.	Battalion relieved by 1/5th Manchester Regt and went into Divisional Reserve in billets at HINGETTE. Night relief.	WRP (1) oo 61
Jany 4th to Jany 14th	Battalion in Divisional Reserve. Whole Battalion on work in the line every 3rd day. Company training during the remainder of the time.	WRP
Jany 15th GIVENCHY	Battalion relieved 1/6th Lancs. Fusiliers in front line - Left Sub-sector of GIVENCHY Sector. Daylight relief.	WRP (2) oo 62 (cancelled) & (3) oo 63
Jany 19th 20th 21st 22.	Quiet. Work chiefly wiring and draining trenches.	WRP
Jany 23rd	Attempted enemy raid on No 5 Post (Left Post of B Coy) at 4-30 am. Enemy entered our line but were driven out leaving 1 Officer and 1 NCO killed and 2 privates wounded. Our casualties Nil.	WRP

WAR DIARY
or
INTELLIGENCE SUMMARY.
(Erase heading not required.)

Army Form C. 2118.

Hour, Date, Place	Summary of Events and Information	Remarks and references to Appendices
1918		
January 23rd WINDY CORNER	Battalion relieved by 1/5th East Lancs Regt and went into Supports in the Keeps and at WINDY CORNER. Night relief.	(H) O.O. 6pp WRP
Jany 24th to Jany 29th	Work on Keeps and with Tunnelling Companies.	WRP
Jany 29th GIVENCHY	Battalion relieved 1/5th East Lancs Regt in the Front line (Left Sub-Sector). Daylight relief.	(5) O.O. 65 WRP
Jan 29th 30th and 31st	Quiet in the line. Work, wiring and repairing trenches.	WRP

W R Peel
Lt-Col.
Commanding 1/10th Manchester Regt

OPERATION ORDERS. No. 61.   (1)   Copy No. 11

SECRET.   by

Lieut:Col: . R. P L. D.S.O. Commanding 1/10th. Manchester Regiment.

Ref: Sheets.   January 1st. 1918.
BETHUNE. 1/40.000 & 36.b.N.E. & 36.c.N.W. 1/20.000

1. The Battalion will be relieved by the 1/5th. Manchester Regiment, on the 3rd.inst.

2. "A" Coy. will be relieved by "A" Coy. 1/5th. Manchester Regiment.
   "B" "   " "   "   " "B" "   "
   "C" "   " "   "   " "C" "   "
   "D" "   " "   "   " "D" "   "

3. GUIDES. Each Coy. will send Three guides per Coy. and 1 per Battalion Headquarters, to meet the incoming Unit at Brigade Headquarters at 12 noon.

4. ADVANCE PARTY. An advance party of the incoming Unit of 1 Officer per Coy. and 1 N.C.O. per Platoon, and 3 signallers for Battalion Headquarters will arrive on the evening of the 2nd.inst, and remain until the incoming Unit arrives.
   The Coy. cooks of the incoming Unit will be accommodated with our Coy. cooks on the night of the 2nd, until the arrival of their Unit.

5. All working parties will continue work until 12 noon.

6. On relief Coys. will march to the Brigade Reserve Area at HINGETTE. Route: Along South bank of Canal.
   GORRE.
   Road junction.   F.5.b.4.5.
       "   "   X.27.c.1.6.
       "   "   X.27.a.7.7.
       "   "   X.20.c.4.7.
       "   "   X.20.c.7.2.
       "   "   X.18.d.2.8.
       "   "   W.18.d.8.9.
       "   "   W.17.b.9.8.
   Where guides will meet Companies 200 yards will be maintained between Platoons on the East of a line BEUVRY — LOCON.

7. Lewis Gun Limbers will be at WESTMINSTER BRIDGE at 2-30 p.m. Each Coy. will have their Lewis Guns at this point and 4 men per Coy. Lieut. Hird will superintend the loading of these guns and march the party to billets after the guns are loaded.

8. Blankets, petrol tins, dixies etc will be left at each Coy. ration dump in the charge of 2 men per Coy. Any officers trench kit and signalling stores will be similarly left at these dumps. The Transport officer will arrange for sufficient transport to collect these dumps, and convey to billets.

9. Men will have their mid-day meal before the relief, under arrangements to be made by O.C. Coys.
   Dinners will be issued on arrival in billets.

10. The Quartermaster will allot billets to C.Q.M.S. to-morrow the 2nd inst. The C.Q.M.S. will then meet their Coys. at W.17.b.9.6. and conduct them to billets.
    Coy. cooks in the line and officers servants will march down with their Companies.

11. One runner per Coy. and 2 per Headquarters will report to the Quartermaster to-morrow night, the 2nd inst, and proceed with him to the new area on the 3rd.inst, where they will ascertain the location of Headquarters, Companies, etc.

2.

12. All Defence Schemes, Aeroplane photographs, Programmes of work, Certificates of cleanliness, Trench Stores, etc, will be handed over and receipts obtained.

13. Leather jerkins will be worn over service dress. Greatcoats will not be worn, but rolled and carried round the haversack.

14. Completion of relief will be wired to Headquarters by code word "SINBAD" and arrival in billets notified to Battalion Headquarters by runner.

15. <u>ACKNOWLEDGE.</u>

                                                 Captain.
                                                 Adjutant.

Distribution as under:-

```
No.  1...... O.C. "A" Coy.
 "   2......  "   "B"  "
 "   3......  "   "C"  "
 "   4......  "   "D"  "
 "   5......  "  1/5th.Manchester Regiment.
 "   6...... C.O.
 "   7...... Q.M.& T.O.
 "   8...... M.O.
 "   9...... R.S.M.
 "  10...... H.Qrs.Coy.
 "  11...... War Diary.
 "  12......  "    "
 "  13...... File.
 "  14...... 2nd in Command.
```

1/10th Manchester Batmnls.

Reference Operation Order No. 21.

Reserve supplies of Batm's Stores from ration and other will be handed over to the 1/5th Cheshire Managing Regiment as follows:-
Cartridges S.A.A. will be replaced by Battalion orderly Room by 7 p.m. on the 3/2/18, to be checked by the Battalion Staff. In the event that stores so laid down in O.O./OA/167 of 29/12/17 have been handed over in spare men sent to H.Q. Mons, on the 3/14/17 have been handed over in spare condition. A sufficient of deployment of stores should be indicated from the Receipts for these stores should be obtained from the relieving unit.

Mobile Reserve will not be carried on slanding of march.
The Quartermaster will take over the Mobile Reserve of the 1/5th Cheshire Regiment, will hand over the mobile Reserve of this Batt. Baggage wagons from the 1/5th Ches. Regt. will report at the following.

S.O. Stores at 3 p.m. on the following.
1 Lewis will be sent to Billets, and nine will be at Battery Station (an employed parties in the area of the Battery. Off. will detail Guides to meet this party.

January 2nd, 1918.

To :- O.O./ O.D.

Bn.Lieut.
Adjutant.

OPERATION ORDER No.64.

by

Lieut:Col: W.R. PEEL. D.S.O. Commanding 1/10th.Manchester Regiment.
----

1. The 1/10th.Manchester Regiment will be relieved by the 1/5th.
   East Lancs. Regt. in the Left Battalion Sector of the Left
   Brigade on the morning of the 23rd. inst.
   On Relief the 1/10th. Manchester Regiment will move into Brigade
   Support and relieve the 1/4th. East Lancs.Regt. (vide
   preliminary Order, dated 21/1/18.)

2. Companies will be relieved as follows :-
   Right Coy. "D"Coy.1/10th.Manchester Regt. by "D"Coy. 1/5th.East Lancs
   Centre "   "B"   "   "   "   "   " "B" "   "   "   "
   Left   "   "A"   "   "   "   "   " "A" "   "   "   "
   Support "   "C"   "   "   "   "   " "C" "   "   "   "

3. One guide per Platoon and one per Coy.H.Q.and One for Battalion
   H.Q. will meet relieving Coys. and Battalion H.Q. at ESTAMINET
   CORNER at 10 a.m. on the 23rd.

4. All Trench Stores, maps, aeroplane photograps, work and defence
   schemes must be carefully handed over to relieving Companies
   and receipts obtained (in duplicate).

5. Completion of relief will be wired to Battalion Headquarters by
   code word "IKEY".

6. On relief Companies will march independently to their positions
   in the Support Line and will relieve Coys. of the 1/4th. East
   Lancs. Regt. as follows :-
   "A"Coy. 1/10th.Manchester Regt will relieve"D"Coy.1/4th. E. L.
   "B" "   "   "   "   "   "   "B" "   "   "
   "C" "   "   "   "   "   "   "A" "   "   "
   "D" "   "   "   "   "   "   "C" "   "   "

7. Men will wear gum boots on going out of the Line and carry
   their boots. Unserviceable gum boots will be carried and
   returned to Battalion H.Q. on arrival in the new localities.
   Great care must be taken to ensure, that all periscopes, wire
   cutters, and petrol tin containers in packs are brought out
   on relief, and the periscopes must be returned to Battalion
   H.Q. on arrival in Support.

8. Advanced Parties of 1 Officer and 2 N.C.Os.per Coy, and 1
   Officer and 1 N.C.O.per Battalion H.Qrs.will report to their
   respective Coy.and Battalion H.Qrs. of the 1/4th.East Lancs.
   Regt. at 8 a.m. on the 23rd. inst. to take over.

9. One cook per Coy. with sufficient dixies and men to carry them
   should proceed with the Advanced Party and prepare tea for the
   mid-day meal. The remaining cooks and dixies to proceed
   with their Coys.
   Company S.Bs. will draw clean socks as the Companies pass the
   present Battalion H.Qrs. on relief and will be changed on
   arrival in the Support Line.
   Companies will make their own arrangements about carrying down
   Mess Panniers, but it must be borne in mind that the trucks
   cannot be used in daylight.

10. Completion of the relief of the Support Line, will be wired
    to Battalion H.Qrs. by code word "POPOFF".

2..........

11. Copies of Dispositions (with rough sketch) and copies of trench stores &c (in duplicate) will be forwarded to reach this office not later than 9 a.m. on the 24th. inst.

12. ACKNOWLEDGE.

January 22nd. 1918.

Captain.
Adjutant.

Distribution :-

No. 1. O.C. "A" Coy.
" 2. "   "B" "
" 3. "   "C" "
" 4. "   "D" "
" 5. C.O.
" 6. 2nd in Command.
" 7. O.C. "H.Qrs"Coy.
" 8. Q.M.& T.O.
" 9. R.S.M.
" 10. O.C. 1/4th.East Lancs.Regt.
" 11. "   1/5th. "   "   "
" 12. Adjutant.
" 13. File.
" 14.)
" 15.) War Diary.

OPERATION ORDERS No. 63.

by

Lieut:Col: W.R.PEEL. D.S.O. Commanding 1/10th. Manchester Regiment.

1. Operation Order No. 62. is cancelled.

2. The Battalion will relieve the 6th. Lancashire Fusiliers on January 17th. in the Line.

3. "A" Coy. will relieve "B" Coy. 6th. Lancashire Fusiliers.
   "B" "   "   "   "C" "   "   "   "
   "C" "   "   "   "D" "   "   "   "
   "D" "   "   "   "A" "   "   "   "

4. Starting Point for "A" "B" & "D" Coys. the Crucifix at W.6.c.99.50.
   Route. LOCON – PONT TOURNANT along Canal Bank to bridge at K.13.d.6.8. GORRE. TUNING FORK Rd. S. ESTAMINET CORNER.
   Head of "A" Coy. pass Starting Point at 9 a.m.
   Order of march "A" "B" "D". 200 yards between Platoons.
   Starting Point for H.Qrs. and "C" Coy. Drawbridge. AVELETTE.
   Route. Along Canal Bank to LE QUESNOY. GORRE TUNING FORK Rd. S. ESTAMINET CORNER.
   Order of march :- "C" Coy. "H.Qrs".
   Head of "C" Coy. pass Starting Point at 9 a.m.
   200 yards will be maintained between Platoons. Usual hourly halts up to ESTAMINET CORNER.

   DRESS. Fighting Order. Greatcoats rolled and carried round the haversacks. Leather jerkins worn over the tunic. If wet, ground sheets will be worn.
   Guides will meet Coys. at ESTAMINET CORNER.

5. The Lewis Gun limbers will leave the Q.M.Stores at 8-30 a.m. under the T.O. "A" "B" & "D" Coys. will not send men to accompany them. "C" Coy. will detail 12 men to report to the T.O. at 8-29 a.m. The Lewis Guns will be unloaded at ESTAMINET CORNER where Coys. will pick them up.

6. Companies will draw Gum Boots at the Gum Boot Store at A.1.a.3.3. These the men will carry up. They will change their socks in the trenches and put on the Gum Boots. Sacks will be issued to Coy. S.Bs. for the purpose.

7. All packs containing surplus kit and caps, blankets and Officers valises and surplus Mess Stores will be dumped at Coy.H.Qrs. at 7-30 a.m.

8. All maps, Defence Schemes, etc. Trench Stores, etc. will be taken over and receipts given. Copies of which will be forwarded to reach Orderly Room by 9 a.m. 18th. inst.

9. Completion of relief will be wired to Headquarters by code word "AGREED"

10. ACKNOWLEDGE.

Distribution : – No.1. O.C. "A" Coy.   No.8. Q.M.& T.O.
                   2. "   "B" "   9. R.S.M.
                   3. "   "C" "   10. O.C.1/6th.L.Fs.
                   4. "   "D" "   11. A/Adjt.
                   5. C.O.   12. File.
                   6. 2nd in Command.   13.)
                   7. O.C."H.Qrs"Coy.   14.) War Diary.

January.18th.1918.

2nd/Lieut,
Act/Adjutant.

1/10th. Manchester Regiment.

OPERATION ORDER No.22.

Unless further orders are received the following corrections should be made:-

For 14th read 16th.
For 15th read 17th.

January 15th, 1915.

H. Fearne.
2nd/Lieut:
Act/Adjutant.

OPERATION ORDER No. 62.

by

Lieut: Col: W.R. PEEL. D.S.O. Commanding 1/10th. Manchester Regt.

1. The Battalion will relieve the 6th. Lancashire Fusiliers in the front line on January 15th.

2. "A" Coy. will relieve "B" Coy. 6th. Lancs.Fusiliers.
   "B" "   "   "   "C" "   "   "   "
   "C" "   "   "   "D" "   "   "   "
   "D" "   "   "   "A" "   "   "   "

3. An advance party of 1 officer per Coy: and 1 N.C.O. per Platoon and 1 officer for Battalion H.Qrs will parade at the Cross Roads LES CHOQUEUX at 9 a.m. and proceed to ESTAMINET CORNER F.6.a.4.0. where they will meet guides. They will remain with the respective Coys: of the 6th. Lancs Fusiliers till the arrival of the Battalion.

4. The Companies will pass the Starting Point at the Cross Roads at LES CHOQUAUX in the following order :-
   "A" "B" "C" "D" H.Qrs.
   Head of "A" Coy. to pass the Starting Point at 9 a.m.
   Route. GORRE TUNING FORK ROADS. F.6.a.4.0. where guides will meet the Battalion at 11-30 a.m.
   Distances of 200 yards between Platoons will be maintained.
   DRESS. Fighting order. Greatcoats rolled, and carried round the haversacks. Leather jerkins will be worn over the tunic.
   Unexpended portion of the days ration will be carried in the haversacks.

5. Lewis Guns will be carried in limbers to ESTAMINET CORNER F.6.a.4.0. where they will be unloaded. Companies will pick up their guns as they pass.
   O.C. Coys. will detail 4 Lewis Gunners per Coy: to accompany the Lewis Gun limbers. These men will parade under the Lewis Gun officer who will take charge of the Lewis Gun limbers at LES CHOQUAUX at 8-50 a.m. on the 15th inst.
   Lewis Guns will be loaded on limbers by 5 p.m. on the 14th.inst.

6. The Tea Ration for the mid-day meal for the 15th.inst.will be sent up on the afternoon of the 14th Inst. and 1 cook per Coy: and 1 H.Qrs. will proceed with the limbers.
   They will parade at the Q.M.Stores at 2 p.m. on the 14th.inst.
   The Q.M. will arrange to send up sufficient Dixies.
   Any Officers Mess stores to be sent up to-morrow night, should be stacked at the Q.M.Stores by 1-30 p.m.

7. All packs containing surplus kit and caps, blankets rolled in bundles of 10, officers valises and surplus Mess kit will be stacked at Company Q.M. Stores by 8 a.m., 15th inst.

8. "A" & "B" Coys. will put on Gum Boots at the Gum Boot Store A.17.4.

9. All Maps,etc., and Trench stores will be taken over, and receipts given, copies of which will be sent to the Orderly Room by 9 a.m. on the 16th.inst.

10. Completion of relief will be wired to Battalion Headquarters by code word "AGREED".

11. ACKNOWLEDGE.

Distribution:- No.1. O.C. "A" Coy.   No.8. Q.M.& T.O.
              2 "   "B" "   9. R.S.M.
              3 "   "C" "   10. O.C.1/6th.L.Fs.
              4 "   "D" "   11. A/Adjutant.
              5 C.O.   12. File.
              6 2nd in Command.   13. War Diary.
              7 O.C.H.Qrs.Coy.   14. "   "

January 15th.1918.

                                        2nd/Lieut: A/Adjutant.

OPERATION ORDERS No.65.
by
Lieut.Col. W.R.Pugh, D.S.O. Commanding 1/10th. Manchester Regiment.

SECRET. (5)

1. The Battalion will relieve the 1/5th.East Lancs.Regt. in the Line on January 28th. 1916.

2. Companies will relieve corresponding Companies.

3. Companies will move as follows:-
   "A" Coy. will leave the Keeps at 8-30 a.m.
   "B" "   will leave as soon as "A" Coy. is clear.
   "C" "   as soon as "B" Coy. is clear.
   "D" "   will move independently. They will be clear of the O.B. Line by 9-45 a.m.

4. An advance party of 1 Officer per Coy. and 1 N.C.O. per platoon will report at the respective H.Qrs. of the Coys. of the 1/5th. East Lancs Regt. at 8-30 a.m. to take over Trench Stores, etc.

5. Men will march in gum boots carrying their boots with them.

6. Blankets rolled in bundles of 10 will be dumped at Battalion H.Qrs. by 8-0 a.m. The Q.M. will arrange to have a guard over these until taken down by the transport at night.

7. One ration for the mid-day meal and meat rations for dinners for the 28th. will be taken to PETOGNET CORNER and left under a guard until O.C. "D" Coy. can arrange to take them to their respective Cookhouses.
One cook per Coy. and the necessary fatigue will go to the new Cookhouses to-morrow night and take charge of the rations when delivered by "D" Coy. The dry rations for the 29th. will be issued tomorrow night the 28th.inst.

8. Each Coy. will leave a responsible N.C.O. to hand over and obtain receipts for all Trench Stores taken over by the 1/5th. E.L.R. in the present area. Certificates of cleanliness and receipts for Trench Stores (in duplicate) to be rendered to Battalion Orderly Room by 7 a.m. on the 30th.inst.

9. O.C. "H.Qrs"Coy. will arrange for a party to take up all surplus Signalling Equipment, Reserve Lewis gun S.A.A. and H.Qrs.Mess Stores to-morrow night.

10. Periscopes will be issued on the 28th. as follows:-
    "A" Coy.   1.   "B" Coy.   1.   "D" Coy.   1.

11. All Trench Stores,etc. will be taken over and receipts given. Copies will be forwarded to Battalion Orderly Room by 7 a.m. on the 30th.inst.

12. Dispositions of Coys. will be sent to Battalion Orderly Room at the same time.

13. Completion of relief will be wired to Battalion H.Qrs. by code word "BLOAY"

14. ACKNOWLEDGE.

January 27th. 1916.

J.C.Rowbotham
Captain.
Adjutant.

Distribution:- No.1. O.C. "A" Coy.
              2. "   "B" "
              3. "   "C" "   No.11. T.O.
              4. "   "D" "   12. R.S.M.
              5. "   "H.Qrs" "   13. Adjutant.
              6. " 1/5th. E.L.R.   14.)
              7. C.O.   15.) War Diary.
              8. 2nd in command.   16. File.
              9. Q.M.& T.O.
             10. R.S.M.

Vol. 13

War Diary.

of

Officer Commanding 1/10th Battn Manchester Regt.

Kept by

Capt. J. C. S. ROWBOTHAM (Adjutant)

From Feby 1st 1918. To Feby 28th 1918.

WAR DIARY
INTELLIGENCE SUMMARY

Army Form C. 2118.

Ref. Sheets 36a S.E.4, 36 S.W.3, 36 c.N.W.1, 36 b N.E.2

Place	Date	Hour	Summary of Events and Information	Remarks and references to Appendices
GIVENCHY	1918 Feby 1st to Feby 3rd		Battalion in line. Everything quiet. Work chiefly wiring and draining trenches.	I
GORRE	Feby 4th		Battalion relieved by 1/5th East Lancs Regiment and went to billets in GORRE.	
	Feby 5th to Feby 9th		Battalion in billets. Usual cleaning up.	
GIVENCHY	Feby 10th		Battalion relieved the 1/5th East Lancs Regt on the left sub-sector of GIVENCHY. Daylight relief.	II
	Feby 11th to Feby 13th		Everything quiet in the line. Usual wiring parties. On the evening of the 11th, one Company of the Battalion on our right (1/9 Manch Rgt) raided the enemy trenches and brought back prisoners.	
	Feby 13th		Battalion relieved by 1/5th Battn Kings Liverpool Regt of the 55th Divn QR and proceeded by Route March to billets at BETHUNE, proceeding to BUSNES on the 14th.	III

WAR DIARY
or
INTELLIGENCE SUMMARY.
(Erase heading not required.)

Army Form C. 2118.

Place	Date 1918	Hour	Summary of Events and Information	Remarks and references to Appendices
BUSNES	Feb 1st to Feb 15th		Battalion in billets at BUSNES. Divine service. Battalion receiving a large draft of men and nine officers from the 2/10 Manchester Regt.	O-O 69 JW JCR JCR
	Feb 16			JCR
	Feb 17 to Feb 21		Usual training programme.	JCR
HINGETTE	Feb 22		Battalion relieved the 1/5th East Lancs. Regt. at HINGETTE.	O-O 40 JCR I
	Feb 23 to Feb 28		Battalion now under C.R.E.	JCR

O. Whitham Capt. Adjt.
for Major
Comdg 1/10 Manchester Regt.

OPERATION ORDER No.66.   Copy No......

by

Lieut:Col: W.R.PEEL.D.S.O. Commanding 1/10th.Manchester Regiment.

Ref Sheet.BETHUNE. 1/40.000 RICHEBOURG. 36 S.W.3.   Febr:2nd 1918.
1/10.000
LA BASSEE. 36.C.N.W. 1. 1/10.000.

1. The Battalion will be relieved by the 1/5th.East Lancs.Regt.on the morning of the 4th.inst.

2. Coys.will be relieved by corresponding Coys.of the 1/5th. E.L.R.

3. On relief Coys.will march into Brigade Reserve at GORRE.
Route. BARNTON ROAD. RATION CORNER. ESTAMINET CORNER, southern road of TUNING FORK. Coy cooks in the line and Officers servants will march down with their Coys.
A distance of 200 yards between Platoons will be maintained.
Coys. will bring out all Gum Boots and hand them in at the Store at RATION CORNER. They will obtain receipts for those handed in.
Remaining dixies will be carried to ESTAMINET CORNER.

4. Breakfast and dry rations for the 4th inst.will be brought up tomorrow night. The remainder of the ration for the 4th inst will be kept at the Q.M.Store. The T.O. will arrange for 1 limber to be at ESTAMINET CORNER at 10-30 p.m tomorrow for transport of canteen &c and surplus mess stores and kits. All dixies not required for breakfast will be taken down tomorrow night.

5. The T.O. will arrange for 4 limbers to be at ESTAMINET CORNER at 1 p.m. on the 4th inst. for transport of Lewis Guns and ammunition, signalling stores,Officers mess stores and trench bundles.
Each Coy. will leave 1 man per gun at ESTAMINET CORNER to load the guns and limbers. Sergt. Bradshaw will superintend this.

6. One cook per Coy.and 1 per Battalion H.Qrs.will remain until the Battalion is relieved. The others will proceed to GORRE immediately after breakfast. Dinners will be issued on arrival in billets.

7. Lt.Haslewood will allot billets to C.Q.M.S.tomorrow the 3rd inst.
C.Q.M.S. will meet Coys. at the Eastern boundary of billeting area, and conduct them to billets.

8. All Defence Schemes,Aeroplane photographs, programmes of work, Trench Stores &c will be handed over and receipts obtained. The orders re relief of A.A.Posts and exchange of anti-tank drums and handing over remaining anti-tank S.A.A.will be carried out. All receipts,in duplicate will be forwarded to this office by 12 noon,5th inst.
All anti-gas Trench Stores will be stated in detail in the Trench Store list (para 6.of S.S.195) Certificates of cleanliness will be obtained.

9. Leather jerkins will be worn over service dress. Greatcoats will not be worn, but rolled and carried round the haversack.

10. Completion of relief will be wired to Headquarters by code word "TOK SPROT" and arrival in billets notified to Battalion H.Qrs.by runner.

11. ACKNOWLEDGE.

for Captain.
Adjutant.

Distribution:-No.1. O.C. "A"Coy.   No. 8. M.O.
" 2. " "B" "   " 9. R.S.M.
" 3. " "C" "   " 10. O.C."H.Qrs"Coy.
" 4. " "D" "   " 11. War Diary.
" 5. " 1/5th.E.L.R.   " 12. " "
" 6. " C.O.   " 13. File.
" 7. " Q.M.& T.O.   " 14. 2nd in command.
   " 15. R.Q.M.S.

OPERATION ORDER No. 47.

SECRET.

Lieut/Colonel .... 2nd.L. D...... Commanding 1/18th. Manchester Regiment.

1. The Battalion will relieve the 1/5th. East Lancs. Regt. in the Line on February 10th. 1918.

2. Companies will relieve corresponding Companies.

3. Companies will march out of billets at COMMS in the following order :-
"A" "B" "D" "H.Qrs" Coys. "A" Coy. will march out at 9-30 a.m. Companies will march by Platoons with 200 yards between Platoons. Sufficient distance will be left between "D" Coy. and H.Qrs.Coy. to allow "D" Coy. (stationed at INDY COLLEGE) to get clear.

4. An advance party of 1 Officer per Coy. and 1 N.C.O. per Platoon and 1 Officer and 1 N.C.O. per Battalion H.Qrs. will report at the respective H.Qrs. of the Coys. they are relieving at 9 a.m. to take over trench stores etc.

5. "B" Coy. will march to the line in their gum boots and carry their ankle boots. O.C. "C" Coy. will arrange to draw 250 pairs of gum boots from the Div. Gum Boot Store first thing tomorrow morning, and will issue to "A" "B" & "D" Coys.& H.Qrs.Coy. as they pass in the following proportions:-
"A" Coy...... 80
"B" Coy...... 70   Coys. will carry these gum boots and change at Coy.
"D" Coy...... 70   H.Qrs. in the line.
H.Q.Coy...... 30

6. Blankets properly rolled in bundles of 10 and labelled, mens valises, Officers valises and mess panniers will be stacked outside the front on the Chateau by 9 a.m. on the 10th and the Quartermaster will arrange to collect and convey to the Q.M.Stores on departure of the Battalion.

7. Men ration for the mid-day meal and meat rations for dinners on the 10th will be conveyed to ESTAILLET COMMS tonight the 9th inst. Also all surplus Battalion equipment, reserve L.G. S.A.A. Orderly Room boxes and H.Gren. stores will be sent with those rations. The T.O. will arrange to collect those en route to ESTAILLET COMM H.
O.C. "B" Coy. will detail a party of 14 men to meet the above and convoy to the line tonight.
One cook per Coy. and sufficient fixive will proceed to the new cookhouses tonight and take charge of the rations when delivered by "C"Coy.
The dry ration for the 10th will be issued tonight the 9th inst.
L.Gollowath will draw 9 periscopes tonight and issue to Coys. with the L.Gs in the following proportion:- "A" Coy.......
"B" Coy.......1
"D" Coy.......3
H.Q.Coy.......1

8. Dress for the line :- Fighting Kit - greatcoats rolled round the haversack. Caps will **not** be taken into the line.

9. All Trench Stores &c. will be taken over and receipts given, copies will be forwarded to Battalion Orderly Room by 7 a.m. on the 11th inst. These will be accompanied by a rough sketch map showing disposition of Coys.

10. Completion of relief will be wired to Battalion H.Qrs. by code word "QUID"
11. ACKNOWLEDGE.

Distribution:-
No.1. O.C. "A" Coy. &c. 6. 1/5th.E.L.R. 10.11. I.O.
2. "   "B" "   7. G.O.C.   12. H.Q.M.S.
3. "   "D" "   8. General in command. 13. M.P.
4. "   "H" "   9. Q.Q....T.O.   14.)
5. " L.G. " 10. M.B....   15.) War Diary.
                                     16. File.

Captain
Adjutant

OPERATION ORDER.   No. 68.   Copy No.

SECRET.   by

Lieut. Col. W.R. PEEL. D.S.O. Commanding 1/10th. Manchester Regiment.

February 12th/18.

1. The 126th. Brigade is being relieved by the 185th. Brigade on the 15th. inst.

2. The Battalion will be relieved by the 5th. Kings Liverpool Regt.
   "A" Coy. will be relieved by "A" Coy.
   "B" Coy.   "   "   "   "B" Coy.
   "C" Coy.   "   "   "   "C" Coy.
   "D" Coy.   "   "   "   "D" Coy.

3. O.C. Coys. will each detail four guides (1 per Platoon) to report at Battalion H.Qrs. at 10-45 a.m. O.C. H.Qrs Coy. will detail 2 men as guides. These guides Lt. Howarth will take to ESTAMINET CORNER to be there at 11-30 a.m. to meet the incoming unit.

4. On relief Companies will march to FERME-DU-ROI.
   Route – GORRE. Thence along Canal Bank. Distances of 200 yards between Platoons will be maintained.

5. Lewis Gun Limbers will be at ESTAMINET CORNER at 2-30 p.m. Each Coy. will detail 4 Lewis Gunners to remain with the guns and to load them. Lt. Howarth will supervise this. He will also take from Coys. as they pass :- periscopes, wire cutters & very pistols noting how many are returned by each Coy.

6. Gum Boots will be carried down and handed in to the Gum Boot Store and receipts obtained.

7. All maps, aeroplane photographs, defence schemes, programmes of work and anti-tank ammunition will be handed over and receipts in duplicate obtained.

8. The mid-day meal will be served to the men at 11-30 a.m.

9. Men will not wear greatcoats.

10. Completion of relief will be wird to Battalion H.Qrs. by code word "GHYPER" and arrival in billets will be notified by runner.

11. ACKNOWLEDGE.

                                                    Captain.
                                                    Adjutant.

Distribution:-
No. 1. O.C. "A" Coy.   No. 10. R.S.M.
    2.   "B" "   11. I.O.
    3.   "C" "   12. R.Q.M.S.
    4.   "D" "   13. Adjt.
    5.   H.Qrs. "   14.)
    6. C.O.   15.) War Diary.
    7. 2nd in command.   16. File.
    8. 5th. K.L.R. 185 Bde.
    9. Q.M.& T.O.

ADDENDUM No. 1 TO

OPERATION ORDER. No. 68.
----

1. A billeting party composed as under will proceed to BUSNES on the 13th, after seeing the Battalion in billets at FERME-DU-ROI and will report to the Sub-area Commandant there, who will allot them billets for the Battalion. They will be accomodated for the night of the 13th by the Sub-area Commandant. They will meet the Battalion at the entrance to BUSNES.

   2nd/Lieut. H.J.Fearne.
   4 Coy. Clerks.
   Sgt. Bowers for H.Q.

2. In addition to receipts for Trench Stores, certificates of cleanliness must be obtained from the relieving Companies and all gas proof dug-outs must be handed over as such, and receipts obtained. These together with Anti-Tank S.A.A. must be shown seperately.

3. Supply wagons will report at the CHURCH at P.31.b.90.85 at 4 p.m. on the 14th.inst. and 2nd/Lieut.Fearne will arrange to meet them there with one of his Advanced Party and guide to the new Quartermaster Store at BUSNES.

4. Administrative Orders for the move from FERME-DU-ROI to BUSNES will be issued at FERME-DU-ROI.

February 12th.1918.

Captain.
Adjutant.

Distribution as Operation Order No. 68.

SECRET.

OPERATION ORDER. No. 69.   COPY NO....

by

Lieut.Col. W.R. PEEL. D.S.O. Commanding 1/10th. Manchester Regiment.

---

1. The Battalion will move by march route to BUSNES on the 14th. inst.

2. The Battalion will be formed up in fours head of column at E.6.c.2.9. at 11-15 a.m.
   Order of March :- H.Qrs. A B C D Coys. 1st Line Transport.
   Route :-   E.11.b.4.9.
               Canal Bank.
               D.5.a.20.60.
               LES QUARTRE VENTS.
               Road Junction W.27.d.8.7.
               ROBECQ.
               BUSNES.
   Distances of 100 yards will be maintained between Coys. and 100 yards between the rear Coy. and 1st Line Transport.
   Dress. Full marching order. Steel helmets to be worn. Caps in the supporting straps of packs.
   Rifle covers will not be worn.

3. There will be a halt of 1 hour from 1 p.m. - 2 p.m. for the mid-day meal.

4. Pack Cobs will march behind their respective Companies.

5. Blankets rolled in bundles of 10 and securely labelled will be stacked outside Coy. billets by 8 a.m. 7·30 AM
   Officers valises and Mess Stores by 9 a.m. 8 AM
   Leather jerkins will be tied in bundles of 10 and stacked with the blankets at 8 a.m. 7·30 AM

6. Parade states will be handed to the Adjutant at the Starting Point.

7. O.C. Coys. will take steps to ensure that their men are turned out clean with their packs properly packed.
   Special attention is to be paid to the cleaning of clothing and boots.

8. Billets will be left scrupulously clean and a certificate to that effect will be given to the Adjutant at the Starting Point.

9. Arrival in billets will be reported by runner to Battalion Headquarters. Also a billet distribution list will be sent at the same time.

10. **ACKNOWLEDGE.**

February 13th. 1918.

                                                    Captain.
                                                    Adjutant.

Distribution:-
No. 1. O.C. "A" Coy.
    2. "   "B" "
    3. "   "C" "
    4. "   "D" "
    5. "   H.Qrs "
    6. C.O.
    7. 2nd in Command.
    8. I.O.
    9. Adjutant.
    10. R.S.M.
    11. Q.M.& T.O.
    12. R.Q.M.S.
    13.)
    14.) War Diary.
    15. File.

OPERATION ORDER No. 70. Copy No......

by

Lieut-Col. T.R. PELL. D.S.O. Commanding 1/10th. Batt. Manchester Regiment.

Febr: 21st/18.

1. The Battalion will relieve the 1/5th. East Lancs.Regt. at HINGETTE to-morrow, the 22nd inst.

2. An advance party of 1 N.C.O. per Coy. and 1 .C.O per Battalion Headquarters will proceed under Lieut. Street to the new area. This party will report to the Orderly Room at 1-30 p.m. 21st inst.

3. Head of column will pass the Starting Point at 8-15 a.m.
   Starting Point = Crossing of Canal at M27.E.8.9.
   Order of March :-   Band.
                         H.Qrs.
                         "C" Coy.
                         "A" "
                         "D" "
                         "B" "
                         1st. Line Transport.

   Route :- Via Canal Bank unless otherwise ordered.

   DRESS. Full Marching Order. Helmets to be worn. Caps in the supporting straps of the pack. No rifle covers.

4. Lewis Guns will be loaded tonight under arrangements to be made by the Lewis Gun Officer.

5. Blankets rolled in bundles of 10 securely tied and labelled will be stacked at Coy. H.Qrs. by 6-30 a.m. Leather Jerkins in similar bundles will be stacked at the same place and time.
   Officers valises will be stacked at Coy.H.Qrs. by 7-30 a.m.
   The Transport Officer will arrange to collect the above.
   Officers Mess Panniers will be ready at the following times :-
                "C" Coy.   7-15 a.m.
                "A" "   7-30 "
                "D" "   7-50 "
                "B" "   8-10 "
                H.Q.   8-30 "

   The Transport Officer will send round to Coys. tonight for any valises that are not being used. Officers not using their valises will have them ready by 8-30 p.m. tonight.
   Similarly all wash bowls issued to Coys. will be returned to Q.M.Stores not later than 8-30 p.m. and the Q.M. will return to Town Major.

6. O.C. Coys. will take special care that all billets and the vicinity of billets are left clean. They will render a certificate to this effect to the Adjutant at the Starting Point.
   Marching out States will be rendered to Orderly Room by 7 a.m.

7. A rear party of 1 N.C.O. and 7 men will be detailed by the Adjutant and will remain behind to clean up the billeting area. They will report to Major Tetley. P.N. D.S.O. at the Orderly Room at 8-30 a.m.

8. Four G.S. Wagons, in addition to baggage wagons, will report at the Q.M. Stores at 7-30 a.m. to-morrow.

Distribution:-
 1. O.C. "A" Coy. 5.O.C."D".Coy. 10. T.S.
 2. "   "B" "   6. O.O.   11. Q. &T.O.
 3. "   "C" "   7 2nd in Command. 12. R.Q.M.S.
 4. "   "D" "   8 I.O.   13&14 War Diary.
                  9 Adjutant.   15. M.O.
                                     16. 1/5.E.L.R.
                                     17. Town Major. BUSNES.

Captain.
Adjutant.

42nd Division.
126th Infantry Brigade

1/10th BATTALION

MANCHESTER REGIMENT

MARCH 1 9 1 8

Attached:-

Appendices I & II.

Army Form C. 2118.

126/42

10:- Mob Lancasters 2/General.
AQMG
126 K Box

Herewith War Diary of the
unit for the month of June 1918.

W Hulewood Lt
for Lieut Col
Commdg Mob Lancasters Regiment

1/4/18

Place	Date	Hour		Remarks and references to Appendices
HINGETTE	1st June 1918			
-do-	2nd			
-do-	3rd			
	4th	11AM		appx I
LAPUGNOY	5th			
	6th			
LAPUGNOY	7th			
	8th			
	9th			
LAPUGNOY	10th			
LAPUGNOY	11th			
	15th			
LAPUGNOY	16th			
LAPUGNOY	17th			
LAPUGNOY	18th			
LAPUGNOY	19th			
LAPUGNOY	20th		Battalion attack Relieve	
LAPUGNOY	21st		Battalion Training	appx II

Army Form C. 2118.

WAR DIARY

of

O.C. 1/10 Lancashire Regt.

(Kept by Lieut W A HASKEWOOD the officer
detailed by him for that purpose)

From March 1st to 31st 1918 inclusive.

VOL XXV

Place	Date 1918	Hour		Remarks and references to Appendices
HINGETTE	1st			
-do-	2nd			
-do-	3rd			appendix I
-do-	4th	11AM		
LAPUGNOY	5th			
	6th			
LAPUGNOY	7th			
	8th			
	9th			
LAPUGNOY	10th			
LAPUGNOY	11th			
	15th			
LAPUGNOY	16th			
LAPUGNOY	17th			
LAPUGNOY	18th			
LAPUGNOY	19th			
LAPUGNOY	20th			Battalion attack scheme
LAPUGNOY	21st			Battalion Training appendix II

Army Form C. 2118.

or

INTELLIGENCE SUMMARY.

(Erase heading not required.)

Instructions regarding War Diaries and Intelligence Summaries are contained in F. S. Regs., Part II. and the Staff Manual respectively. Title pages will be prepared in manuscript.

Place	Date 1918 April	Hour	Summary of Events and Information	Remarks and references to Appendices
HINGETTE.	1st		Battalion Training	
-do-	2nd		-do-	
-do-	3rd		Divine Service	
	4th	11AM	Battalion proceeded by march route to billets in LAPUGNOY. Billets dirty & insufficient	Appx I
LAPUGNOY	5th 6th		Battalion re-arranging billets & cleaning up.	dtd
LAPUGNOY	7th 8th 9th		Battalion Training.	
LAPUGNOY	10th		Divine Service	
LAPUGNOY	11th to 15th		Battalion Training.	
LAPUGNOY	16th		Battalion Bathing & Training.	
LAPUGNOY	17th		Divine Service	
LAPUGNOY	18th		Batt. Training. 4 Platoons in A.R.A. Competition on Range.	
LAPUGNOY	19th		Batt. Training	
LAPUGNOY	20th		Battalion Attack Scheme	
LAPUGNOY	21st		Battalion Training.	Appx II

Army Form C. 2118.

WAR DIARY
or
INTELLIGENCE SUMMARY.
(Erase heading not required.)

Instructions regarding War Diaries and Intelligence Summaries are contained in F. S. Regs., Part II. and the Staff Manual respectively. Title pages will be prepared in manuscript.

Place	Date 1918	Hour	Summary of Events and Information	Remarks and references to Appendices
LAPUGNOY	March 22	9.15	Battalion Training. Orders received to be prepared to move by Tactical train at short notice.	
LAPUGNOY	23	8 am	Battn ordered to be prepared to entrain at a later hour. Battalion, less 1st Line Transport marched to BURBURE where it entrained. 1st Line Transport proceeded by road to ADINFER WOOD. Proceeded by bus to ADINFER WOOD.	
ADINFER	24th	6 AM	B.O. & Coy Commanders reconnoitred ground East of COURCELLES.	
		11 AM	Orders received to be prepared to move at short notice.	
		2.15 pm	Battalion marched to ROBERT WOOD forming Advanced Guard to the Brigade (2 S 1 S) remained at ADINFER WOOD.	Emma Stone or Nielson
		9.30 pm	Battalion moved to Railway cutting immediately West of GOMMIECOURT.	
	25th	1 AM	Battalion ordered to stand to and to move at once to a position immediately West and S.West of ERVILLERS as immediate support to positions of 40th & 59th Divisions. Info. on advanced that situation at ERVILLERS and immediately EAST obscure.	
		1.15 am	Battn. marched near GOMMIECOURT. B Coy acting as advanced Guard forming flank guard to the Battalion.	
			On arriving at ERVILLERS "D" Coy took up position R.13.6.15.15. — R.13.C.0.4. where connected with right Battalion of 3rd Division was established. "B" Coy. Brig a 2.6 — R.13.C.15.15. "A" Coy on the right of "D" Coy. R.19 a.t.4 — R.19 a.2.6. while "A" Coy was in touch with & Bat. Inniskns whose road at A.20 a.	
		8 AM	Hostile shelling heavy on approach to ERVILLERS. Battn ordered to send two Coys to N.East and East of ERVILLERS. "B" Coy took up position R.13 d.9.5 — R.13 d.4.4. "A" Coy B.19 6.81 — R.13.d.9.5. the left of "D" Coy 3/60 Rifles on right of "B" Coy took up position on the edge of the village. These two Coys had some approx 100-150 yards in advanced by 3/41, 20/L & 59th Division positions. "C" Coy moved to "D" Coys position Batn HQrs. to "B" Coys position. During the morning continuous enemy shelling on ERVILLERS and immediately west of the village.	
		3.20 pm	Enemy attacked along the whole of the front line, immediately to the EAST of ERVILLERS	

WAR DIARY or INTELLIGENCE SUMMARY

Army Form C. 2118.

Place	Date 1918 April	Hour	Summary of Events and Information	Remarks and references to Appendices
	25		The front line withdrew to B & D Coys positions. On night of D Coy front line troops withdrew. 1 Platoon of A Coy sent at 5 pm to fill the gap between B Coy & A Coy right flank. Troops immediately moved expand. The enemy gained possession of BEHAGNIES. A local counter attack at R25 d.2.2 prevented the enemy from enveloping the right flank of the defence of ERVILLERS until relief. The enemy never approached nearer than 200 yards being prevented from doing so by rifle & machine gun fire, no artillery support being forthcoming.	MW
		6.30 pm	Mobile shelling on ERVILLERS and front line very intense.	
		8 pm	Message received that Bn. Drum were falling back at 9 pm to Railway NW of GOMIECOURT.	
		9.30 pm	The Bn. & troops of Bn. HQR & SGR Reserve withdrew from ERVILLERS immediately East to a position linking up with 3rd Divn on left extending East of BOMIECOURT Station Road to road A29 d.8.6. to B Coy covering the withdrawal.	
	26.	1 AM	Orders received to withdraw to A10 c 7.2. Zero hour 2 am. The Battalion withdrew taking up an intermediate position at RAILWAY CUTTING at 22 d. New position at A10 d. taken up at 4 am. Troops dug in.	MW
		7 AM	Orders issued to withdraw to line BUCQUOY — AYETTE.	
		8 AM	Bn. moved thro' ground covered by rear guard of 2 Platoons of D Coy & 2 Platoons of A Coy. Enemy slowly pressed rear guard as far as COURCELLES WEST. D Coy took up next position on line F 23 a 4.0 – F 23 a 40.99. C.A.R Corps on the flank. D Coy in support. A little enemy shelling when taking up position. Bn. Position by 11 AM. 8/L Lancashires on the RIGHT. 31st Divn on the left. Evening & night quiet.	

Army Form C. 2118.

WAR DIARY
or
INTELLIGENCE SUMMARY
(Erase heading not required.)

Place	Date 1918	Hour	Summary of Events and Information	Remarks and references to Appendices
	27		Enemy sniping machine gun fire from ABLAINZEVILLE WOOD. Two sections of our Northern edge of wood. Their sections drove back the enemy but our two heavy counter attacks forced us to withdraw. At about 11 a.m. the enemy attacked the troops on our left who withdrew. No attack developed on our front. After the withdrawal by the troops on our left a gap of 400 yds was left on our left flank. D. Coy. was sent up to fill this gap, a company of the 1/5th East Lancs Regt came up in support of Irish Guards on our left located. Enemy occupied ABLAINZEVILLE-AYETTE Road.	W.H.
	28.	6.30 p.m	In early morning COLDSTREAM GUARDS took over portion of front held by D Coy up to BUCQUOY-AYETTE Road. 1 Platoon D Coy withdrawn to support Line. During the whole day parties of enemy advanced from COURCELLES & ABLAINZEVILLE-AYETTE Road. Heavy casualties inflicted on enemy by machine gun fire. Enemy shelling gas fumes during the day intense. Day spent in improving trenches & getting up supplies of S.A.A. etc. Enemy shelling intense at times. Enemy moves & little sniping.	W.H.
	29.		Very quiet morning with little sniping.	W.H.
	30th	6.30 a.m	Battn relieved by 19th Middlesex Regt (Pioneers) after relief Battn marched to trenches at ESSARTS LES BUCQUOY.	W.H.
	31st		Battalion at ESSART. Battalion rested & congratulated by Divl Commander. In approx trenches from Road Bucq – Road 31st inclusive. Casualties June 9	W.H.

	Killed	Wounded
Officers	1	4
O.R.	7	68

Total casualties 6

W.H. Sherwood Lt.
for Lieut Col.
Commdg 1/10 Lancashire Regiment

A P P E N D I C E S   I & II.

SECRET.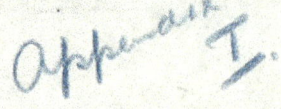

OPERATION ORDER. No. 72.   Copy No........

by

Major F.E. TETLEY. D.S.O. Commanding 1/10th. Battalion Manchester Regiment.
----

1. The Battalion will proceed to LAPUGNOY tomorrow the 4th inst. by march route.

2. Starting Point will be at W.16.a.50.75 at 1 p.m. Coys. are reminded that they must be there at 12-50 p.m. to allow the 10 minutes halt.

3. ROUTE. HINGES CROSS ROADS W.14.d.4.7. L'ABBAYE Road Junction D.6a.95.25 - Road Junction D.6.a.20.45 ESQUE.

4. Order of march will be :- Band, H.Qrs. "C" "D" "B" "A" Coys. 1st. Line Transport. Distances of 100 yards will be maintained between Companies and Transport. The usual hourly halts will be observed.

5. DRESS. Full marching Order. Steel Helmets, particular attention to be paid to the packing of packs and fitting of equipment. Chin straps on the point of the chin.

6. An advanced party composed as under will rendezvous at Battalion Orderly Room at 7 a.m.
    2nd/Lieut. H.J.Fearns. 1 N.C.O. per Coy. 1 N.C.O. per Battalion H.Qrs. and 1 N.C.O. for Transport Section - to be able to ride cycles last named to proceed on horseback.

7. A Rear Party composed as under will remain behind and ensure the billets are left clean to the satisfaction of the Officer detailed. Lieut. E.R.Streat. Cpl.Smith and 2 men per Coy. Lieut. Streat to report to the Adjutant at 12-30 p.m. for instructions.

8. Officers kits, blankets properly rolled in bundles of ten, securely tied and labelled and leather jerkins also in bundles of ten securely tied will be stacked outside Coy. H.Qrs. at 8 a.m.

9. Baggage Wagons will report to Battalion H.Qrs. at 7-30 a.m. 1 Motor Lorry will report at Battalion H.Qrs. at 8 a.m.

10. Hot dinners will be served at 11 a.m. and tea on arrival at LAPUGNOY The watercarts will refill the cookers of "A" & "B" Coys. after the meal.

11. The Mess paniers of "A" & "D" Coys. will be ready for collection at 11-30 a.m. Mess paniers of H.Qrs. "B" & "C" Coys. to be at H.Qrs. Mess at 12-30 p.m. The Mess cart will collect.

12. The Transport will rendezvous on road outside Orderly Room and all vehicles with exception of "B" Coy will rejoin these with exception of "B" Coy. cooker, watercart and mess cart which will rejoin as column passes the Estaminet Corner at W.11.c.10.10.

13. Railhead remains at LILLERS.

14. Refilling Point will be at HAUT.RIEUX approx W.23.c.8.2 from the 5th inst exact locality will be notified later. Hour for refilling 9 a.m.

15. D.A.D.M.S. remains at BUSNES.

16. INSTITUTIONS. CHOQUES.   Y.M.C.A.
                LILLERS. (Army Cinema) on Square.
                LABEUVRIERE. 1st. Corps Rest Station.
                BUS RIEUX.

17. Marching out states and certificates that billets have been left clean will be handed to the Adjutant at Starting Point.

18. Watches will be synchronised from Battalion Orderly Room at 11 a.m.

19. Coys. will report arrival in billets in new area by Orderly.

20. ACKNOWLEDGE.

March 3rd. 1918.

                                                          Captain.
                                                        Adjutant.

```
              No.1.
Distribution :-  O.C. "A" Coy.
              2.    "B"  "
              3.    "C"  "
              4.    "D"  "
              5.   H.Qrs"
              6.   C.O.
              7.   I.O.
              8.   Q.M.& T.O.
              9.   R.Q.M.S.
             10.   R.S.M.
             11.   Adjutant.
             12.)  War Diary.
             13.)
             14.   File.
```

SCHEME.

Appendix II

The enemy have strongly attacked and captured the line D.29.c.
- D.28.b.0.5. - D.28.d.1.2. - D.22. central.

A Battalion of the X Brigade which have suffered heavily
is holding the line D.27.d.5.0. - D.27.central. - D.21.c.0.0.

On the morning of the 20th March the 126th. Bde group at
GAIONNE - RICQUART is ordered to counter-attack and drive the
enemy from his position on the line D.29.a.2.0. - 29.b.95.40.
- D.28.b.60.90.

The 10th. Manchester Regt. is ordered to attack the enemy
in his position D.28.b.95.40. - D.28.b.60.90.

OPERATION ORDER No. 1.

by

Lieut.Col: E.R.PEEL. D.S.O. Commanding 1/10th.Batt: Manchester Regt

Ref. Map. 1/20.000 sheet 36.B. N.E.

Information. 1. The enemy is holding the position on a line
D.29.b.95.40. - D.29.b.60.90.
Y Battalion is holding a line D.27.d.5.0. - D.27. central.

Intention. 2. The 10th.Manchester Regt. is ordered to attack the enemy position D.29.b.95.40. - D.29.b.60.90. at Zero hour on March 20th.
The 8th.East Lancs.Regt. are ordered to attack on the Right of the 10th Manchesters and Z Battn. on the Left.

Dispositions. 3. "B" & "D" Coys. will form the attacking line.
"A" Coy. in support to "B" Coy.
"C" Coy. in support to "D" "
"B" Coy. will attack on the Right of the Battalion Front. "D" Coy. on the Left.

Boundaries. 4. Right Boundary of "B" Coy.
D.27.d.0.5.   True bearing 72 deg:
D.27.d.85.70.
D.29.b.05.20.
D.29.b.95.40.

Left Boundary of "B" Coy.
D.27.d.90.60.
D.29.b.20.90.
D.29.b.70.70.   Track inclusive.
Left Boundary "D" Coy.
D.27.a.80.10.
D.27.b.90.45.
D.28.c.60.90.   True bearing 75 deg:

Line of S.
Deployment. D.27.d.9.2. - D.27.a.8.1.

(2)

Formation. 6. Coys. forming the attacking line will advance
in two waves preceeded by the Battalion Scouts.
Leading Section of each platoon will extend.
Remainder of platoon, sections in file.
Coys. in Support, half platoons in Artillery
Formation.
Distances, Battalion Scouts.
150 yards in advance of leading sections.
50 yards distance between lines.
100 yards distance between waves.

Consolidation.
7. Line to be consolidated approx: on the line
captured from the enemy.
Coys. will organize defence in depth.

Report
Centre. 8. Battalion Headquarters previous to Zero hour
at D.27.c.5.5. At Zero plus 25 move to
D.27.b.8.1.

Contact
Aeroplane. 9. A contact aeroplane will fly over at 11 a.m.
and 11-30 a.m. Flares will be lit when
called for.

Zero Hour. 10. Zero hour will be notified later.

Watches. 11. Watches will be synchronised at 8 a.m.

(Signed) J.C.S. ROWBOTHAM.

March 19th, 1918.

Captain.
Adjutant.

126th Inf.Bde.
42nd Div.

1/10th BATTN. THE MANCHESTER REGIMENT.

A P R I L

1 9 1 8

Attached:

Appendices 1 to 11.

Vol 15

WAR DIARY

of

Officer Commanding 1/10th Manchester Regt.

from April 1st 1918. To April 30th 1918.

Volume 3et

April 30th 1918

Army Form C. 2118.

WAR DIARY
or
INTELLIGENCE SUMMARY.
(Erase heading not required.)

Instructions regarding War Diaries and Intelligence Summaries are contained in F. S. Regs., Part II. and the Staff Manual respectively. Title pages will be prepared in manuscript.

Place	Date	Hour	Summary of Events and Information	Remarks and references to Appendices
ESSARTS.	1918. April 1st	8 a.m.	Marched to Front Line and relieved 23rd MIDDLESEX REGT in Left Brigade Sector, immediately E. of BUCQUOY - AYETTE ROAD. 429 Field Coy. R.E. attached to Battalion.	W.R.P.
	" 2nd		Heavy hostile shelling of Front & Support Lines. Battalion H.Qrs. moved to firm Pit. W. of BUCQUOY-AYETTE.	W.R.P.
	" 3rd		Front quiet, back area shelled. AYETTE heavily shelled at 11 a.m. Enemy aircraft active in the morning. 429 Field Coy R.E. relieved by 1 Coy. 9th Northumberland Fusiliers.	W.R.P.
	" 4th		Quiet. Battalion relieved by 45th Marshalls Regt. Relief not completed till 2.15 a.m. on the 5th.	W.R.P. No 1
	" 5th		After relief Battalion marched to reserve trenches at ESSARTS. The last Company arriving at 5 a.m. Intense hostile barrage on reserve trenches from 5.30 a.m. - 10.30 a.m. 8 in. 5.9 and large amount of gas shells used. Casualties heavy. 3 Killed. 9 Wounded. 4 Officers + 66 O.R. gassed. Very wet night.	W.R.P.
	" 6th		Wet night. Quiet day, except for intermittent shelling of ESSARS.	W.R.P.
SOUASTRE. PAS.	" 7th		Battalion relieved by 2/5th West Yorks Regt. Relief completed by 4.30 a.m. Battalion moved to SOUASTRE. 4 p.m. Battalion marched to PAS. During period March 24th to April 7th the following Officers commanded Companies:- CAPT. J.A.C.TAYLOR A.Coy. CAPT. T. BLETCHER & Lieut. W. CHAPMAN. B.Coy. CAPT. A. BUTTERWORTH. C. Coy. CAPT. R.V. STANFORD & 2/Lieut. W. H. HODSON. D. Coy.	W.R.P. No 2 & No 5
	" 8th		In Rest.	W.R.P.
	" 9th		In Rest. Reconnaissance of RED LINE & SWITCH. Capt. J.C.S. RONDOTHAM assumes command of D. Coy. Lieut. F. HOWARTH assumes duties of Adjutant. Lieut. E.H.FINCH assumes command of B. Coy.	W.R.P.

Army Form C. 2118.

WAR DIARY
or
INTELLIGENCE SUMMARY.
(Erase heading not required.)

Instructions regarding War Diaries and Intelligence Summaries are contained in F. S. Regs., Part II. and the Staff Manual respectively. Title pages will be prepared in manuscript.

Place	Date	Hour	Summary of Events and Information	Remarks and references to Appendices
	April 10th	3-25 a.m.	Battalion ordered to be prepared to move at ½ hours notice.	WRP
	11th		Battalion training. Battalion inspected by G.O.C. 142nd Division.	WRP
	12th		Training.	WRP
	13th		IV Corps Commander visits Battalion. Training.	WRP
	14th		Battalion moved at 4-40 a.m. to Bivouac at HENU. Cool & foggy day. In afternoon, Commanding Officer reconnoitred front held by 8th Somerset Light Infantry. Advance parties sent up at night.	WRP No 5
	15th		Battalion moved from Bivouac at HENU at 6-15 p.m. and marched via SOUASTRE – FONCQUEVILLERS and GOMMECOURT, meeting guides at GOMMECOURT. Heavy shelling of FONCQUEVILLERS for 10 minutes on the Battalion passing thro'. Capt. T.E.S. ROWBOTHAM & Lt. E.T. FINCH wounded. Lt. W. CHAPMAN assumed command of D. Coy. 2/Lt. H.J. NORRIS of B. Coy. Battalion held immediately N.E. of ROSSIGNOL WOOD. 5th West Lancs Regt. on Left & 125th 73rd on Right (8th L.F.'s) Line in hand condition. B. & D. Coys in front Line. C in support. A. Coy. in Reserve. Quiet night with slight burst of machine gun fire. Battle surplus under Capt. J.A.C. TAYLOR proceeded to PAS. Transport Lines & Quartermaster Stores at COIGNEUX.	WRP No 6
	16th		Quiet morning. Intermittent 10.5cm shelling during the day. Considerable movement near ROSSIGNOL WOOD. This was dealt with by our Artillery. Work at night on new Support Line & on existing trenches. Enemy artillery active at times during the night.	WRP
	17th		Intermittent shelling (Rifle) otherwise quiet. At night 5th F.L.R. took over our front line. D. Coy. remained near Sunken Road. C. Coy. in CHUB TRENCH. A.B. Coys. in SAP ON TRENCH. Work continued on support line. Wet afternoon & night. Warning received from Corps that attack operation on 18.15	WRP

Army Form C. 2118.

WAR DIARY
or
INTELLIGENCE SUMMARY.
(Erase heading not required.)

Instructions regarding War Diaries and Intelligence Summaries are contained in F. S. Regs., Part II. and the Staff Manual respectively. Title pages will be prepared in manuscript.

Place	Date	Hour	Summary of Events and Information	Remarks and references to Appendices
	April 18th		Wet misty. Advance party sent to 5th East Lancs Regt. Enemy artillery active at times. Patrols sent out. No enemy attack developed.	WRP
	19th		Orders received to relieve 5th E.L.R. on 19/20th. B. Coy on Right. A. Coy in Centre. C. Coy on Left. D. Coy in Support. Hostile shelling during day & night more intense than usual.	WRP No 8.
	20th		Night Quiet. Less enemy shelling during the day. Our artillery very active. Enemy machine guns active.	WRP
	21st		Our artillery active. Enemy quiet.	WRP
	22nd		Quiet day. Warning orders to extend front a.a. take over 500 yards from 62nd Division.	WRP
	23rd		D. Coy. relieved B. Coy. 5th K.O.Y.L.I. at 10 pm. B. Coy. of 8th Manchester Regt. under orders of C.O. 10th Manchester & took up position in BASS TRENCH & ROACH TRENCH. Four Battery Commanders visited Battn. S.O.S. Lines. Headquarters moved to CHUB TRENCH.	WRP No 9.
	24th		Relieved by 8th Manchester. D. Coy. under orders of O.C. 8th Manchester in immediate Support. B. Coy. in IVAAC TRENCH. C. Coy. CHUB TRENCH. A. Coy. SALMON TRENCH.	WRP No 10.
	25th		Heavy shelling at 4 a.m. otherwise quiet day. Relieved at night by 5th E.L.R. Battalion goes into Reserve at GOMMECOURT.	WRP No 11.
	26th		Battalion in Reserve. Work on JULIUS POINT and Carrying to Front Line.	WRP
	27th		Battalion in Reserve. Work on JULIUS POINT and Carrying to Front Line.	WRP

Army Form C. 2118.

WAR DIARY
or
INTELLIGENCE SUMMARY.
(Erase heading not required.)

Instructions regarding War Diaries and Intelligence Summaries are contained in F. S. Regs., Part II and the Staff Manual respectively. Title pages will be prepared in manuscript.

Place	Date	Hour	Summary of Events and Information	Remarks and references to Appendices
	April 28th		Battalion in Reserve. Work on Julius Point and carrying to front line.	ARP
	29th		Battalion in Reserve. Work on Julius Point and carrying to front line.	ARP
	30th		Battalion in Reserve. Work on Julius Point and carrying to front line.	ARP

W.R. Peel Mac
Comg 1/10 Manchester Regt

APPENDICES

1 to 11 .

Copy / Operation Order No 10. I

1). The 1/5 Manchester Regt will relieve the Battn in the Line tonight 4/5th inst.

2.) A Coy will relieve A Coy.
   D . . . . B
   C C
   B . . . . D

3. OC Coys will send 3 Guides to Battn. H.Q. at 7-30 p.m. These guides will proceed under 2/Lt Whitehead to where they will meet the incoming Unit at F.14.d.0.0.

4. After relief Coys will march to ESSARTS
ROUTE :- Along northern edge of C.T. running through Square F.22.d and F.21.b. F.15.d and F.15.c. crossing this trench in F.14.d to Cross Road. at F.14.d.0.0 thence to Cross Roads F.19.c.7.2.
A Coy takes over from B Coy.
   C C
   D . . . . D
   B . . . . A
Battn HQrs will be at E.24.c.7.9

Lewis Guns.

5.) Coys. will leave their Lewis Guns at the ration dump F.21.b.9.7 where O.C. Coys. will leave them under the charge of 4 men per Coy. Limbers will arrive at this point at 12-30 a.m and take the Guns to ESSARTS.

6.) Coys. will Collect all petrol tins and dixies and will send them to the ration dump by 9-30 pm Officers may send their mess Stores to the same place at the same time with one Servant per Coy.

7.) Salved Rifles will be Sent down at the same time as in para. 6.

8.) Coys will carry out with them all Very Pistols, tools, periscopes etc.

9.) Coys will ensure that they very Carefully hand over the Defence Scheme.

10) The Completion of relief will be notified to Battn H.Q. by Code word. "CHIC".

11). On arrival at the destination Coys will send a runner to Battn. H.Qrs.
This runner will guide Battn H.Qrs runner back to Coys.

Distribution
No 1 OC 1/5 Manchester Regt
   2   . A Coy
   3   . B .
   4   . C .
   5   . D .
   6   . T.O.
   7   . H.Qrs
   8   War Diary
   9
   10   File.

April 4th/1918.

(Signed) F. Howarth.
Lieut &
a/Adjt.

Copy

Operation Order No 11. II

1.) The Battalion will be relieved by 75th West Yorks Regt. tonight.

2.) A Coy relieves A Coy
    B   ·   B ·
    C   ·   C ·
    D   ·   D ·

3) O.C. Coys. will ensure that all dispositions in case of attack are carefully handed over.

4.) All Very Pistols, Petrol tins, etc will be taken out by Coys.

5. After relief Lewis Guns & Lewis Gun equipment will be taken to 'C' Coys. H.Qrs. and there dumped. The parties carrying the above will report to 2/Lt MALTBY, C. Coy who will superintend the loading of limbers (which arrive at the ration point at about 1 a.m.) He will then march the party with the limbers to the destination of the Battalion, and there issue Guns to Coys.

In the same way he will superintend loading of dixies. etc.

6. On completion of relief Coys. will march to SOUASTRE.
Route:- GOMMECOURT - FONQUEVILLERS - SOUASTRE (Valley Camp) Guides for incoming units will lead Coy. out.

7. Completion of relief will be sent to Battn. HQrs by runner.

8. Acknowledge.

(Signed) F. Hogarth.
Lieut &
A/Adjt.

6/4/18.

Copy

Operation Order. No 75.
by
Lieut. Col. W.R. Peel. D.S.O. Commanding.

1. The Battalion will proceed by march route to PAS & be billeted there today 7/4/18.

2. Order of march. Band. HQrs. A. B. C. & D Coys. 1st Line Transport. Route:- Old Wind Mill - HENU - PAS.

3. Starting point will be D.21.b.5.0. Head of column will pass Starting Point at 3-50 p.m. Distances of 200 yards between Coys will be maintained. Usual Lewis lasts to be observed.

4. Dress:- Fighting Kit. Steel Helmets. Box Respirator over right Shoulder. Leather jerkins to be worn over the tunic.

5. Blankets in bundles of 10 properly labelled. Officers Kits & Mess Panniers will be stacked at QM Store at 2-30 p.m. Transport Officer will arrange

- 2 -

to collect the Officers Kits at 10% Billet.

6. OC Coys will render a marching out state to the Adjutant at the Starting Point & Arrival in billets will be notified by runner.

7. Time will be synchronized at 3 p.m.

8 Acknowledge.

7/4/18.

(Signed) J.C.S Rowbotham
Captain
& Adjt.

OPERATION ORDER NO.76.

by

Lieut.Col. W.R. PEEL. D.S.O. Commanding 1/10th Batt: Manchester Regt.

1. The 42nd Division is now in Corps Reserve.

2. In the event of a heavy enemy attack the Division will assemble in the RED LINE.

3. The 126th.Infy Bde will assemble in positions of readiness between SQUATRE inclusive and BOIS DU WARNICOURT exclusive.

4. From the RED LINE portions of the Division may be ordered forward to counter-attack any bodies of enemy who may have penetrated the PURPLE LINE to reinforce any threatened point or to occupy if necessary the PURPLE LINE SWITCH from SAILLY LES BOIS to rough CHATEAU DE LA HAIE.

5. In the first instance the 5th.E.Lancs.Regt. will take up a position from BOIS DE MARTIMONT exclusive to ROAD JUNCTION J.4.0.0.2.
1/8th.Manchester Regt. J.4.0.0.2.
IV Corps Boundary.
1/10th. Manchester Regt. in valley, J.1.s.2.0.

Mewart
Lieut. &
a/Adjutant.

April 12th.1918.

OPERATION ORDER No. 77.

by

Lieut. Colonel. W.R. PEEL. D.S.O. Commanding.

1. The Battalion will move into tents at HENU to-morrow, the 15th.inst. D.13.b.5.3.

2. The Battalion will pass the Starting Point at 4-40 a.m. at O.16.d.9. Road Junction.
Order of March :- Headquarters. "D" "C" "A" "B" Coys. 1st Line Transport. Distances of 100 yards will be maintained between Coys. and 1st Line Transport.
DRESS. Full marching Order.

3. O.C. Coys. will arrange for their men to have tea before marching off and breakfasts on arrival in the new area.

4. Blankets rolled in bundles of 10 and Officers valises will be stacked at Coy. H.Qrs. by 3-30 a.m. Officers Mess Stores at the same place at 3-45 a.m.

5. Lewis Gun limbers will be loaded to-night. O.C. Coys. will detail 1 man to accompany each limber.

6. The Transport Officer will ensure that the water carts are full before leaving.

7. Sick Parade will be held immediately on arrival in the new area.

8. The working parties of "C" & "D" Coys. will move off after breakfast from the new area.

9. An advance party of 1 N.C.O. per Coy. and Transport will report to Major T.H.Astley.D.S.O. at 4-45 a.m. at D.13.d.6.2. Road and Pack Junction.

Lieut. &
/Adjutant.

April 15th.1918.

Copy.

Operation Order No. 78.
by
Lieut. Col. W.R. Peel. D.S.O. Commanding.
_____

1. The Battalion will relieve the 8th Somerset Light Infantry in the Line tonight 15/16th inst.

2. B. Coy. relieves C Coy. 8th Somersets.
   D Coy.   "   A Coy.   "   "
   With 2 platoons each in the front line and one platoon each in immediate Support.
   C Coy relieves D Coy. in Support.
   A. Coy   "   B   "   Reserve.
   Battn. H.Qrs at K. 6. c. 4. 7.

3. Battn will march out at 6-15 p.m.
   Order of march :-
        D. B. C. HQrs. A. Coy.
   ROUTE :- Via SOUASTRE FONQUEVILLERS
   Distances of 200 yds between platoons.

4. Guides will meet Coys. at O.G. Line E. 28. c. 60. 35 at 9 p.m.

5. Lewis Gun limbers will take the Lewis Guns to the point of rendezvous. The Guides to be there at 8-45 p.m. OC Coys. will detail one man per gun to go with the limbers. The party will

-2-

march under Sergt. AINSWORTH.

6. All men of the leading two Coys. will carry two bombs each.

7. Men without leather jerkins will carry greatcoats.

8. The rations for tomorrow will be carried on the man.

9. Water will be taken in limbers to a place to be notified later.

10. The battle Surplus will be under the orders of Capt. J.C.Taylor & will proceed today to BOIS-ST-PIERRE One cooker will accompany them.

11. Relief Complete will be notified to Battn. HQrs. by Code word "ROBEY"

Distribution

No 1 ac A
  2   B
  3   C
  4   D
  5   HQ
  6   QM.T.S.
  7   RSM
  8   War Diary
  9   "
 10   File.

15/4/18.

Signed. F. Howarth.
Lieut & A/adjt.

Operation Order 79.

VII

1. The Battalion will be relieved in front line trenches by 5th E.L.R tonight 17-18. inst.

2. "B" Coy 5th E.L.R will take over No 7 & 8 posts at present held by D Coy. at dusk this evening. A Coy 5th E.L.R. will take over Nos 1 to 4 posts inclusive held by B Coy & posts 5 & 6 held by D Coy at about 2-30 a.m 18th inst.

3. After relief the whole of B Coy will take up a position in Salmon Trench on left of "C" Coy.
D Coy will occupy the trench where its and B Coys support platoons are at present located & also a portion of the Dam Trench at present occupied by a platoon of 5th E.L.R.
OC D Coy will move his HQ to those occupied by B Coy by 10 p.m this evening.

-2-

4. All bombs S.A.A. S O S rockets in front line will be handed over. All tools Very pistols periscopes etc will not be handed over.

5. OC A Coy will arrange to show advance party of B Coy the position B Coy is to take up & to accommodate the officers of B Coy if possible in the dug out at present occupied by machine gunners

6. Working parties will continue as for last night with the exception that they will report to 2/Lt Norris & not 2/Lt Chapman. In the event of an attack whilst these parties are out digging they will occupy the trenches they are digging. They will come under the orders of 2/Lt Chapman.

7. A Coy will carry up rations as for last nights to C & D Coys.

- 3 -

The rations for B Coy Hqrs will hand over to B Coy's advance party in Salmon Trench.

8. OC. C. Coy. will arrange to place some of his Coy men in the northerly end of CHUB TRENCH so as to cover the valley which runs along the south westerly edge BIEZ WOOD.

Copies to:-
1 OC A Coy
2   B
3   C
4   D
5 C.O. /5th Bed: Lancs
6 File

J Howarth
Lieut &
a/Adjutant

17/4/18.

ADDENDA TO OPERATION ORDER No 77.

1. "A" Coy. will occupy the Strong Point from K.5.c.8.y - 4.9 to K.5.c.5.1. to 6.a.3.2.
O.C "A" Coy will accommodate as many men as possible in the Strong Point which is not yet completed. The remainder of the Coy. must be prepared to take up positions in this Strong Point in the case of an attack. O.C "A" Coy. will therefore think out disposition for his troops.
All platoon Commanders must thoroughly reconnoitre this position.

17/10.

H Howarth
Lieut &
Adjutant

Operation Order No. 80   VIII

1) The Battalion will relieve the 1/5 E. Lancs. Regt in the line tonight.

2) 'B' Coy relieves 'A' Coy 1/5. E.L.R on the RIGHT
   'A'   "   " 'B'   "   "   "   CENTRE
   'C'   "   " 'D'   "   "   "   LEFT
   'D'   "   " 'C'   "   "   "   SUPPORT

3) RIGHT Coy. 2 Platoons in Front line
               1 Platoon in Support
               Coy Hqrs   K.6.d.75.15

   CENTRE Coy. 2 Platoons in Front Line
               1 Platoon in Support
               Coy Hqrs   L.7.a.65.45.

   LEFT Coy.   2 Platoons in Front line
               1 Platoon in Support
               Coy Hqrs   L.7.a.65.10.

   Support Coy. 2 Platoons N half BASS TR.
                1 Platoon   ROACH TR.
                Coy Hqrs   N.6.d.65.25.

2

4) Rations will be carried by Coys tonight and the relief will not commence till rations have been drawn and each man has been issued with them.

5) Guides will meet the Battn at 10-pm or after at 5th E.L.R. Hdqrs.
'B' Coy will march direct to 'A' Coy. 5th E.L.R. ~~Hdqrs~~ to be there at 10-pm if rations are issued in time
'C' Coy will march to Battalion H. Qrs, 5th E.L. Rgt. to be there at 10-pm if issue of rations permits.
'D' Coy will march direct to the Support Coy. as soon as rations are drawn.
A Coy will arrive at 5th ELR HQ at 10-30 PM.

6) Battalion Hdqrs will move so as to arrive at Battn Hdqrs 5th E.L.R. at 10-30 pm.

7) 1 Runner per Coy and 4 for Battn Hdqrs will report at 5th E.L. Rgt. at 8-30 pm to learn the routes to the various Companies.

8) All tools, S.A.A, Bombs, S.O.S Rockets etc. will be handed over to 5th E.L. Regt. and receipts obtained.
Very Pistols, Periscopes etc will not be handed over.
In the same way the above will be taken over from the 5th E.L. Regt and receipts given.

9) Completion of Relief will be notified by code-word RUM.

10) Acknowledge

19/4/1918.

F. Howarth
Lieut
A/Adjutant
REGAIN

Operation Order No. 81

1. On night 23/24th the Battn. will extend its front and take over the portion of the 5th K.O.Y.L.I. front from L.76.25.15 as far north as L.2.c.20.18. This portion of the line is now held by B. Coy 5th K.O.Y.L.I.

2. D. Coy will take over this front being relieved by a company of the 6th Manchesters who will come under command of O.C. 1/10th Manchester Regt.

3. Time and place of rendezvous of guides to meet the Company of 6th Manchesters will be notified later.

4. Guides for D. Coy will meet the Company at B. Coy 5th K.O.Y.L.I. headquarters. D. Coy moving here as soon as relieved by 6th Manchesters.

5. Battn. Headquarters will move at a time to be notified later to dugouts in Chu B TR at approx. K6.c.9.5. Present Battn Headquarters will remain as an exchange and in addition will be occupied as Coy. Hdqrs of Company of 8 Manchesters.
A Runner Relay Post will also be established at this point. The R.A.P. will remain as at present.

6. The Sign. Officer will arrange at dusk to connect D Coys new Hdqrs to present Battn. Hdqrs.

7. All trench stores etc. will be taken over by O.C. D Coy and receipts given.

8. Completion of relief will be reported to Hdqrs by code word INEY.

P.T.O.

No 1 Copy. File
2. O.C. A
3.   B
4.   C
5.   D
6. Hdqrs Coy
7. 1/8 Manchester Regt
8.   Coy 1/8 Manchester Regt

IX

Reference Operation Order No 81.

Para.1. for "as far North as L.2.c.20.18"
read " L.2.c.9.1.

Para 5. is Cancelled.

J Howarth
Lieut &
A/Adjt.

23/4/18.

OPERATION ORDER No 82.
by
Lieut. Col. W R Peel. DSO. Commanding.

1. The Battalion less D Coy will be relieved by the 8th Manchester Regt. tonight 24/25th And will go into Support. 'D' Coy. will go into immediate Support to the 8th Manchesters & on completion of relief will come under the orders of the 8th Manchesters.

2. A Coy. will be relieved by A Coy.
   B " " " " " C "
   C " " " " " B "
   D " " " " " D "

3. OC. C. Coy. will arrange details of relief with OC. C Coy 8th Manchester who is at present in WAACS TRENCH OC. D. Coy. will arrange details of relief with OC D. Coy. 8th Manchesters. These two reliefs will commence as soon as visibility permits. After relief "B" Coy will move into WAACS TRENCH and 'D' Coy. into BASS TRENCH & ROACH TRENCH coming under the orders of OC. 8th Manchesters OC C Coy & OC. A Coy will send

Guides to report to Battn. H.Q. at 8-30 p.m.
One guide per Coy. H.Q. & one guide per platoon.

After relief 'C' Coy. will move into CHUB TRENCH and A Coy into STRONG POINT in SALMON TRENCH.

4. An advance party of one officer from 'B' Coy & one officer from A. Coy 8th Manchesters will be sent to C & A H.Qrs. respectively at 8-30 p.m.

5. Each Coy will send an advance party to the trenches they go to, to take over trench stores. These advance parties will arrive at their respective trenches at 8 p.m.

6. All trench stores will be handed over & receipts obtained. Tools, periscopes & Very Pistols will not be handed over.

7. Ration parties of 1 N.C.O & 12 men per Coy will report at the ration point at 10-45 p.m. & carry rations to the new position of their Coys.

- 3 -

8. On completion of relief "D" Coy. will commence working on HERRING TRENCH and the platoon of "B" Coy. on PIKE TRENCH.

9. On completion of relief Battn. H.Q. will move to SALMON TRENCH.

10. Completion of relief will be wired to Battn. H.Q. by code word FRANK.

Distribution. No 1 OC A Coy
2   B
3   C
4   D
5   HQ
6   D Coy 8th Manchesters
7   War Diary
8   "
9   File.

F. Howarth
Lieut &
a/Adjt.

24/4/18.

Copy OPERATION ORDER N° 83   XI
              by
Lieut. Col. W.R. Peel. D.S.O. Commanding.

1. The Battn. will be relieved by the 5th
   E.L.R. tonight 25/26th and will
   move into Reserve in GOMMECOURT.

2. A Coy is relieved by B Coy. 5th E.L.R.
   B "   "   "   " C "   "   " "
   C Coy. 5th E.L.R. will be disposed as
   follows :— 1 platoon WAAC TRENCH.
              1   -   PIKE TRENCH.
              1   -   HIGH STREET.
   C Coy will be relieved as follows
   1 platoon & Coy HQrs by 1 Platoon
   & Coy HQrs of "A" Coy. 5th E.L.R.
   2 platoon by 2 platoon 'D' Coy.
   5th E.L.R.

3. After relief Coys will move to their
   Battle positions in the GOMMECOURT LINE
   After every man knows his position
   Coys will then move into dug outs.
   Battn. HQrs will be situated in
   E.29.a.35.75. The personnel will
   be prepared to man the trench
   in which the dug outs are situated.

A Coy. takes over the positions & dug outs occupied by C Coy. 5th E.L.R. the centre Coy and takes over Post 8 in RUM. TRENCH with Support Platoon and Posts 21 & 22 in the GOMMECOURT LINE with the two leading platoons.

B Coy takes over Post No 17 in RUM TRENCH (1 Platoon) & No 20 Post in the GOMMECOURT Line at present occupied by B Coy 5th E.L.R. on the right.

C Coy. takes over No 19 Post in RUM. TR. (1 platoon) And Nos 23 & 24 Post GOMMECOURT LINE at present occupied by 'D' Coy. 5th E.L.R. on the left.

D Coy. after rejoining the Battn will be in reserve & takes over from A Coy 5th E.L.R.

4. The advance party which proceeded this afternoon will meet Coys at present Battn H.Q. in SALMON TRENCH & will conduct them to the new positions.

3.

5. Working Party. A Coy will find a carrying party of 1 Officer & 50 O.R. to report to Sergt BOUCHEY at junction of O.G. front line and FONQUEVILLERS - GOMMECOURT Road at 10 p.m. and will carry material to SALMON POINT. Probable hour of return 4 a.m.

6. A pushing party of 2 NCO's & 20 men from 'C' Coy will report with all equipment at present Battn HQ at 9 p.m. and will be guided to GOMMECOURT where they will push trucks containing rations of 8th Manchesters to the unloading point.

7. All trench stores, including tools, will be handed over and receipts obtained. Periscopes & Very pistols will not be handed over.

8. Completion of relief will be wired to these HQ. by code word "RUM" and when Coys are in their new positions notification will be sent to Battn HQrs.

4.

9. D. Coy. After the reorganization of the front line will be informed by O.C. 8th Manchesters where they may move. They will then march straight to GOMMECOURT.

10. ACKNOWLEDGE.

Marratt
Lieut &
A/Adjutant.

25/4/18.

1/10th North Lancashire Regiment

12/2/4

Vol 6.

WAR DIARY of
O.C.

1/10th Lancaster Regiment

Aug 1st to 31st 1918

Volume 34

Army Form C. 2118.

WAR DIARY

or

INTELLIGENCE SUMMARY.

(Erase heading not required.)

Instructions regarding War Diaries and Intelligence Summaries are contained in F. S. Regs., Part II. and the Staff Manual respectively. Title pages will be prepared in manuscript.

Place	Date 1918 MAY	Hour	Summary of Events and Information	Remarks and references to Appendices
FONQUEVILLERS	1st		Warning order that Battalion would be relieved by 5th EAST LANCS Regt on night 2/3rd.	KRP
			Advance party came up in afternoon, an also also advance party of 51st Divn who are coming in to take over.	KRP
-do-	2nd		Battalion relieved by 1/5th EAST LANCS Regt and went into bivouacs at J.6.d. "5 am" Appendix I	Stat 51°NE 1/20000 KRP
J.6.d.	3rd		Rest of Battalion on working parties. Battalion ordered to move up to BEER TRENCH on 4th.	KRP
BEER TRENCH	4th		Battalion moved to BEER TRENCH at 5 am. On Working parties. appendices	KRP
-do-	5th		On Working parties	KRP
-do-	6th		Battalion relieved by 1/5th LOYAL NORTH LANCS Regt and moved into camp in WOOD near PAS. Appendix II	Sqt 51° NE 1/40000 KRP

WAR DIARY
or
INTELLIGENCE SUMMARY.

Army Form C. 2118.

(Erase heading not required.)

Instructions regarding War Diaries and Intelligence
Summaries are contained in F. S. Regs., Part II.
and the Staff Manual respectively. Title pages
will be prepared in manuscript.

Place	Date 1918	Hour	Summary of Events and Information	Remarks and references to Appendices
PAS	May 7th		Arrived in Camp 2.30 a.m. Reconnaissance of RED LINE by C.O. and Company Commanders in the afternoon.	WRP
- do -	8th		Training	WRP
- do -	9th		Battalion mans RED LINE for practice, marching out at 8.30 a.m and returning to camp at 6 p.m.	WRP
- do -	10th		Battalion Training	WRP
- do -	11th		— do —	WRP
- do -	12th		— do —	WRP
- do -	13th		— do —	WRP
- do -	14th		— do —	WRP
- do -	15th		— do —	WRP
- do -	16th		— do —	WRP
- do -	17th		— do —	WRP

Army Form C. 2118.

WAR DIARY
or
INTELLIGENCE SUMMARY.
(Erase heading not required.)

Instructions regarding War Diaries and Intelligence Summaries are contained in F. S. Regs., Part II. and the Staff Manual respectively. Title pages will be prepared in manuscript.

Place	Date 1918 May	Hour	Summary of Events and Information	Remarks and references to Appendices
PAS	18th		"L" Coy 3rd Battn. 304th Inft REGT U.S.A. attached for training	1st RPP
-do-	19th		Battalion on Working parties	6th RPP
-do-	20th		— do —	6th RPP
-do-	21st		— do —	6th RPP
-do-	22nd		Brigade Tactical Exercise	6th RPP
-do-	23rd		Training	6th RPP
-do-	24th		Major F.E. TETLEY D.S.O. leaves Battalion and goes to 1/5th MANCHESTER Regt.	6th RPP
-do-	25th		Training	6th RPP
-do-	26th		Presentation of Medal Ribbons by G.O.C. 42nd Division (Appendix IV)	6th RPP

Army Form C. 2118.

WAR DIARY
or
INTELLIGENCE SUMMARY.
(Erase heading not required.)

Instructions regarding War Diaries and Intelligence Summaries are contained in F. S. Regs., Part II. and the Staff Manual respectively. Title pages will be prepared in manuscript.

Place	Date 1918 Jan.	Hour	Summary of Events and Information	Remarks and references to Appendices
PAS	27ᵗʰ		Battalion Training	APP
-do-	28ᵗʰ		Battalion on Working Parties	APP
-do-	29ᵗʰ		—do—	APP
-do-	30ᵗʰ		—do—	APP
			—do—	APP
PAS	31ˢᵗ		Battalion Training	APP

L. R. Peel Lieut Col
Commdg 110ᵗʰ Lancaster Regt.

APPENDIX III

Bar to D.S.O.   Lt.Col. W.R. PEEL. D.S.O.

D.S.O.   Captain. J.A.C. Taylor.

M.C.   Captain) F. Howarth.
                           & Adjt.)

M.M.   L/Sergt. Robinson. B.
                           Pte. Spink, E.
                           Pte. Hutchins. E.
                           Pte. Davies. J.
                           Pte. Hulme. S.

Belgian Croix de Guerre.
                           Sergt. Haslam. S.
                           Pte. Coulson. J.

Lieut.Col. W.R. PEEL. D.S.O. received the V.C. ribbon awarded to
No. 375499 Pte. Mills. W. late of this unit.

Operation Order No 85 File 2

1) The Battalion will move into
BEER TRENCH on the morning
of 4-5-18.

2) A Coy will take up a
position from E28a 5.10 to
E28c 20.55

B Coy from E28c 20.55
to E27d 8.2

C Coy from E27d 8.2
to K3b 85.80

D Coy from K3b 85.80
to K3d 1.1.

All Coys will be
disposed of in depth

Battⁿ H Q^{rs} will be
at E27d 99.60

3) Coys will leave their
area in the following

10. Completion of relief will be sent by runner to Bere Hove by code "G.D.S.O.A.B."

Companies will report arrivals in Camp.

11. ACKNOWLEDGE

5/18

F Howarth.
Lieut & Adjt
REGAIN

Distribution
Copy No 1 A Coy
" 2 B "
" 3 C "
" 4 D "
" 5 HQ "
" 6 2nd in Command
" 7 T.O. & Ord
" 8 1/5th Loyal N.L. Regt
" 9 Rear Guard
" 10 File
" 11 File

1 Limber will be at the Cookhouse at 10 pm and will convey back all dixies and empty petrol tins. The Cooks will accompany this limber.

1 Limber will be at A Coy's Ration Dump at 10 pm to convey officers mess stores & Signalling equipment. 1 S[?] and 1 Officer's servants to be detailed will accompany this limber.

6. Officers chargers will be on the SOUASTRE Rd at D 23 c 4. 5.

7. All Trench Stores will be handed over and receipts obtained. These will be sent in to Orderly Room by 12 noon 7-5-18

8. Rear HQrs will arrange for an advance party to billet over the camp

9. The Rear will arrange for a hot meal on arrival in camp

Operation Order No 86
by Lt Col W.R. Reed M.C. Commanding
───────────────

1. The Battalion will be relieved by 1/5th Loyal North Lancs. Regt on the evening of 6th May 1918.

2. Corresponding Coys will relieve each other.

3. 4 guides per Coy and 1 per Battn H.Qrs will report to these Hd. Qrs by 7.30 pm and will proceed under an Officer to be detailed later to junction SAILLY - au - BOIS Road and Mule Track to meet incoming unit at 8.30 pm.

4. On completion of relief, Companies will march by platoons to PAS via SOUASTRE and HENU.

5. Lewis Gun Limbers
   1 Limber for guns of C & D Coys will be on the HEBUTERNE Rd at 10 pm. 4 men per Coy will accompany these limbers. 1 Limber for A and B Coys guns will be on the GOMMECOURT Rd at junction with Mule Track at 10 pm. 4 men per Coy will accompany these limbers.

7) One runner per Coy will move with Batt. H.Qrs. in order to locate the new position.

8) Coys will report their arrival in their new area by runner to Bn HQrs.

9) ACKNOWLEDGE

Distribution

Copy No	1	A
	2	B
	3	C
	4	D
	5	E Coy
	6	Lewis gun (?)
	7	T.O. & Lieut
	8	War Diary
	9	File

(Signed) F HOWARTH
Lt & Adjt

5/18

the Battalion Cook-house
at E27 b 15 95 at 6-30 am

OC Coys will ensure
that breakfast is drawn
at this time in order
that working parties are
able to turn out as per
working Table annexed

5) Officers Valises & mens
Packs will be stacked
at Battn Orderly Room
at 4 am.

6) Tools will be drawn
by 4 am. from Battn
Stores as follows:-
   A Coy 70 ⎫
   B Coy 70 ⎬ Shovels
   C Coy 70 ⎭
   These will be taken
to the new area where
Coys move into position

other :-

D Coy at 4-30 am

Route :- across country
through K2 a and b

A Coy at 4-35 am

Route :- SAILLY au BOIS Road
— FONQUEVILLERS

B Coy at 4-40 am
C Coy at 4-50 am

Route :- through K2a & b
(across country)

Batln H.Qrs Coy 5 am

Route :- across country
to SAILLY au BOIS - FONQUEVILLER.
Rd — FONQUEVILLERS

4) Tea will be issued
at 4 am. and breakfast
will be drawn from

CONFIDENTIAL

12/2/4

Vol 17

1/10th Battalion Manchester Regiment.

WAR DIARY.

June 1st to June 30th 1918.

Volume No. 35.

1/10th Manchester Regt.

WAR DIARY
or
INTELLIGENCE SUMMARY.
(Erase heading not required.)

Army Form C. 2118.

Place	Date	Hour	Summary of Events and Information	Remarks and references to Appendices
	1918 June 1		1 Battalion Training Warning Order for Battn. to relieve 1st Otago Regt. on night 7/8th inst.	LCW
	2			
	3			
	4		1 Battalion Training.	LCW
	5		Battalion Training. C.O. & O.C. Coys reconnoitred line.	LCW
	6		Advance Party went up into line. On Working parties. 3rd Batt. 107th Infantry Regt. U.S. left.	LCW
	7		Order to relieve 1st OTAGO Batt. N.Z. in the time K27 B7 D (Sheet 57d NE) Batt. embussed at PAS at 5.30 p.m. debussed at BUS and marched to relieve the above Batt. in the left Sector of the Right Brigade Sector. "D" Coy on the left, "C" Coy on the Right, "A" Coy in Support, "B" Coy in Reserve. Relief complete by 11.55 p.m.	LCW LCW
	8		At 2.30 a.m. intense hostile bombardment on Left Platoon Sector of "C" Coy. Casualties 2/Lt. S. GREGORY Killed. 6 OR killed 6, 9 OR wounded. Day quiet. Patrols went out at night.	LCW
	9		Quiet night and day.	LCW

1/10th Manchester Regt.

WAR DIARY
or
INTELLIGENCE SUMMARY.

Army Form C. 2118.

Place	Date	Hour	Summary of Events and Information	Remarks and references to Appendices
1918	June 10		Quiet night and day. Reorganised positions of Support and Reserve Coys.	LCV
	11		Daylight patrol attempted to obtain identification but failed. Relieved by 1/8th Manchester Regt.	LCV
II	12		Relief completed at 12-30 a.m. Battalion went into Support.	LCV
	13		In Support finding Working Parties.	LCV
	14		In Support finding Working Parties.	LCV
	15		Night of 15th Batt. moved into Right Sector relieving 5th E.L. Regt. "B" Coy on the Right, "A" Coy on Left, "C" Coy Right Support, "D" Coy Left Support. Considerable amount of hostile shelling during the night.	LCV
III	16		Day and night quiet. Own patrols active.	LCV

1/10th Manchester Regt.

WAR DIARY
INTELLIGENCE SUMMARY.
(Erase heading not required.)

Army Form C. 2118.

Place	Date	Hour	Summary of Events and Information	Remarks and references to Appendices
	1918			
	June 17		Working Party of "C" Coy caught by hostile shell fire. 4 Other killed 3 Other Wounded. At 9-45 p.m. Enemy shelling on L/Coy sector intense. 2/Lt BANKS Wounded. Our artillery retaliated.	L Coy
	18			L Coy
	19	1 A.M.	Enemy shelling intense. At midnight 5th E.L. Regt. carried out a raid on WATLING ST. Assembly in our front line. Day quiet.	L Coy
	20		Daylight raiding party of 1 N.C.O & 4 O.R. rushed an enemy post under cover of a T.M. Barrage. garrison however fled before raiding party reached the post. Lt. W.R. Pool D.S.O. on leave to U.K. Major L.C. Wilde D.S.O. Commanding.	L Coy
	21		Hostile shelling greatly increased. Receive orders for relief by 5th Manchesters. C.O. & Adj. of relieving unit visit sector prior to relief. Company Commanders & Advance Party of 5th Manchesters arrive.	L Coy
	22		Day and night quiet.	L Coy

1/10th Manchester Regt.

Army Form C. 2118.

WAR DIARY
or
INTELLIGENCE SUMMARY.
(Erase heading not required.)

Instructions regarding War Diaries and Intelligence Summaries are contained in F. S. Regs, Part II. and the Staff Manual respectively. Title pages will be prepared in manuscript.

Place	Date	Hour	Summary of Events and Information	Remarks and references to Appendices
	1918			
	June 23		Relieved by 15th Manchester Regt & moved into Divisional Reserve at	Cos
V	24		BUS WOOD. Relief quiet. Bathing and cleaning up.	Cos
	25		2 Coys working under 428th Field Coy R.E. and 2 Coys Training	Cos
	26		2 Coys working under 428th Field Coy R.E. and 2 Coys Training	Cos
	27		2 Coys working under 428th Field Coy R.E. and 2 Coys Training	Cos
	28		2 Coys working under 428th Field Coy R.E. and 2 Coys working under 42nd Div. Signal Coy.	Cos
VI	29		2 Coys working under 428th Field Coy R.E. and 2 Coys working under 42nd Div. Signal Coy. Orders received to relieve 1/6 & 1/7 Manchester Regt in the front Line.	Cos

1/10 Manchester Regt.

Army Form C. 2118.

WAR DIARY
or
INTELLIGENCE SUMMARY.
(Erase heading not required.)

Instructions regarding War Diaries and Intelligence Summaries are contained in F. S. Regs., Part II. and the Staff Manual respectively. Title pages will be prepared in manuscript.

Place	Date	Hour	Summary of Events and Information	Remarks and references to Appendices
	30th		2 Coys working under 428th Field Coy R.E. 2 Coys working under 42nd Divisional Signal Coy. Commanding Officer & Company Commanders reconnoitre Sect:- 57.D. N.E. K.27.C. Area to be taken over.	A.o.s

June 30th 1918.

L.C. White Major
Commanding 1/10th Manchester Regt.

NIGHT   W A R N I N G   O R D E R.

1. The Battalion will relieve the 1st OTAGO Regt. (N.Z.) in the Left Battn. Sector, Right Sub-Sector, II Corps Front on the night of 7/8 June 1918.
Battalion Hd-Qrs........ Sheet 57 D, N.E. T 20 d 45. 25.

2. Prior to the above relief the 198th Inf. Brigade is being relieved in Divisional Reserve, Left Reserve Division, by the 118th Inf. Brigade on the 7th inst.

                                                           F. Howarth
                                                          Capt. & Adjt.
4/6/18.   1/10th Manchester Regiment.

Distribution :- Normal.

SECRET   1/10th Manchester Regiment.

1. Reference Warning Order issued 4/6/18.

2. The following Advance Party will proceed to the Line and will await the arrival of the Battalion:-

    A Coy..... 2/Lt. W.H.GREGORY.
    B " ..... Lieut A.F.ALLEN.
    C " ..... 2/Lt. S.GREGORY.
    D " ..... 2/Lt. H.J.BANKES.
and 1 N.C.O. per platoon (4 per Company)

    H-Q Coy.... 1 Officer and 1 N.C.O.

A Bus will take this party starting from the Town Hall, PAS, at 4 p.m. Wednesday, 5th inst. and will proceed to BERTRANCOURT.

2 days rations to be carried   *F. Howarth*

                                         Capt and Adjt,
4/6/18   1/10th Manchester Regiment.

ADMINISTRATIVE INSTRUCTIONS.   No.88

by

Lieut.Colonel. W.R. PEEL. D.S.O.   Commanding.

---

1. The Transport of the Brigade less vehicles proceeding to BUS will march to LOUVENCOURT under the Brigade Transport Officer on the 7th. inst.
    Starting Point - Rd Junction.   C.16.d.8.4.
    Time :-   2-30 p.m.
    Route :-   Via PAS & AUTHIE.
    20 yards distance will be maintained between every 6 vehicles and 200 yards between Transport of Battalions.

2. The vehicles accompanying the unit.i.e. 3 Cookers.
                                        5 limbers.
                                        1 water cart.
    will march to BUS. Brigaded.
    Starting Point:- Rd Junction. C.16.d.8.4.
    Time :-   2-0 p.m.
    Route :-   Via PAS & AUTHIE.

3. Battle Surplus will march to Halloy under orders to be issued by Major L.C.Wilde. D.S.O.   1 Cooker will accompany this party.

4. **TENTAGE.** All tents will be struck and dumped at C.17.d.5.0. by 10-30 a.m. Lieut.W.A.Haslewood will hand these over to and obtain a receipt from Major L.C. Wilde. D.S.O.

5. Officers valises will be dumped at the Q.M.Stores by 9-30 a.m.

6. Each Coy.Lewis gun limber will carry 7 dixies, 5 Lewis guns and Officers trench Mess kit. "C" Coy. limber will in addition carry 1 H.Qrs.Lewis Gun. The limbers will be loaded by 1-30 p.m.

7. 2 cooks per Coy. will go into the line.

8. The T.O. will detail 1 limber to take the kits of the Officers on the Battle Surplus to HALLOY.

9. Mess Stores not taken into the line will be stacked at the Q.M.Stores at 2 p.m.

10. O.C. Coys. will detail 1 Lewis gunner to accompany each limber to BUS. These men must be ready to march off at 1-30 p.m.

11. A rear party under Lieut.W.A.Haslewood, consisting of 1 N.C.O. & 8 drummers will remain behind to ensure that the camp is clean after the Battalion has marched off.

12. **SUPPLIES.**   Railhead - ORVILLE.
                    Refilling Point - T.36. central.

- 2 -

13. **WATER**   Water for troops in the line is obtained from BERTRANCOURT, and for Transport and personnel at Rear Headquarters at LOUVENCOURT.

    Water Carts   I.34.b.3.2.
    Water Bottles.   I.34.b.3.2.
       "   "   O. 4.b.2.7.
    Horse Troughs.   O. 4.b.2.7.

    Times of watering.
    6-30 a.m. to 7-0 a.m.
    11-0 a.m. to 11-30 am.
    4-0 p.m. to 4-30p.m.

14. **ACKNOWLEDGE.**

June 6th. 1918.

                                                F. Howarth
                                                  Captain.
                                                  Adjutant.

Distribution. O.C. "A" Coy.
                    "B" "
                    "C" "
                    "D" "
                    H.Q. "
        C.O.
        2nd in Command.
        Q.M.
        T.O.
        R.S.M.
        War Diary.
        File.

1/10th. Battalion Manchester Regiment.

Reference OPERATION ORDER NO.88.

1. The Battalion will proceed by busses to BUS where the evening meal will be served.
Coys. will parade at 4-45 p.m. ready to march off and march to the PAS - COUIN Road . The rear of the column will rest on the Cross Roads at 0.23.b.15.70.
   Starting from head of column parties of 25 per bus will be told off, a distance of 80 yards for every 6 parties and 25 yards between groups of 6 will be maintained.
   On a long whistle blast men will embus.

2. On arrival at BUS the evening meal will be served.

June 7th. 1918.

F. Howarth
Captain.
Adjutant.

OPERATION ORDER NO. 88.

SECRET.
by
Lieut.Colonel. W.R. PEEL. D.S.O. Commanding.

1. The Battalion will relieve the 1st OTAGO Battalion in the front line on the night of 7/8th of June.

2. "D" Coy. will relieve No. 4 Coy. on the Right.
   "C" Coy. will relieve No.10 Coy. on the Left.
   "A" Coy. will relieve No.14 Coy. in Support.
   "B" Coy. will relieve No. 8 Coy. in Reserve.

3. One Headquarter Lewis Gun team will be attached to "C" Coy. and will come under the orders of O.C. "C" Coy.

4. The Lewis Gun Limbers will proceed by march route under 2nd/Lieut. S.G.Maltby to K.26.c.5.6. where they will be unloaded and stacked by Coys. 200 yards between the guns of each Coy. O.C. Coys. will detail 1 man per gun to accompany these limbers. These men should be instructed in what order Platoons will march, in order that the Platoon guns may be kept separate.

5. The Battalion will proceed to the trenches either by :-
   (1) Busses to Bertrancourt, and by march route from there, or
   (2) By march route.
   In either case the order of march will be :-
   "C" Coy.
   "D" Coy.
   "A" Coy.
   "B" Coy.
   H.Qrs.
   Intervals of 200 yards will be maintained between Platoons.

6. One guide per Platoon and two guides per Battalion H.Qrs. will meet the Battalion at a place to be notified later.

7. DRESS:- Fighting Order.
   O.C. Coys. will ensure that all water bottles are filled and that men are not allowed to drink from these without orders.

8. All Trench Stores, Maps, Defence Schemes,etc., will be taken over and receipts given. A list,in duplicate, of Stores, etc., taken over will be sent to Battalion Orderly Room by 7 a.m. on the 8th inst.

9. Completion of relief will be wired to Battalion Headquarters by code word "BAND".

10. ACKNOWLEDGE.

F. Howarth
Captain.
Adjutant.

June 6th.1918.

Distribution:- O.C. "A" Coy.
              "B" "
              "C" "
              "D" "
              H.Q. "
         C.O.
         2nd in Command.
         Q.M.
         T.O.
         R.S.M.
         War Diary.
         File.

OPERATION ORDER No. 20.
by
Major L.B. Little, D.S.O., Commanding.

1. The Battalion will relieve one Coy. and one platoon 1/7th Manchester Regt. in the Right Divisional Sector, Left Sub-Sector, and one Coy. and 3 platoons of 1/7th. Manchester Regt. in Support, Right Divisional Sector.
On completion of relief the Battalion will be in the Left Divisional Sector, Right Sub-Sector.

2. Coys. will relieve as follows:-
"B" Coy. 1/10th. Manchester Regt. will relieve "B" Coy. 1/7th. Manchester Regt. in the Front Line.
"D" Coy. 1/10th. Manchester Regt. will relieve one platoon "B" Coy. 1/7th. Manchester Regt. in K.28.B.7.6. and surrounding area.
"C" Coy. 1/10th. Manchester Regt. will relieve "D" Coy. 1/7th Manchester Regt. in K.28.d.
"A" Coy. 1/10th. Manchester Regt. will relieve 3 platoons "D" Coy. 1/7th. Manchester Regt. in Fort Charles.
Battalion Headquarters will be at K.19.d.7.6.

3. Advance parties composed as under will parade at Battalion Orderly Room at 2 p.m. July 1st ready to proceed to the line where they will await the arrival of their Coys.
One Officer per Coy. and 1 N.C.O. per platoon.
2 N.C.O's. 1 Bomber and 1 Gunners for Battalion L.T.M.
"B" Coy. will send 1 N.C.O. and the No.1 Lewis Gunners up to the line at 5 a.m. July 2nd, where they will take over the gun positions, and await arrival of their Coys.
Advance parties will take over all maps, programmes of work aeroplane photographs, etc. which concern the area they are relieving.
List of Trench Stores in duplicate will be rendered to Battalion Orderly Room by 6 a.m. July 2nd.

4. Coys. will leave this camp in the following order:-
"B" Coy.   4-0 p.m.
"D" Coy.   4-40 p.m.
"A" Coy.   7-0 p.m.
Batt.H.Qrs.   7-10p.m.
"C" Coy. will leave Camp at 8-30 p.m. and will meet guides at crossing of river track and road J.35.c.70.15. at 9-30p.m.
This being a daylight Relief it is essential that 200 yards distance is kept between platoons.

Operation Order No 89
by Lt Col W R Peel DSO Comdg
_____

1. The Battalion will be relieved by the 1/8th Manchester Regt tonight 11/12th inst and will move into support on the right flank of the Brigade

2. Coys will be relieved by corresponding Coys of the 1/8th Manchester R[egt].

3. Guides (1 per platoon) will be at Coys HQ's by 9-30 p.m.

4. All patrol line, tools, Trench Stores etc will be handed over to incoming unit and receipts obtained.

5. The two Front Line Coys will each leave 1 Officer to remain in their sector for 24 hours with the incoming unit. The Scout Officer will leave 1 Scout (L-Cpl) to remain for 24 hours.

6. Coys after relief will take
over Coy localities as follows:-

A Coy will take over locality
occupied by C Coy
1/8 Manch Rgt

B Coy will take over from
D Coy
1/8 Manch Rgt

C Coy will take over from
B Coy
1/8 Manch Rgt

D Coy will take over from
A Coy
1/8 Manch. Rgt

7. An advanced party of 1 Officer,
1 NCO & 4 men (to act as
guides) will rendezvous at
these HQrs at 1-30 pm.
They will be taken from
there to their Coy and
platoon localities after which
they will return to their
own Coys.

and guide platoons to their new localities after relief. The men should be specially good at this since course the routes will be fairly hard to find at night.

8. OC Coys will ensure that sufficient water is left at their Coy cookhouses for the 8th Manchester Rgt to keep them supplied up to midday tomorrow, and in the same way the 8th Manchesters are leaving a supply for our Coys.

9. Rations will be taken to the new localities where they will be handed over to the NCO mentioned in para. 7. Coys should send after the evening meal a cook to their new localities leaving one cook behind to hand over Coy cookhouse to

9. ...ary kits Coys will carry out with them their Mch-guns, Lewis guns, magazines, Very Pistols, periscopes, etc.

10. Lists of Trench Stores handed over and taken over will be forwarded to Battn HQrs by 9am 13th inst.

A certificate of cleanliness will be obtained and copy sent to Battn HQrs

11. Completion of relief will be sent to Bhere HQrs by code-word "MAUD" and arrival in new locality will be sent to Battn HQrs by code-word "ALLAN"

12. Position of Battn HQrs will be K25 b 1.6.

13. ACKNOWLEDGE

11/6/16

J Howarth
Capt
& Adjt

Distribution
———————

Copy No 1   OC   A
       2   B
       3   C
       4   D
       5   HQ
       6   Lewis & TO
       7   OC   1/5 Manch Rgt -
       8   O
       9   R Sem
      10   War Diary
      11   — do —
      12   File

Operation Order No 70
by Lt Col C.F.R. Rea Dso Comg

I. The Battalion will relieve the 1/5th Bn East Lancs Regt tonight 15/16th in the Right Battalion Sector.

II. Coys will relieve as follows

B Coy 1/10 Manch Regt will relieve D Coy 1/5 E.L.Rgt
D Coy   —do—   —do—   A Coy   —do—
C Coy   —do—   —do—   C Coy   —do—
A Coy   —do—   —do—   D Coy   —do—

III. Guides (1 per platoon) will be at 1/5 East Lancs Regt HQrs by 9-45 pm

Coys will march out from their areas so as to arrive at 5th East Lancs HQrs as follows
(K 34 a 3 B)

B Coy   9-45 pm
A Coy   9-55 pm
C Coy   10-5 pm
D Coy   10-15 pm

4. An advance party of 1 Officer and 4 NCOs per Coy will report to 5th East Lancs HQrs at 2.30 pm. Each Officer will take over all Disposition Maps, Trench Stores, etc in his Coy area.

5. One guide per Coy will report to 5th East Lancs Bn HQrs at 11 am in order to conduct their advance party to this area. All patrol teams (circa 15 per Coy which will be carried up to the line) tools, Trench Stores disposition maps etc will be handed over to advance party & receipts obtained also certificates of cleanliness

6. Sufficient water must be left at each Coy HQrs for the 5th East Lancs Regt to keep them supplied till breakfast

7/ Rations and water will
be brought to Left Support
Coy HQrs each evening via
the exception of Batt.n
Stores which will be left
at the CHALK PIT.

Coys will send down
their own ration parties
with empty petrol tins at
4 p.m.

8/ Coys should send after
the evening meal a cook
to their cookhouse.

Coys will carry up
with them their mess-tins,
Lewis gun magazines, Very
Pistols, Periscopes, etc.

9/ List of Trench Stores
handed over and taken over
will be forwarded to
Batt.n HQrs by 9am.
11th inst.

10/ Position of Batt.n HQrs will

be K 32 a 3 1

III. Completion of relief will
be made to Batt. H.Qrs.
by code-word "BABY BOY"

IV. Acknowledge.

F. Howarth
Capt + Adjt

15/8

Distribution.

Copy No 1   OC A Coy
     2   B
     3   C
     4   D
     5   H.Q.S.
     6   Adm + TO
     7   C.O.
     8   OC 1/8 East Lan Regt
     9   RSM
    10   war diary
    11   war diary
    12   File

SECRET.

Operation Order. No 91.
by Lt-Col. W.R. Peel. DSO. Commanding.

IV

1. The 5th East Lancashire Regt. will carry out on night 18/19th a raid on WATLING ST. between K.34.c.60.65 and K.34.c.30.95 and the trench junction at K.34.c.55.90.

2. The Company carrying out the raid will assemble in our front line between posts 13 and 19. On their arrival the garrisons of 6 to 19 Posts will withdraw. Those of Posts 6.7.8.9. will move to a flank. Those of posts 11.12.14 down MOUNTJOY TR. and 17 & 19 to Northern Flank.

3. After the Raid the 1/5th East Lancs. will hold the posts till relieved by our garrison. This relief will be carried out as soon as possible after the raid is over.

4. The 1/5th East Lancs. will assemble as in para 2. at ZERO – 60 minutes

The raid will commence at ZERO and the raiding party will return to our front line at ZERO + 20 at latest.

5. ZERO hour will be notified later.

6. When the posts mentioned above have been withdrawn A & B Coys will wire code word "CHICK". When the posts have been taken over by us after the raid code word "EN" will be wired.

Fullerphone only to be used.

Howarth
Capt
Adjt.

18-6-18.

Distribution No 1 OC A Coy
2 . B
3 . C
4 . D
5 C.O.
6 adjt.
7 Sigs Officer
8 I.O
9 War Diary
10 -do-
11 File.

SECRET

Ref. Operation Order No 91

Zero hour :- 12 midnight

Para 3   As the right of the
5th Bns RIF only extends to
No 13 Post D Post 120 M.G.
S.P. 6. will not withdraw
till Zero - 20. 14 Post will
not withdraw from MOUTNOY
TRENCH but to the Northern
flank as does 19, 18 and 17 —
19, 18, 17 & 14 withdraw as soon
as the 5th Bn Leins RIF are
in position. The signal
for the raiding party to
withdraw from the enemy line
will be the old S.O.S rocket
2 white and 2 green stars.
This will be sent up at
not later than Zero + 20
    As soon as possible after
the raiding party are back
in our trench our guns
will register down on the

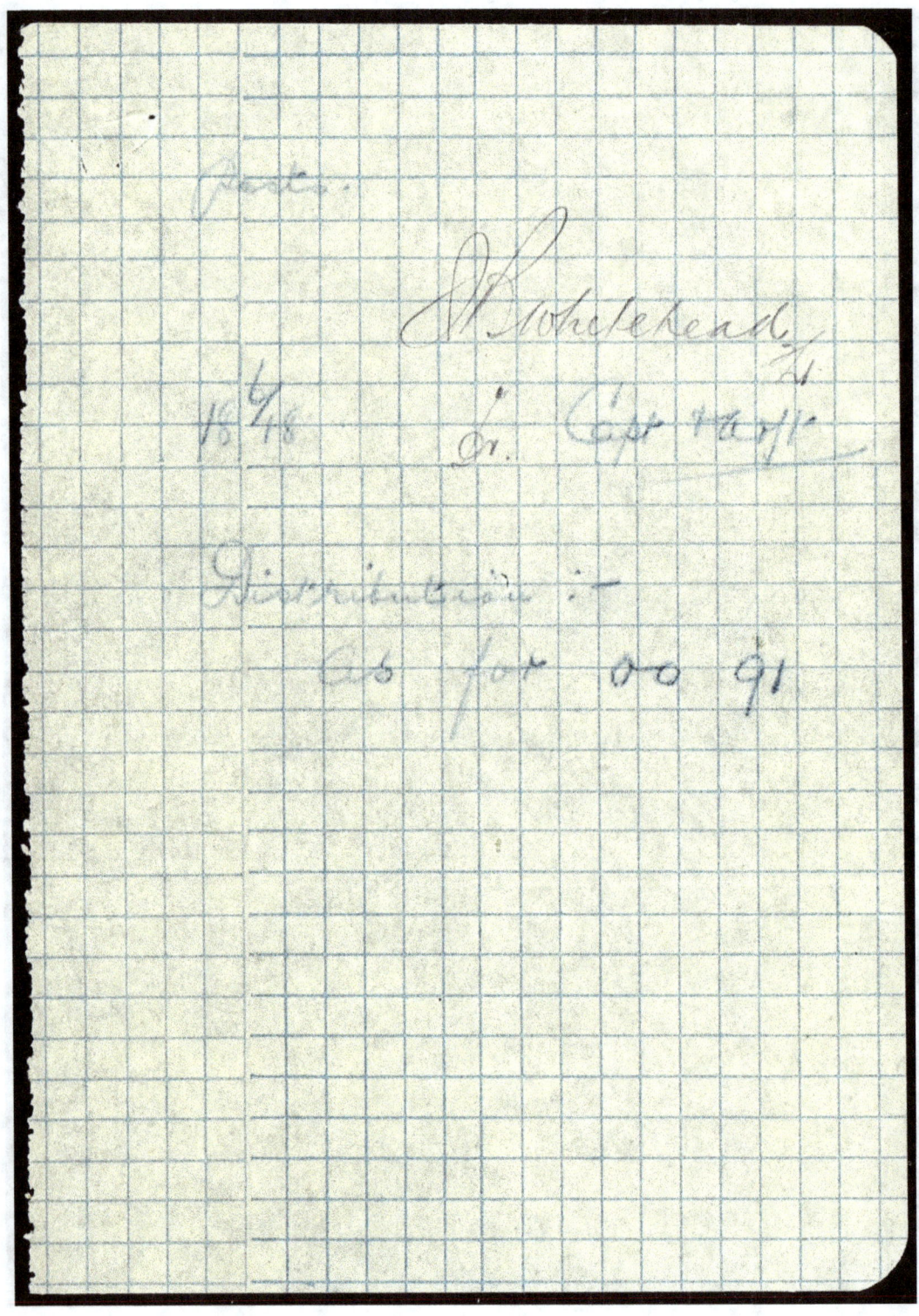

1. Operation Order No 92.
by
Major C. C. [Vivian] O/C Camp

June 21/1918

1. The Battalion will be
relieved by the 1/5th Devon
[Home] Bn on the night
22/23rd inst.

2. Coys will be relieved
as follows :-

A Coy 1/4 Devon R by A Coy 1/5 Devon Regt
B Coy —"—   by D Coy —"—
C Coy —"—   by C —"—
D Coy —"—   by B —"—

3. One guide per platoon,
one per Coy HQrs and one
per Batln HQrs will report
to the Intelligence Officer at
Batln HQrs at 8-30 am
on 23rd inst.

4. An advance party of
1 Officer and 4 NCO's per

Company and 1 NCO per Battalion Hqrs will report to Bttn Hqrs at 9am on the 23rd inst.
This advance party will proceed in charge of the Senior Officer to take over the camp occupied by the 1/5th Manch Regt in BUS WOOD (J20 c 9.5 approx).
Coy advance parties will take over as follows:—

A Coy 1/10 Man Regt from C Coy 1/5 Man Regt
B Coy — " — from B Coy — " —
C Coy — " — from A Coy — " —
D Coy — " — from D Coy — " —

A guide will meet this party at J26 b 9.0 (cross roads). Offr in charge of this party will also take over any maps, counter attack schemes, etc which may have to be handed over.
This advance party will be at road junction J27 d 45.50 at 11-30 pm in order to

guides (?) Coys to the new area.

5. All patrol tins, tools, Thunder
Stones, disposition maps, Grid
references etc will be handed
over to the Advance Party
of 1/5th March. R/C and
receipts obtained and signatures
of thoulieurs. These will be
spent on to Battn Orderly
Room by runner, 24th inst.

Coys will carry out with
them one Bren-sticks, Bomber
grids, magazines (?), pistols,
prismatic, etc to Coy's
tips where Coy interior fire
bunkers will be available
to collect them.

One tradesman per Coy
will be detailed to go
down with limbs/lorries to
the new area.

6. The Lieut and TO will
arrange to visit the new
area tomorrow and ascertain
what arrangements are in

firms with regard to cooking rations, water etc.

If considered advisable the 2nd will arrange for the Field Kitchens to be brought up and the Transport Officer for the stabling of the mules belonging to the water carts and will give full instructions to the Water Corpl as to where he will bring the water carts after the last journey to the lines on the 23rd inst.

The Transport Officer will also arrange for the 4 Coy Lewis Gun limbers 'C' move to D Coy HQrs by 10 pm 23rd inst and the limbers to report to Battn HQrs

7. An advance party of the relieving unit, 1 Officer and 4 NCOs per Coy will report to each Coy HQrs about 8 pm 22nd inst.

8. Consolidation & relief
    will be sent to Bde
    HQ by code word
    "TOSKIBA" and on
    arrival in camp by
    runner.

9. ACKNOWLEDGE.

                                J Howarth
                                Capt
                                & Adjt
                                R.S.N.H

    Distribution

    Copy No 1   OC A
         "   2   B
         "   3   C
         "   4   D
         "   5   HQ
         "   6   2nd & TO
         "   7   CO
         "   8   OC 1/1 Man Rgt
         "   9   RSM
         " 10   Near Adamy
         " 11   do
         " 12   File

1/10 Manch Regt.

Army Form C. 2118.

WAR DIARY
or
INTELLIGENCE SUMMARY.
(Erase heading not required.)

Vol 18

Instructions regarding War Diaries and Intelligence
Summaries are contained in F.S. Regs., Part II.
and the Staff Manual respectively. Title pages
will be prepared in manuscript.

Place	Date 1918	Hour	Summary of Events and Information	Remarks and references to Appendices
COLINCAMPS & BERTRANCOURT	July 1st	—	All four Companies working under R.E's in and near the front line	1/5 RP — I
	" 2nd	—	A B & D Coys moved up and relieved Coys of the 1/6th and 1/7th Manchesters in Support positions. This relief was complete by 9-30 p.m. C Coy relieved B Coy 1/5th Manchesters in front line. This relief was complete by 11-35 p.m. Night quiet.	1/5 RP
Arras	" 3rd	—	Intermittent shelling of Support during the day. 9 days 120 other ranks than been admitted to hospital with influenza.	1/5 RP
R.P	" 4th	—	Day and night quiet. Companies work on their front line & supports	1/5 RP 1/5 RP
"	" 5th	—	Work on wiring continued	—
Stacks	" 6th	—	2 Coy relieved C Coy in the front line. relief complete by 9-30 pm.	1/5 RP — II
57 D NE	" 7th	—	Heavy shelling of our Support line. During this period day & night patrols have been carried out continuously. Coy work on wiring trench.	1/5 RP
and	" 8th	—	Enemy put over mustard gas about 2.7 pm on Ruizey Card Batln Hqrs. This faith had to be evacuated by 9 am A Coy moved to a position about 400 yards in near (CORNISH TRENCH) and Batln Hqrs to SAILLY-AU-BOIS	1/5 RP
57 D SF	" 9th	—	One we occupied by 10 pm same evening. Day and night quiet. Our patrols put over small quantities of gas and Supports of Coy V.C & Capt G.B. TAYLOR injured from V.C & D Coy	1/5 RP
	" 10th	—	D Coy relieved in the front line by B Coy and C Coy relieved in Support by A Coy. C & D Coy moved into Reserve.	1/5 RP
	" 11th	—	Day quiet. Little talk between Coy's and Batln V.N.Grs. during the night. No shelling or Reserve Coy's out.	1/5 RP
	" 12th	—	Support Coy's work on their Supports. Suffering near trenches & wiring. Day and night quiet.	1/5 RP
	" 13th	—	1/5 L.R. Regiment relieved us from here and moved command of the Battalion.	1/5 RP
	" 14th	—	Daylight patrol at 2 pm. Enemy post located. Enemy Artillery very fully working	1/5 RP
	" 15th	—	Sniping patrol at 9 am by C Coy in the front line. Enemy fired on B Coy. Countable first on B Coy Main battn at patrol. Capt T.E.L. ROWBOTHAM wounded Capt G.B. TAYLOR and Lieut E.R. STREET evacuated. A Coy on 2nd in Command Command	1/5 RP — III
	" 16th	—	Very wet morning. Day light Patrol.	1/5 RP

WAR DIARY
or
INTELLIGENCE SUMMARY.
(Erase heading not required.)

Army Form C. 2118.

Place	Date	Hour	Summary of Events and Information	Remarks and references to Appendices
	July 17th 1918		Quiet day. Patrols out at night.	W.R.P.
	18th	-	Quiet day. Patrols out at night.	W.R.P.
	19th	-	Battalion relieved by 9th Manchesters (and provided two Coys (A & B) in Brancho: Coys (A & B) in billets at Bivouacs at BERTRANCOURT. Enemy aeroplanes bombed BERTRANCOURT at 11·45 pm and burned to own (1 Killed)	W.R.P.
	20th		Last platoon arrived 3·45 am. 3 Coys working. 1 Coy training.	W.R.P.
	21st 4 22nd		3 Coys working 1 Coy Training.	W.R.P.
	23rd		A and B Coys relieved C and D Coys. Coys on work as above.	W.R.P.
	24th		3 Coys working. 1 Coy Training.	W.R.P. VI
	25th		Warning orders to relieve 8th Lancs Fusiliers in the Supports area of the Rifle Brigade	W.R.P.
	26th		Battalion relieved 8th Lancs Fusiliers in Supports to the Rifle Brigade Sector Sheet 57D NE J 30 d 6.1. Relief completed by 8 pm. Following officers commanding Coys:- A – Capt G.B. TAYLOR D – Capt W.J. NORRIS C – Capt P. STOTT D – 2/Lieut. J.C.S. ROWBOTHAM	W.R.P.
	27th & 28th		Battalion on working parties on platoon posts and Knuckling dugouts.	W.R.P.
	29th		Hostile shelling at 9am. Hostile shelling at 8pm. Work as above. No casualties	W.R.P.
	30th		Our artillery carried out short Retaliation shoot. Coys on work as above. Enemy shelling on H.Q.s 1pm.	W.R.P.
	31st		Quiet day. Orders received to relieve 8th Manchester in Left Battn on 3rd inst.	W.R.P.

W.R. Peel
Lt Col
Comdt
1/10th Manchesters B/-

OPERATION ORDER No. 95.
by
Major L.C. WILD. D.S.O. Commanding.

1. The Battalion will relieve .... Coy. and one Platoon
1/5th. Manchester Regt. in the Right Divisional Sector,
Left Sub-Sector, and one .... and 2 Platoons 1/7th.
Manchester Regt. in .... Right Divisional Sector.
On completion of Relief the Battalion will be in the Left
Divisional Sector, Right Sub-Sector.

2. Coys. will relieve as follows :-
"C" Coy. 1/10th. Manchester Regt. will relieve "B" Coy.
   1/5th. Manchester Regt. in the Front Line.
"D" Coy. 1/10th. Manchester Regt. will relieve one platoon
"B" Coy. 1/5th. Manchester Regt. in K.34.B.8.1. and
surrounding area.
"B" Coy. 1/10th. Manchester Regt. will relieve "D" Coy.
1/7th. Manchester Regt. in K.27.c.
"A" Coy. 1/10th. Manchester Regt. will relieve 2 Platoons
"B" Coy. 1/7th. Manchester Regt. in Fort Charles.
Battalion Headquarters will be at K.19.c.4.9.

3. Advance parties composed as under will parade at Battalion
Orderly Room at 2 p.m. July 1st. ready to proceed to the
line where they will await the arrival of their Coys.
One Officer per Coy. 1 N.C.O. per Platoon.
Two N.C.O's. 2 Scouts and 2 Runners for Battalion H.Qrs.
"C" Coy. will send 1 N.C.O. and the No.1 Lewis Gunners
up to the line at 9 a.m. July 2nd. where they will await
arrival of their Coys .... take over gun positions and await
arrival of their Coys.
Advance parties will take over all Maps, Programmes of
work, aeroplane photographs, etc. which concern the
area they are relieving.
List of Trench Stores in duplicate will be rendered to
Battalion Orderly Room by 9 a.m. July 3rd.

4. Coys. will leave this Camp in the following order :-
   "D" Coy.   6-0 p.m.
   "B" "   6-30 p.m.
   "A" "   7-0 p.m.
   Batt. H.Qrs.   7-15 p.m.
"C" Coy. will leave Camp at 8-30 p.m. and will meet guides
at crossing of KIWI track and Road J.04.d.70.15. at 9-30 pm

- 2 -

This being a daylight r[elief it] is essential that 300
yards distance is kept be[tween] Platoons.
O.C. "A" "B" & "D" Coys. wi[ll i]ssue o[r]ders as to where
their own advance parties [wil]l meet them when moving into
the line.
Coy. Lewis Gun limbers wil[l be] loaded by 4 p.m. July 2nd.
Each Coy. Lewis Gun limber w[il]l proceed in advance of
its own Coy. The point at which they will unload being
selected by each O.C. Coy.
2 Lewis Gun limbers will report to Battalion Orderly Room
at 6-30 p.m. for H.Q. Coy.
The Transport Officer will get in touch with the Transport
Officer of 1/6th. Manchester Regt. and obtain information
as to rations. The water cart will be stationed in
BERTRANCOURT.

5.
Packs will be stacked by Coys. opposite the Battalion
Guard Tent by 9-0 a.m. July 2nd.
Officer's valises and surplus Mess stores will be stacked
in the same place by 4 p.m.
The Transport Officer will arrange to have these conveyed
to the Quartermasters Stores.
Battle Surplus and all men under 18½ years of age will
parade in front of Battalion Orderly Room at 9-30 a.m.
July 2nd, for inspection by the Adjutant.
DRESS :- Full Marching Order.

6. Petrol tins, 7 dixies per Coy. and Officers mess stores
will be taken up on Coy. L.G. limbers.

7. Completion of relief will be sent to Battalion Headquarters
in code as follows :-

    "A" Coy.   C.S.M. Bathe.
    "B" Coy.   C.S.M. Simms.
    "C" Coy.   Sergt. Pilling.
    "D" Coy.   C.S.M. Toogood.

8. ACKNOWLEDGE.

June 30th.1918.

                                            Captain,
                                            Adjutant.

ADDENDUM to OPERATION ORDER No.93.
by
Major L.G. WILDE. D.S.O. Commanding.

Para 1. After 'Battalion will relieve' add 'on the
night of 2nd/3rd.'

July 1st 1918.

                                            Captain,
                                            Adjutant.

OPERATION ORDER No.94.

Copy No. 11

by

Major L.I. WILDE. O.C.C. Commanding.

1. "D" Coy. will relieve "C" Coy. in the front line upon the night 6/7th July 1916. After relief "C" Coy. will occupy the area vacated by "D" Coy.

2. All details of relief will be arranged between O.C. Coys. concerned.

3. Maps, Trench models, maps, Aeroplane Photographs, etc., will be taken over and receipts sent in to Battalion H.Qrs. by noon July 7th.

4. Advance parties composed as under will be sent by each Coy. to their new area, by 10 a.m. July 6th.
   1 officer per Coy. 1 N.C.O. per Platoon.

5. Completion of relief will be wired to Battalion Headquarters by code word :-

       "C" Coy........"Tails"
       "D" Coy........"Up".

6. ACKNOWLEDGE.

July 5th. 1916.

                                        Howarth
                                        Captain.
                                        Adjutant.
Distribution :-
No.1. O.C. "A" Coy.   No.8. O. 127th.Brigade Headquarters.
No.2. O.C. "B" Coy.   No.9. O.C. 1/7th.Manchester Regiment.
No.3. O.C. "C" Coy.   No.10. "   1/8th.Manchester Regiment.
No.4. O.C. "D" Coy.   No.11.)
No.5. O.C.   No.12.) War Diary.
No.6. I.O.   No.13.)
No.7. Asst.I.O.   No.14. File.

AMENDMENT TO BATTALION ORDER No.95.

by

Major [illegible] [illegible]. [illegible]. Commanding.

---

1. Para. [illegible] substitute - "A" & "C" Coy. reliefs to be completed by [illegible] p.m.
   "B" Coy. will not commence to relieve until [illegible] p.m.

2. All patrol [illegible] will be handed over on relief and not taken out by Coys.

II

July 10th. 1916.

J. Howarth
Captain,
Adjutant.

OPERATIVE ORDER NO. 94.

by

Lieut.Col. W.A. PILE. D.S.O. Commanding.

Copy No........

1. "A" Coy. will relieve "B" Coy. in the front line on the night 14/15th July. After relief "B" Coy. will occupy the area vacated by "A" Coy.

2. All details of relief to be arranged between O.C.Coys. concerned.

3. Maps, Panoramas of works, Aeroplane Photographs, Patrol time/Trench Stores, etc., will be taken over and receipts sent in to Battalion Headquarters by noon July 15th.

4. Advance parties composed as under will be sent by each Coy. to their new area by 10 a.m. July 14th.

   1 Officer per Coy. 1 N.C.O per platoon.

5. Completion of relief will be wired to Battalion Headquarters by code word "FERN"

6. Acknowledge. (Coys. only.)

July 13th 1916.

                                                    Captain.
                                                    Adjutant.

Distribution:- No. 1.   O.C. "A" Coy.
               2.   "   "B" "
               3.   "   "C" "
               4.   "   "D" "
               5.   C.O.
               6.   2.O.
               7.   Adjt. & M.O.
               8.   Major L.O. Wilde. D.S.O.
               9.   145th Bde H.QTrs.
              10.   M.O. 1/5th. West Lancs Regt.
              11.   M.O. 1/5th. Loyal Fusiliers.
              12.   War Diary.
              13.   "
              14.   File.

16. The Transport Officer will arrange for sufficient water for breakfast 27th instant, to be delivered to-morrow evening to each Company and Battalion Headquarters.

17. Completion of relief will be reported by code word "DOVER".

18. Acknowledge.

(signature)
Lieut.,
A/Adjt.,
1/10th Manchester Regt.

25/7/18.

Distribution:-

```
No.  1. O.C. "A" Coy.
 "   2. O.C. "B"  "
 "   3. O.C. "C"  "
 "   4. O.C. "D"  "
 "   5. Headquarters.
 "   6. Q.M. & T.O.
 "   7. C.O.
 "   8. 2nd in Command.
 "   9. O.C.1/8th Lancs. Fusiliers.
 "  10. O.C.1/7th Lancs. Fusiliers.
 "  11. R.S.M.
 "  12. War Diary.
 "  13.  "   "
 "  14. File.
```

WAR DIARY

of

Officer Commanding

1/10" Manchester Regiment.

From:- August 1st 1918

To:- August 31st 1918

Volume 37

Army Form C. 2118.

WAR DIARY
or
INTELLIGENCE SUMMARY.
(Erase heading not required.)

Instructions regarding War Diaries and Intelligence Summaries are contained in F. S. Regs., Part II. and the Staff Manual respectively. Title pages will be prepared in manuscript.

Place	Date	Hour	Summary of Events and Information	Remarks and references to Appendices
COLINCAMPS	1918 Aug 1st		Battalion on working parties	
	2nd		— ditto —	
	3rd		Working parties. Relieved 8th Manchester Regt. in the left sector D and C Coy in Front Line.	
	4th		Quiet day. Patrols out day and night	
	5th		Quiet day. Our artillery fire on WATLING ST.	
	6th		Quiet day. Gas projectors by us. Staffords patrols found WATLING ST abandoned.	
	7th		D Coy relieved by A Coy and C Coy relieved by B Coy in the Front Line.	
	8th		A Coy relieved by D Coy. C Coy relieved by 1 Coy 8th Manchester Regt. and 1 Coy 8th Manchesters Regt. took over left support Coys. positions. A + C Coys came back to COLINCAMPS.	
	9th		Rehearsal for attack on WATLING ST and VALLADE Tr. with A and C Coys.	

Army Form C. 2118.

WAR DIARY
or
INTELLIGENCE SUMMARY.
(Erase heading not required.)

Instructions regarding War Diaries and Intelligence Summaries are contained in F. S. Regs., Part II. and the Staff Manual respectively. Title pages will be prepared in manuscript.

Place	Date	Hour	Summary of Events and Information	Remarks and references to Appendices
	1918 Aug 10		A and C Coy's relieve attack. WATLING ST shelled.	#
	11th		Two day fixed for 11th. Two put off owing to unfavourable weather for Gas Projector. Weather still unfavourable. Daylight patrol from WATLING ST	#
	12th		(North of SERRE Rd) movement. 1 Platoon occupies Ten the Marshalls Regt relieve Battalion.	IV
		3 pm.	During relief enemy attacks three times on WATLING ST but is repulsed.	#
BERTRANCOURT	13th	4-25 am	Relief completed at 4-25 am. Battalion for rest billets at BERTRANCOURT. Day spent in rest, bathing and cleaning up	#
	14th		Close order drill – Musketing up drill, etc	#
	15th		– ditto – one Coy on the range. At 1 pm orders received that Battalion in placed at disposal of 127 Bde. Battalion moves up at 6-15 pm and takes up position	V
COLINCAMPS			as follows :– 1 Coy BEAUSSART SWITCH 3 Coy's East and South of COLINCAMPS	#

WAR DIARY
INTELLIGENCE SUMMARY.
(Erase heading not required.)

Army Form C. 2118.

Place	Date 1918	Hour	Summary of Events and Information	Remarks and references to Appendices
	16th		Training and Bathing	#
	17th		ditto	#
	18th		Battn. found 2 and a half Coys. for work on making road at BEAUMONT HAMEL. Warning Order that Brigade is going to relieve 125 Brigade on night 20/21st	# #
	19th		Battn. on working parties	#
	20th		Battn. for working parties at night	#
K27 – K26 and K25 (sheet 57 D NE)	21st		Battn. moved forward 2 Coys. Tew 12th & 125 Brigades have attacked. Battalion placed at disposal of 127 Brigade. At 2 am Battalion ordered to be prepared to move at short notice. Orders received to move to K27c and there assemble and to attack MIRAUMONT in conjunction with 5th Australia Rgt. Battn. moved at 6.30 pm from Railway Avenue arriving at K26 and K27 at 8.30 pm. attack cancelled by Brigade. Battn. took up position in K27 – K26 and K25. The 125 Bde in front	#

WAR DIARY or INTELLIGENCE SUMMARY

Army Form C. 2118.

Place	Date	Hour	Summary of Events and Information	Remarks and references to Appendices
	Aug 1918 22nd	5.15 am	Enemy attacked at 5.15 am. 2 platoons of "C" Coy moved up in close support to 5th Lanc. Fusiliers. The enemy attack was covered by very heavy shelling. At 6 pm enemy attacked on the left but the attack was successfully driven off. Others received from 12th R.I.R. to attack trench in K.33. A and B Coys detailed for this.	
	23rd	2.30 am	when a barrage attack delivered by A and B Coys and objective taken. Outposts pushed out in front and touch obtained with Lancs Fusiliers on the left and 7th Manchesters on the right. Casualties 2/Lieut ELLIOTT and 7 other ranks killed. 28 other ranks wounded. 4 prisoners taken. Remainder of garrison driven into the Lancs Fusiliers. Remainder of day quiet. At 10 pm came under orders of 126 Brigade. Patrols pushed out to see	

Army Form C. 2118.

WAR DIARY
or
INTELLIGENCE SUMMARY.
(Erase heading not required.)

Place	Date	Hour	Summary of Events and Information	Remarks and references to Appendices
	2nd		it possible to establish Bridgeheads over the ANCRE. All three patrols encountered machine gun fire. 2 platoons of C Coy pushed forward to NW edge of MIRAUMONT but held up by machine guns. The 5th East Lanc. Rgt on the left of the Battalion sent 2 Coys to IRLES at 1-30 pm. At 1-30 pm B Coy was sent to R3 and orders to work up the North bank of the ANCRE to MIRAUMONT. At 3-30 pm A & C Coys advanced from R5 NE of MIRAUMONT into the village. All 3 Coys met in the village and then advanced over the ANCRE to the high ground in R12a. 40 prisoners and 18 machine guns taken in MIRAUMONT also other war material (rifles etc.). At 7 pm other recent Nos. of the East Lancs Rgt and 8th Manchesters would advance on LOUPART Rd and that this Battalion would wait en route	✗

Army Form C. 2118.

WAR DIARY
or
INTELLIGENCE SUMMARY.
(Erase heading not required.)

Instructions regarding War Diaries and Intelligence Summaries are contained in F. S. Regs., Part II. and the Staff Manual respectively. Title pages will be prepared in manuscript.

Place	Date 1918	Hour	Summary of Events and Information	Remarks and references to Appendices
PYS.	Aug 24th (cont.)		Cont. Battalion took up a position known PYS. in position at 10 pm.	
	Aug 25		Battalion in same position resting	
	Aug 26		Battalion moved at 4/30 a.m. to M 2 a and c area of concentration. Warning order received to be prepared to relieve 189th Brigade.	
WARLINCOURT	Aug 27		The Brigade which the 189 Brigade in the line The Battalion in reserve immediately west of WARLINCOURT. Looli't shelling has during the day by Ditch and Lanpart wood	
	28		The Battalion moved up to WARLINCOURT	
	29		Battalion moved to WARLINCOURT. Heavy enemy shelling during the night.	

Army Form C. 2118.

WAR DIARY
or
INTELLIGENCE SUMMARY.
(Erase heading not required.)

Instructions regarding War Diaries and Intelligence Summaries are contained in F.S. Regs., Part II. and the Staff Manual respectively. Title pages will be prepared in manuscript.

Place	Date 1918	Hour	Summary of Events and Information	Remarks and references to Appendices
EAST of THILLOY	Aug 30	—	At 3-15 am Battalion moved to East of Thilloy in front of an advance. 12 noon orders received that Battalion would attack REINCOURT in the evening. A and D Coys. with C Coy in Support assembled just South of BAPAUME. Zero hour 7pm. Enemy put down heavy barrage. A Coy got in alright on the left. D Coy suffered terribly from M.G. barrage and from machine gun fire from NW of Village. The Company however managed to cope with machine guns & eventually the village was taken. Later during the night the Batn. took over the front of 8th Gordons Rgt. to enemy — 2 Machine guns — 2 Field guns and other war material captured.	※
	31	—	Casualties of Previous day Lt E B GREGSTEN 2Lt J B WHITBIRD 2Lt W. WIGNALL wounded & 8 other ranks killed and 80 wounded. Enemy heavily shelled REINCOURT during the morning. Battalion left of the line 700 yards. Others reinforced Year. Congratulatory. telegram received from Major Genl SOLLY-FLOOD CMG. DSO. The following officers rejoined Batn on Aug 30th LtCol M. R. PEEL DSO — Capt F. Hanson MC — 2Lt webstirfield — 2Lt authorised — WCook (wounded) — Capt Bayley (France) — Capt L. A. C. Taylor MC — 2Lt Lt Williams — 2Lt Capt E. S. Taylor — Lt C. A. Allen — 2Lt A. Cooper — 2Lt Theily — Capt A. Butterworth to Wignall (wounded) — 2Lt E. G. Matby — 2Lt B. Harrop — 2Lt D. Thaw — 2Lt Earl Cooper — 2Lt E.B. Griselin (wounded)	VII ※

M. R. Peel LtCol
Comdg 1/10 K. Manchesters Regt.

Operation Order No 1 105
by
Lt Col WR Peel. DSO Comdg

VI

I. The Battn will vacate present position tomorrow morning 26th inst, and will occupy the area in M 3 a and c (Sheet 57 C SW) before 9 am.

II. D Company will pass Road junction M 2 d 7.9 at 7-45 am
C Company will pass at 8 am.
B Coy will leave their present position at 7-15 am and A Coy at 7-30 am
HdQrs will leave at 7 am

III. Coys will meet guides at Cross-roads (M 2 d 7.9) and 1 Officer per Coy will meet Commanding Officer at these Cross-roads at 7-15 am.

Battn HQrs will join at A and B Coys limbers

IV Coys will send guide to Battn HQrs at 5-45 am to conduct Lewis Gun limber to their Coy area.

V Battn HQrs will be at M 3 a 2. 2. and Coys will report there by runner when in position

VI Disposition sketches will be sent to Battn HQ by 10 am

VII acknowledge F. Howarth

25/9/18   Capt + Adjt

Operation Order No 109

by

Lt Col W R Pike DSO Comdg.

I. The Batn will be relieved tonight in the Forward Line by the 1/5th Manchester Rgt.. On completion of relief the Batn will be in Divnl Reserve.

II. After relief Coys will be guided by their own runners to Batn HQrs where all Lewis Guns, SAA & petrol tins will be loaded on Coy & Coy limbers.

III. Coys will march down via N 3 b and C — N 9 a to road running through LIGNY THILLOY and LA BARQUE halting in MISTY way (N 6 d 3 3) for hot tea & rum issue. After tea has been issued Coys will proceed to MARK

their Lt Coy areas in
M T Cs

Officer chargers will be
switching off the valley
at N¼ to 5. 7.

IV All patrol teams Mot.
Stones etc will be brought
out on relief

V Te Co's will report to
Bakra HQ'S immediately
they arrive in their
new areas.

VI ~~Capt~~ Luce will arrange
for breakfast to be
cooked in Coy kitchens
by Q men tomorrow
morning.

J Howarth

31/5   Capt Adjt

OPERATION ORDER No. 18.

by

Lieut. Col. W.R. PEEL, D.S.O, Commanding.
_____

1. The Battalion will move this evening at 6-15 p.m. and will take up a position in the COLINCAMPS area.

2. Guides will meet Coys. at the WINDMILL (BERTRANCOURT) at 6-45 p.m.
   Order of March:- "A" "B" "C" "D" Coys. H.Q.Coy.
   A distance of 100 yards will be maintained between platoons.
   "A" Coy will move out at 6.15 p.m.

3. Evening meal will be issued by 5 p.m. and Coys. will arrange for tomorrows fresh meat to be cooked immediately it arrives tonight. Dry rations will be issued before moving out.

4. All water bottles will be filled by 4 p.m. and petrol tins sent round to the Transport billet and handed over to the water Corporal. Dixies will be taken up on the L.G.limber together with the cooked meat and tea ration.

5. The Transport Officer will arrange for the Coy.L.G.limbers to report to respective Coys.H.Qrs. by 5 p.m. (18 mags.per gun will be taken) 3 limbers to report to Battalion H.Qrs by 5 p.m. also.
   Cookers must be ready to move with the Battalion on receipt of such orders.
   The watercart will move up with the Battalion.
   The R.S.M. will arrange for the 28 petrol tins in the Battalion to be loaded and placed on the limber and these will move up with the water cart tonight.

6. "C" Coy. will find the working party for tomorrow as per separate instructions issued.

7. The Battle surplus will remain in billets tonight under command of Major L.C. Wilde, D.S.O.
   Each Coy. will send one Officer or N.C.O. to receive instructions from Major L.C.Wilde, D.S.O. at 6-30 p.m. tonight.

8. O.C. Coys and the Transport Officer will report to Battalion Orderly Room at 6-30 p.m. this evening ready to proceed to the Line.

9. Marching out "states" will be rendered to Battalion Orderly Room by 5 p.m. tonight.

10. ACKNOWLEDGE.

August 15th 1918.

Capt & Adjt.

Distribution:- No.1. O.C. "A" Coy.
              2. " "B" "
              3. " "C" "
              4. " "D" "
              5. " H.Q. "
              6. 2nd in command.
              7. Q.M.
              8. T.O.
              9. R.S.M.
             10. Medical Officer.
             11. War Diary.
             12. " "
             13. File.
             14. C.O.

SECRET.

OPERATION ORDER No 10
by
Lieut.Col. W.R. PEEL, D.S.O., Commanding,

1. The Battalion and two attached Companies of 1/8th Manchester Regt. will be relieved to-day, August 13th, 1916.

2. Companies will be relieved as follows:-

   "A" Coy. 1/10th Manchester Regt., by "A" Coy. 1/7th Manchester Regt.
   "B" "   "   "   "   " "B" "   1/8th   "   "
   "B" "   "   "   "   " "C" "   1/7th   "   "
   "C" "   "   "   "   " "C" "   1/8th   "   "
   "D" "   "   "   "   " "D" "   1/8th   "   "
   "A" "   1/8th   "   "   " "A" "   1/8th   "   "
   "C" "   "

3. An advance party of 1 Officer and 4 N.C.O's per Company from relieving units will report this morning, and will take over all Trench Stores, gas appliances, including gas protection suits, and receipts obtained in duplicate.
   Maps, plans, Programmes of Work, and Defence Schemes will also be handed over, and receipts obtained in duplicate.
   These receipts, together with certificates of cleanliness, also in duplicate, will also be sent to Battalion Orderly Room by 8 a.m. August 13th.
                                  cutters
   Petrol tins, Food Containers, and wire/will not be handed over

4. All Companies, excluding attached Companies, will send 4 guides per Company to meet relieving units. Guides will report to Battn. H.Q., 1/10th Manchester Regt., as follows:-

   "D" and "B" Coys., 1/10th Manchester Regt, at 3.30 p.m.
   "A" and "C" "   "   "   "   " 4 p.m.

5. Companies will proceed after relief as follows:-

   1/10th Manchester Regt. to Billets, BERTRANCOURT.
   Company Quartermaster Sergeants will meet their respective Companies (1/10th Manchester Regt.) at BERTRANCOURT WINDMILL, J.34. a.2.6.

6. Companies will have evening meal before relief.

7. Lewis Gun Limbers for "A" and "C" Companies, 1/10th Manchester Regt., will report to their respective Headquarters at 5.30 p.m..
   Limbers for "B" and "D" Companies, 1/10th Manchester Regt. will report 200 yards West of Support-Double Company Headquarters (K.22.d.9.2.).
   2 Limbers for Battn. H.Q. will report at 9 p.m.
   1 Limber will report to O.C. "B" Company at 5 p.m. for transport of special L.G. ammunition. Limbers for attached Companies of the 1/8th Manchester Regt. will report in accordance with orders issued by O.C. 1/8th Manchester Regt.

8. "A" and "C" Companies, 1/10th Manchester Regt. will stack all Bombs, S.A.A., tools required for special purpose, at Battn. Headquarters, and hand in inventory (in duplicate) to Adjutant on completion of dump.

9. The Transport Officer will arrange for delivery of water to be carried out to-morrow until water tanks in present area are replenished.

10. A minimum distance of 200 yards will be maintained between platoons during relief.

11. Location of Battalion Headquarters, Regimental Aid Post, and the respective Company Headquarters will be notified later.

12. All working parties under R.E. supervision will be carried on without a break by relieving Companies.

13. O.C. Companies will hand over to incoming Companies full details for the withdrawal of troops from positions on occasions of British gas attacks.

14. Completion of relief from present positions will be wired to Battalion Headquarters by code word "GOODRICH".
Completion of occupation of billets will be notified by runner to new Battalion Headquarters by code word "YORK".

15. Acknowledge.

                                                                         Lieut.,
                                                                         A/Adjt.,

12th August, 1918.

Distribution:-
         No.1. O.C. "A" Coy. 1/10th Manchester Regt.
           2. O.C. "B"   "   "   "   "
           3. O.C. "C"   "   "   "   "
           4. O.C. "D"   "   "   "   "
           5. O.C. "A"   "   1/8th   "   "
           6. O.C. "B"   "   "   "   "
           7. O.C. H.Q. "
           8. L.G. T.M.O.
           9. S.O.
          10. 2nd in Command.
          11. O.C. 1/8th Manchester Regt.
          12. R. S. M.
          13. Medical Officer.
          14. War Diary.
          15. "   "
          16. File.

Operation Order No. 102
by
Lt Col W R Peel DSO Comdg.

1. The following reliefs will take place to day the 8th inst.

(a) D Coy will relieve A Coy in the left FRONT sector. Relief will take place after the evening meal. All details of relief will be arranged by OC Coys. After relief A Coy will move to COLINCAMPS and take over the positions at present occupied by C Coy 8th Manchester Rgt.

(b) C Coy will be relieved by A Coy 8th Manchester Rgt and will after relief proceed to COLINCAMPS and take over positions occupied by A Coy 8th Manchester Rgt. A Coy 8th Manch Rgt will not commence relieving until 6 pm.

(c) C Coy 8th Manch Rgt will take over the positions at present occupied by D Coy 10th Manch Rgt (LEFT SUPPORT Coy). They will

not leave their present positions
before 6 pm.

2. Advance Parties
   OC A and C Coys will send
advance parties to take over from
C and A Coys 8th Manchester Regt
in the afternoon.
   OC D Coy will send to A Coy
10th Manchester Regt advance party
to take over trench stores &c
   Advance parties of A and
C Coys 8th Manch Regt will be
sent up this afternoon.

3. All trench stores will be
handed over and receipts in
duplicate forwarded to Batt HQ
by 9am 9th inst
   Petrol tins will be handed over

4. Working Parties: as to be
detailed from Batt H Qrs.

5. Rations The rations of
A and C Coys 10th Manchester
Regt will be delivered

at the new Coy positions. The limbers will then take up cooking utensils &c to the new positions of C and A Coys 8th Manch Rgt. The limbers carrying rations of C and A Coys 8th Manchester Rgt will bring back the cooking utensils &c of A and C Coys 10th Manchester Rgt. OC A Coy 10th Manchester Rgt will have the Coy cooking utensils &c carried down to C Coy present HQ by 6 pm where they will be loaded on to the limbers.

6 After relief C & A Coys 8th Manchester Rgt will come under the orders of OC 10th Manchester Rgt

7 Completion of relief will be sent to Bat HQrs by code word "CATS"

8. ACKNOWLEDGE

8/8/18   Lieut & Act/Adjt
                                          REGAIN

Distribution
———————
Copy No 1 — File
         2 — OC A 8th Man Rgt
         3 — OC C 8th Man Rgt
         4 — " A 10th Man Rgt
         5 — " B 10th Man Rgt
         6 — " C 10th Man Rgt
         7 — " D 10th Man Rgt
         8 — OC 8th Manchester Rgt
         9 —
        10 — 2nd & T O
        11   Sigs & I O

OPERATION ORDER No 101

by

Lieut.Col. W.R.PEEL, D.S.O., Commanding,

Copy No....

1. "A" Company will relieve "D" Company, and "B" Company will relieve "C" Company in the front line on August 7th.
   After relief "D" and "C" Companies will occupy the areas vacated by "A" and "B" Companies respectively.

2. All details of relief to be arranged between O.C. Companies concerned.

3. Maps, Programmes of work, Aeroplane Photographs, petrol tins, Trench Stores, etc., will be taken over and receipts in singlet sent to Battalion Headquarters by noon, August 8th.

4. Advance parties of 1 Officer, and 4 N.C.O's per Company will be sent by "A" and "B" Companies to the new area at 6 p.m. August 6th.

5. Working parties at present furnished by "A" and "B" Companies will be taken over by "D" and "C" Companies respectively from and including all working parties reporting at 7 p.m., August 7th.

6. Completion of relief will be wired to Battalion Headquarters by code word "CHATHAM".

7. Acknowledge (Companies only).

Lieut.,
A/Adjt.

6th August, 1918.

Distribution:-

  No.1. O.C. "A" Coy.
  " 2. O.C. "B" Coy.
  " 3. O.C. "C" Coy.
  " 4. O.C. "D" Coy.
  " 5. C.O.
  " 6. Intelligence Officer.
  " 7. Q.M. & T.O.
  " 8. O.C. 1/5th East Lancs Regt.
  " 9. O.C. 1/8th Lancs. Fusiliers.
  "10. War Diary.
  "11. "   "
  "12. File.

10. Company H.Q. are located as follows:-

"A" & "B" Coys., joint Headquarters, K.34.d.4.2.
"C" Coy., K.35.a.55.10.
"D" Coy., K.27.c.9.3.

11. The Transport Officer will arrange for water to be delivered at the new Company areas by 8.a.m., August 3rd.

12. Dinners will be in the new positions on 3rd inst., and Company Cooks will proceed to new areas immediately after lunch.

13. After relief Battalion H.Q. will be at K.34.b.25.95.

14. The Regimental Aid Post will be established at K.34.d.5.4.

15. All working parties under R.E. supervision will be carried on without a break by relieving Companies.

16. Completion of relief will be wired to Battalion H.Q. by code word "BOSTON".

17. Acknowledge.

[signature]
Major,
Commanding, 1/10th Manchester Regiment.

2/8/18.

Distribution:-

No. 1. O.C. "A" Coy.
2. O.C. "B" Coy.
3. O.C. "C" Coy.
4. O.C. "D" Coy.
5. O.C. Headquarters.
6. O.C. R.E.
7. M.O.
8. O.C. 1/10th Manchester Regt.
9. R.S.M.
10. War Diary.
11. "   "
12. M.O.
13. File.

OPERATION ORDER No.100

by

Major L. O. WHITE, D.S.O., Commanding.

Copy No.......

1. The Battalion will relieve the 1/8th Manchester Regt., on the 3rd August, 1918.
   On completion of relief the Battalion will be on the Left Sub-sector of the Brigade Front.

2. Companies will take over from, and be relieved by, Companies of the 1/8th Manchester Regiment as follows:-

   "A" Coy, 1/10th Manchester Regt. from and by "C" Coy, 8th Manchester Regt.
   "B" Coy,   "   "   "   "   "   " by "D" Coy, 8th Manchester Regt.
   "C" Coy,   "   "   "   "   "   " by "A" Coy, 8th Manchester Regt.
   "D" Coy,   "   "   "   "   "   " by "B" Coy, 8th Manchester Regt.

3. An advance party of 1 officer per Company, and 1 N.C.O. per Platoon will proceed to the new area, reporting for guides to B.H.Q., of 1/8th Manchester Regt., K.31.b.25.05, at 2.p.m. to-day, 2/8/18.
   They will take over Disposition Maps, Trench Stores, Gas Protection suits, Programme of Work, etc., and will remain at the new area.

4. All Companies will send 1 guide per Company to report to the B.H.Q., of 1/8th Manchester Regt., at 10.a.m. on 3rd inst., in order to guide in the advance parties of the relieving Companies.

5. All trench stores, disposition maps, gas appliances, including protection suits, will be handed over to the advance party of the 1/8th Manchester Regt., and certificates obtained in duplicate, together with certificates of cleanliness in duplicate. These receipts will be sent to Battalion Orderly Room by 12 noon, August 4th.
   Patrol line will not be handed over.

6. Guides, one per Platoon, will meet relieving Companies as follows:-

   "A" Coy. at 1/8th Manchesters H.Q., ...
        K.31.b.25.05, at 4.p.m.
   "B" Coy. ....
   "C" Coy. at 1/8th Manchester Regt. H.Q., at 4.30.p.m.
   "D" Coy. at new position Company H.Q., K.31.a.25.10, at 4.p.m.
   "D" Coy. K.27,c.3.5., at 4.p.m.

   Companies will not move before 7.15.p.m., and must be prepared to temporarily postpone relief at the last minute upon receipt of code word "DRYAD". Code word for continuation of relief after postponement will be "BRIGHT".

7. The Left Front platoon of "B" Coy. will not carry out relief until after dark, but will proceed with remainder of Company to new Company area.

8. The Transport Officer will arrange for Company and H.Q. Lewis Gun Limbers (one each per Coy. and H.Q.) to report to present respective Company H.Q., at 6.p.m., for transport of mess stores, Lewis Guns, magazines, and patrol line. One brakesman per Coy. will be detailed to go with each limber.

9. Rations will be delivered to the new Company H.Q., in the case of "A", "B", and "C" Companies on the 3rd inst., and in the case of "D" Company to a point to be fixed by the O.C. Company concerned.

1/10th Battalion Manchester Regiment.

126/7 95M 20

WAR DIARY.

VOLUME No. 38.

CONFIDENTIAL.

Sept. 1918.

Army Form C. 2118.

1/10th Manchester Regiment.

WAR DIARY
or
INTELLIGENCE SUMMARY.
(Erase heading not required.)

Instructions regarding War Diaries and Intelligence Summaries are contained in F. S. Regs., Part II. and the Staff Manual respectively. Title pages will be prepared in manuscript.

Place	Date	Hour	Summary of Events and Information	Remarks and references to Appendices
	Sept			
	1.		Battalion relieved by 5th Manchester Regt. & came down by march route to PYS area & occupied former huts.	
	2.		Cleaning up & reorganisation.	
	3.		Cleaning up. Company inspection. etc.	
	4.		Battalion received sudden orders to move into Battle Positions EAST of HAPLIN COURT WOOD in Q.9.a.&.c.	
	5.		Battalion in readiness to take up position in Corps Reserve.	
	6.		Battalion moved down to LA BARQUE arriving about 2.30 p.m. Billeted in huts & tents. Lieut. J.M. West & 2/Lieut. T.L. Wilson joined unit from Base.	
	7.		Cleaning up. Company inspection.	
	8.		Divine Service	
	9.		Progressive Training Commenced. Battalion parade - Company Training. Arms Drill, saluting - S.B.R. drill. 2/Lieut. E.A. Fraser joined unit from Base.	
	10.		Battalion Training. Special attention paid to Platoon training in Artillery formation.	
	11.		Fire movement - Lost tropping system. "A" Coy in Coy. in attack with M.G's & L.T.M's	
	12.		2/Lt. A. Boyle joined unit from Base. Coy in the attack. Afternoon - Pool shooting - Boxing.	

Army Form C. 2118.

11th Manchester Regiment.

WAR DIARY
or
INTELLIGENCE SUMMARY.
(Erase heading not required.)

Place	Date	Hour	Summary of Events and Information	Remarks and references to Appendices
	Sept.			
	13.		Battalion Training. Capt Higgins + assaulting Ladder machine gun nests.	
	14.		Battalion Receive Warning Order to man Corps Line. Battalion reported ready in 1¾ hours.	
	15.		Brigade Church Parade.	
	16.		Capt. Practices Consolidation & the Attack. "G" Coy gave demonstration in this before	
	17.		Corps & Divisional Commanders & Officers of Brigade. During this period took part in Critical Inter shooting. Football carried out under Battalion & Brigade arrangements.	
	18.		Warning Order to relieve 37th Division on 20th received. Coy. Practices Consolidation.	
	19.		Preparation for relief. Resting.	
	20.		Battalion moves by march route to LEBUCQUIERE. Brigade inspected by Major General in line of march. Battalion later over billets of 10th Somerset. Divisional Reserve.	
	21.		Commanding Officer + Coy. Commanders reconnoitre front line N.15 HAVRINCOURT WOOD move out to relieve 8th Lincoln Regt in the line. Relief complete 10 p.m.	

1/10th Manchester Regiment.

WAR DIARY
or
INTELLIGENCE SUMMARY.
(Erase heading not required.)

Army Form C. 2118.

Place	Date	Hour	Summary of Events and Information	Remarks and references to Appendices
	Sept. 22.		Activity normal. Lieut. Col. W.R. Pickford D.S.O. Capt. F. Hardman, M.C. with 3. O.R. gassed by enemy shell (Mustard) Capt. F. Hardman M.C. evacuated.	ff.
	23.		Lieut. Col. W.R. Pickford D.S.O. evacuated. Major T.T. Keely, M.C. (1/6th Manchester Regt.) taken over command of the Battalion. 5 p.m.	ff.
	24.		Activity normal. Our patrols active.	ff.
	25.		"B" & "C" Coy. push forward the front line. Forward posts established. Strong opposition met with. 1 Casualty. 4" Stokes Mortar Shoot carried out by No. 3 Special Coy. R.E. Front line was evacuated for the Shoot.	ff.
	26.		Advance position from 125 & 127 Brigade recommoitre Battalion Sector in preparation for the Divnl. Assault. 1/5th Manchester Regt. & 1/8th Lancashire Fusiliers, moved into Battalion area at 8.30 p.m. Battalion less 2 Platoon "B" Coy. & 2 Platoon "C" Coy. withdrew at 10 p.m. The 4 Platoon under Capt. J.C. Rowbotham formed protective screen which withdrew at 4 a.m. 27th before the assault was delivered. Battalion marched down via CANAL DU NORD to J. 34. Sheet 57. C. S.E.	ff.

1/10th Manchester Regiment.

WAR DIARY
or
INTELLIGENCE SUMMARY.
(Erase heading not required.)

Army Form C. 2118.

Place	Date	Hour	Summary of Events and Information	Remarks and references to Appendices
	Sept. 27		Battalion at 10 minutes notice to move forward, the idea being to push through attacking Brigades & exploit success. Orders came through at 1.24 p.m. to report to S.O.C. 127th Infy Bde. Battalion reported at 4.15 p.m. at BUTLERS CROSS. moved to dug-outs at Q. H. a. 8. 7. Sheet 57C. S.E. Battalion Headquarters opened in HINDENBURG FRONT LINE.	
	28.	2-30 a.m.	Battalion attacked under heavy artillery barrage at 2-30 a.m. B & C. Coys. on 1st Objective just East of RIBECOURT. A & D Coy. on 2nd Objective 500° EAST. The Battalion then followed up the advance of the enemy to WELSH RIDGE S.W. of MARCOING. A & B Coy in the outpost line. C in support & D Coy in Reserve. Relieved by New Zealand Division at 11 p.m. & moved down into dug-outs in HINDENBURG FRONT LINE. During the operation the Battalion only sustained 3 Officers & 31 OR Casualties - captured 3 Officers & 145 OR. 6 Field Guns. 1 H.5 Howitzer. 5 Minnenwerfers & a large quantity of Light & Heavy M.G's and other war material.	

1/10 Manchester Regt.

WAR DIARY
or
INTELLIGENCE SUMMARY

Army Form C. 2118.

Place	Date	Hour	Summary of Events and Information	Remarks and references to Appendices
	Sept. 29		Battalion marched down to HAVRINCOURT WOOD. Battalion Complimented by Divisional Commander on the good work done during the forenoon. Remainder of day spent in fetching camp.	
	30.		Cleaning up. Coy. inspection + Kit parade. Officers with the Battalion. Major F.T. Kelly M.C. Capt. rayt. L. Hornuck. M.C. Lieut. C.H. Cooper. Lieut. W. Schofield. Lieut. A.L. White. (Medical Officer) Lieut. F.E. Cocke. OC "A" Coy. Capt. J.C.S. Rowbotham. OC "B" Coy. Capt. D. Statt. OC "C" Coy. Lieut. J.F. Beveridge. OC "D" Coy. Lieut. A.F. Allen. Lieut. L.A. Kerr. Lieut. Jno. Jepp. Lieut. W.S. Lawton M.C. 2/Lieut. Sno. Sinialin. 2/Lieut. S.G. Moalthy. 2/Lieut. Wm Gregory. Lieut. C.M. Cooper. 2/Lieut. R.A. Haurof. Lieut. G. Horley. 2/Lieut. E.A. Travis. 2/Lieut. F. Boyle.	

Army Form C. 2118.

1/10th Manchester Regiment.

WAR DIARY
or
INTELLIGENCE SUMMARY
(Erase heading not required.)

Place	Date	Hour	Summary of Events and Information	Remarks and references to Appendices
			The total Casualties for the month are	
			2/Lieut. T.L. WILSON. Killed in Action 28-9-18.	
			Lieut. N.T. NORRIS. Wounded. 28-9-18.	
			Capt. F. HARDMAN. M.C. Gassed. 22-9-18.	
			Lieut. Col. W.R. PEEL. D.S.O. Gassed 22-9-18. Hospital 24-9-18.	
			3. O.R. Killed in Action	
			41. O.R. Wounded.	
			October 1st 1918.	
			W R Peel Lieut. Col.	
			Commanding 1/10th Manchester Regt.	

PROVISIONAL DEFENCE ORDER NO. 2.

by

Lieut. Col. W.R. PEEL, D.S.O. Commanding.

----

1. The Corps Reserve Line is now the NEUVILLE - RUYAUCOURT LINE.

2. The Battalion is responsible for the line from P.13.a.8.3. - P.11.a.0.3.
   Companies will be disposed as on attached sketch.

3. 8th. Manchester Regt. in Brigade Reserve in RUYAUCOURT.

4. 1/5th East Lancs. Regt. on the Right of the Battalion.

5. Administrative Instructions contained in Provisional Defence Order No. 1 will apply.

J. Howarth
Captain.
Adjutant.

September 17th.

Operation Order No. 109.
Lt-Col W.R. Peel DSO Commdg.

1. The 127 Bde are disposed as follows
5th L.F. holding outpost line N & S.
through NEUVE EGLISE, BOUR. TUNNEL
6th L.F. hold a line of resistance through
P.21. central & P.27. central.
7th L.F. are moving up to line of
railway W of YPRES

2. 5th EAST LANCS are moving
forward to positions vacated by
7th L.F. N+W of EOS O.18 +
O.24

3. In the event of enemy counter
attack tomorrow the 5th & 4th 125
Bde are holding a line through
P.21 + P.27 & on a line of supporting
posts. 126 Inf Bde will be disposed
as follows:
1/6 MANCHESTERS on a 2 Coy
front on sq. O.18.
5th EAST LANCS similarly
disposed on sq. O.24.
1/8 MANCHESTER in support
on O.26 b & d.

4. Batt will be disposed as follows
C Coy on LEFT in about
O.18.b. 2 Platoons in front, 2
Platoons in support
B Coy similarly disposed
in O.18.d. The approx. front
line, should run parallel to
road in O.13.A — O.18.d.
A Coy will be in support on
high ground in O.18.A.
D Coy will be in support in
high ground in O.18.C.
M.G. Section 2 guns on
right of B. Coy. covering valley
running to YPRES, & 2 guns
at Batt H.Q. at approx. O.17.b.2.2.

5. On receipt of BATTLE POSITIONS
Coys will at once move to their
locations. Lewis Gun limbers will
move with Coys & as soon as
unloaded will return to present
Batt H.Q. Cookers will
remain at present Batt H.Q.

6. Acknowledge

Howarth
Capt & Adjt

4/9/18

Operation Order No 109
by
Lt Col W.R. Gee DSO Comdg

I. The Bn will be relieved tonight in the trench line by the 1/5th Manchester Rgt. On completion of relief the Bn will be in Divl Reserve.

II. After relief Coys will be guided by their own runners to Bn HQrs where all Lewis Guns, SAA, & petrol tins will be loaded on Coy Coy limbers.

III. Coys will march down via N5b and c — N9a to road running through LIGNY THILLOY and LA BARQUE halting in MISTY way (N6 d 3.3) for hot tea and rum. After tea has been issued Coys will proceed to their old Coy areas in M3a.

Officers chargers will be waiting in the valley at N8b.5.7.

IV. All patrol tins, Mob: stores &c will be brought out on relief.

I. Coys will report to Batn H.Qs. immediately they arrive in their new area.

VI. ~~Coys~~ Qmr will arrange for breakfasts to be cooked in Coy kitchens by 9 am tomorrow morning.

J. Howarth
Capt & A/t

31/9/8.

Operation Order No 110
by
Lt Col W.R. Peel DSO Comdg

In the event of the 5th East Lancs Regt moving forward this Battn will move as follows:—

A Coy to
Position vacated
by A Coy 5th E L Regt
{ 1 platoon P13c 1. 5
  1   "   P19a 0. 7
  1   "   O 18d 6. 6
  1   "   O 24b 7. 7 }

Coy HQrs   O 18d 6. 2

B Coy to
Position vacated
by B Coy 5th E L Regt
{ 3 platoons O24d 7.4 to
              O24d 7.1
  1 platoon O24d 5.7 }

Coy HQrs   O 24 d 5. 9

D Coy to
Position vacated
by C Coy 5th E L Regt
{ 3 platoons P25a 1.5 to
              P19 c 1 2
  1 platoon O 30 b 8. 6 }

Coy HQrs   O 24 d 5. 1

1.

A Coy to } in O.24.c houses
position vacated } about Church and
by D Coy 8th E.L.R. } entrance to B.V8

Batln H.Qrs O.23.d.2.2.

Limbers will accompany Coys
Cookers may be sent up
later

Coys will move up by
sections in artillery formation
across country and not using
roads.

Howarth
Capt & Adjt

5/9/18

Administrative Instructions No 115
issued in Conjunction with O.O. 115
by
Major T. J. Kelly M.C. Commanding.

1. Ammunition. S.A.A. + Grenades.

Right Inf. Bn. Dump.   Q 10. b. 7. 2.
Left   "   Q 10. a. 2. 1.
Support   "   Q 15. a. 1. 9.
                        Q 8. d. 6. 8.

2. Transport Lines.
(a) The ground in all Squares T.30. T.25
c + d + P.5 a + b + P.6 a + b is
reserved for VI Corps Artillery
Squares P.6 c + d & all P.11 + 12
are reserved for 42nd Div. Artillery
D.A.C. Echelon in Squares P.8 + P.9.

(b) "B" Echelon transport will move
forward under orders of B.H.Q.

3. Supply. The normal System of
sending forward Supplies by Limber
from Rear HQrs will be adhered to.
No alteration will be made in the
Railhead or Refilling Points.

A 7000 gallon water tank at approx
Q.7.d.8.8 is reserved for drinking
purposes.
Petrol tins can be refilled.

100 filled petrol tins of water
will be maintained at the advanced
SAA dump at Q.7.d.2.8.
Empty petrol tins will be exchanged
for full ones.

4. R.E. Stores. Main R.E. Dump.
VELU CHATEAU J.25.c.7.7
Adv. Dumps.   P.10.c.5.8
               Q.10.a. central.

5. Police. P/W Cage at P.11. central
P/W Collecting Post Q.10.a.8.8
All prisoners will pass through
Battalion H.Qrs.
Receipts will be obtained
for all prisoners.

6. Supply Tanks. These will be
loaded with S.A.A. bombs etc.
Location notified later.

7. Medical Arrangements.
   notified later.

8. All indents will be forwarded
   by Coys to Battalion H.Qrs.

9. Acknowledge.

26/9/18.

Howarth.
Capt +
Adjt.

War Diary

Provisional Operation Order No 3
by
Major T. J. Kelly. M.C. Commanding.

1. The Battalion is under 10 minutes notice to move.
   All men must be Kept in the vicinity of their Coy. area & Lewis Gun limbers must be Kept ready loaded.
   All water bottles will be filled.

2. On receipt of message BATTLE POSITIONS Coys. will fall in, in their Coy area & send an Officer to Battalion HQrs at once for further instructions.

3. Order of march will be "D" "A" "B" "C" Battn. H. Qrs.
   Coy. L.G. limbers will march at the head of their Coys.
   200 yds distance between platoons will be maintained.

4. ACKNOWLEDGE

27/9/18.

J. Nowark
Capt
Adjt

War Diary

Operation Order No 115.
by
Major T.J. Kell, M.C. Commanding.

1. The Battalion, less 2 platoons "B" Coy & 1 platoon "C" Coy. will be relieved tonight by the 19th Manchester Regt. on the Left & 17th Kings Liverpools on the Right. The dividing line line between 127th & 126th Bdes. will be a line drawn EAST & WEST through Q.5.a.0.5.

2. A. D. Coys & 2 platoons east of C & B Coy under Lieut. Duff will report by Code word "DING" when they are ready to move out, but will only vacate their area on Code word "DON" from Batt. HQ.

3. The front line Consisting of 2 platoons "C" & 1 platoon "B" Coy will pass to the Command of Capt J.C. Rowbotham at 5 p.m. this evening. These 4 platoons will remain here till 4 a.m. 27th inst & proceed by march route to SPOIL HEAP. S.34. picking up

a L.G. limber about Q.9.a.2.8 &
meeting guides at CANAL CROSSING
J.34.d.9.6.

4. A & D Coys with 2 platoons B Coy &
2 platoons C Coy under Lt. Jupp will
pick up L.G. limber about Q.9.a.2.8
& proceed by march route to SPOIL-
HEAP - J.34.
Route will be BUTLERS CROSS -
CLAYTON CROSS - WOOD PLACE
(P.6.b.95.20) crossing Canal J.36.b.95.20
thence along canal Bank to J.34.d.9.6. where
guides will conduct Coys to their
own areas.
200 yds distance will be maintained between platoons.

5. Capt. J.C.S. Rowbotham will arrange
that one officer per platoon is
left with the 2 platoons C Coy &
2 platoons B Coy which are
left to garrison the front line.
Capt. Rowbotham will also
arrange that all the front posts
established by us last night
are withdrawn at dusk tonight.

3

6. All [Remaining?] [?] Pistol [?]
etc will be taken out with Coy.
OC Coys will arrange that spare
men to one out of the line tonight
carrying the following —

[?] S.O.S. [?]   — 1 [?] each
Rifle Grenades — 6 [?]
[?] Flares ([?]) [?] 3 men
No Very Lights — one flare each &
Sentries commanders.
S.O.S. 1 per [?] [?] on Coy H.Q.
Leave for magazines —
  in Contact [?] No [?]
  4 each [?] Nos 3, 4, 5
  2 each [?] [?] 6

[?] [?]
1 [?] [?] each sentries
4 [?] [?] Coy H.Q.
2 [?] [?] Coy H.Q.

7. Signals [?] [?] [?] between
[?] [?] [?] [?] [?]
[?] [?] [?] [?] T.H.Q.
(P.S. [?] sentries).

All the Transport will be
ready to join the Battalion at
short notice after 6 a.m. [?].

-4-

Transport Officers will arrange for L.G. limbers of A. C. & B. Coys. to be at O.G. a 5°° at 6.45 p.m. these to be divided for Batt. H.Q. - Signal Cart to be at BN HQRS about 6.30 p.m. tonight.

He will find transport for B Coys S.G. which is to be at Bdq. H. Q. ? at 4-30 a.m. night wil b met Capt Humberston en route

Officers chargers will b standing out along the road fr every Coy & cross at SHRAPNEL STRR XRD (Q.8.b.3.6.) at 9 p.m. tonight in order for Coll. McClintock at 4-30 am ?? at Bn ? ?

8 MENIN ROAD E

Maworth
Capt
Adjt

2/9/?

WAR DIARY.

5. On arrival Coys will send
   1 runner to Battn Hdqrs.

6. Acknowledge

Mowatt
Capt + Adj

5/18

Addendum to Operation Order N° 1118
by
Major Kelly. M.C. Commanding.
_____

1. Zero night. 24/25th inst. 12 midnight.
   Zero night. 25th. 9. p.m.

2. In the event of weather conditions
   being unfavourable Code word
   NAZIRETH will be sent from
   Hore H.Qrs.

   Howarth
   Capt.
   Adjt.

24/9/18.

SECRET

OPERATION ORDER No 114
by
MAJOR KELLY. M.C. COMMANDING

1. At a day and hour to be notified later No 2 Special Coy. R.E. will carry out a Gas bombardment with 4" Stokes Mortars.
For targets see attached map.

2. All troops, rations, ammunition, water etc will be withdrawn from the area shown in Green & Red by Zero minus 10.
The Right platoon of C Coy will move to the T.P. Q.4.a.6.7.
The forward platoon of A Coy in TRESCAULT TRENCH Q.4.d.7.8 will move to A Coy. H.Qrs.
The whole of B Coy will move into the trench running from Q.4.d.4.5.75 to Q.4.d.8.0. & utilize any convenient trenches in the immediate area.
Care should be taken that fire positions are available for all the men of this Coy.

3. The area shown in Red will be
re occupied at Zero plus 30.
The area shown in Green will not
be re-occupied until declared
safe by an officer of the Special
Coy. R.E

4. The " Stokes Mortar Shoot" may
take place tonight.
Zero hour will be sent round as
soon as it is known.

5. For this operation the following
Code names will be used :-
(1) By telegram stating Zero hour
        received —   TOMMY.
(2) Troops in danger area
        withdrawn —   TURK.
(3) Area marked Red
        re occupied —   NA
(4) Area marked Green
        re occupied —   POO.

6. Acknowledge by Code word BUG.

                                    Howarth
                                    Capt
24/9/18.   2/11

Operation Order No. 46.
by
Major T. J. Kelly. M.C. Commanding

1. The Bde. will exploit through 127th Bde. objective for lines on 8 of N.3.d. Patrols will push forward & take over posts established by our Hussars covering bridges over ESCAUT CANAL.

2. On relief by Infantry, Cavalry will withdraw to Left flank & connect with 62nd Division Headquarters Cavalry Fork Roads G.32.d.2.7

3. 126th Infy Bde will assemble at once as follows:—
   1/8th Manchester Regt. L.3.a.a. (Leading Bn.)
   1/5th Ino Lancs Regt. L.31.central. (Support -)
   with Scout protecting right flank of Bde.
   1/4th Manchester Regt. (Reserve Bn.)
   A + D Coys. in Sunken Rd running from L.34 b.90.95 to R.4 b.9.5.
   A Coy on Left. D Coy on Right.
   Inter Coy boundary junction Sunken Rd & cont'n trench.
   D Coy if not firmly established with the Battalion on its Right, will throw

2.

back slightly & form a defensive Right flank
C Coy. will take up a position in
L.R.33.a.&.c. and R.3.a. so that
it will be able to command the valley.
B Coy. will form on the BLUE LINE
L.32.b.&.d. & R.2.a.
OC A & D Coys. will at once notify Batt:
HQ. when the 5th Manchesters have passed
through their front line.

4. OC Coys will render by this manner
map reference of their Coy HQ in
accordance with this Operation Order
Battalion HQ. is in RIDGE TRENCH
L.31.d.5.2.

5. ACKNOWLEDGE

Howarth
Lt.
Adjt

29/9/18.

Operation Order No 1

1. The Battn. will move to
LIGNY-THILLOY to-morrow
6 A.S.I.

2. Head of column will pass the
Starting Point at 9-15 am
Starting Point Crossroads O9c 19.
Order of march
   H.dqrs
   D.
   A.
   B.
   C.

3. Intervals of 200 yds will
be maintained between platoons

4. Lewis Gun limbers will
march in rear of Coys along
Cookers, Medl limbers & pack
Cobs will march in rear

OPERATION ORDER No.118.

by
Lieut.Col. W.R. Peel. D.S.O. Commanding.

1. The Battalion will relieve the 9th Lincoln Regt. in the Front Line tonight 21/22nd Sept. After relief the Battalion will be in the centre sector, Left Divisional front.

2. "B" Coy.1/10th.Manchester Regt. will relieve "B" Coy. 9th Lincoln Regt.
      (Right Front Coy).
   "C" Coy.1/10th.Manchester Regt. will relieve "A" Coy. 9th Lincoln Regt.
      (Left Front Coy.)
   "A" Coy.1/10th.Manchester Regt. will relieve "C" Coy. 9th Lincoln Regt.
      (Support Coy.)
   "D" Coy.1/10th.Manchester Regt. will relieve "D" Coy. 9th Lincoln Regt.
      (Reserve Coy.)

3. Order of march will be "B" "C" "A" & "D" Coys. Battalion H.Qrs.
   Interval of 100 yards between Platoons will be maintained.
   Head of "B" Coy. will pass Starting Point I.30.b.9.7. at 4.40 p.m.
   Route (follow road) BERTINCOURT - RUYAULCOURT - MATHESON ROAD
   ARTILLERY TRACK to CLAYTON CROSS where guides will meet the Coys. at
   7-15 p.m.

4. Water bottles will be filled before starting.
   Lewis Gun wagons will move at head of each Coy. these will be unloaded in Q.3.c.

5. All trench stores, maps, programmes of work, anti-gas appliances etc., will be taken over and lists in duplicate sent to Battalion Headquarters by 10 a.m. 22nd. inst. also Disposition maps showing Platoon localities and Coy. Headquarters, will be sent in at the same time.

6. As soon as "D" Coy. is in Position they will send an Officer to Battalion H.Qrs to ascertain what carrying parties will be required.

7. Battalion Headquarters will be at Q.3.b.5.2.
   Brigade Headquarters at PLACE MONTMART.

8. Completion of relief will be wired to Battalion Headquarters by code word "DUSTY".

9. Acknowledge.

21/9/18.

Dist: O.C. "A" Coy.
           "B" "
           "C" "
           "D" "
      Lt.Col.W.R.Peel.D.S.O.
      T.O.
      Q.M.
      R.S.M.
      File.
      War Diary.
      "   "

Howarth
Captain.
Adjutant.

PROVISIONAL DEFENCE ORDER No 2
BY
Lt Col. W. R. PEEL. D.S.O. Commanding

1. In event of enemy attack the Battalion will take up a line from P.4.a.7.4 to J.28.c.8.0

2. "B" Coy. will hold the line from J.28.c.8.0 to grid line between J.34.a.9.c.

   "C" Coy. from grid line J.34.a.9.c to J.34.c.8.1

   "A" Coy from J.34.c.8.1 to P.4.a.7.4

   "D" Coy in SUPPORT in J.33.b.

   Battalion H.Q. J.27.d.4.5.

3. Role of Battalion to hold Corps Line of resistance or to counter attack to regain Divisional main line of resistance (Eastern edge of HAVRINCOURT WOOD)

- 2 -

4. Coys. will Stand to on receipt of "BATTLE POSITIONS" and Send O. Officer to Battalion H.Q. immediately.

Transport officer will Send pack & L.G. mules round to Coys. & Battalion H.Q. & in addition 1 S.A.A wagon & pack Cobs loaded with S.A.A. & water to Battalion H.Q.

5. 5th East Lancs will take up a line from P.10.b.9.3. to P.4.a.7.4 H.Q. P.2.d.4.6.

6. 8th Manchester Regt. in SUPPORT in J.26.

7. Acknowledge.

Distribution. OC A Coy.
  B
  C
  D
  HQ
  L.Col. W.R. Rtd. 730.
  Q.M.
  T.O.
  WAR DIARY
  File.

20/4/18.

Capt & Adjt.

1/10th. Battalion Manchester Regiment.

SECRET.   WARNING ORDER.   18-9-18.

Reference Map: 57.Q.1/40,000

1. 42nd Division (less Artillery) is relieving 37th Division (less Artillery) on Sept 20th 21st and 22nd, and will become Left Division IV Corps.

2. The 126th Infy Bde. with 1 Battalion 127th Infy Bde. will take over the Divisional Front.
All 3 Battalions of this Brigade will be in the line.
On 20th inst. Brigade will march to VELU - BEUGNY - LEBUCQUIERE area in relief of 111th Infy Bde.
After dark 21st inst. Brigade will relieve the 63rd Infy Bde.
A bus has been asked for to take a small advanced party from each unit to the Front line on the 20th inst.

3. The boundaries of 42nd Division will be as follows :-

Southern Boundary. Q.7.central - Q.9.c.0.0 - thence due East.
Northern Boundary. K.33.central - K.29.d.0.0.- thence due East.

4. Two Troops 3rd Hussars now attached to 37th Division will be transferred to 42nd Division from midnight 21st/22nd Sept.

5. Command of Left Sector IV Corps will pass to G.O.C. 42nd Division at 12 midnight 21st/22nd Sept.

6. 428th Field Coy. is allotted to 126th Brigade Group.

September 19th 1918.

Distribution.

O.C."A" Coy.
    "B" "
    "C" "
    "D" "
    H.Q."
Lt.Col.W.K.Peel.D.S.O.
Major L.O.Wilde.D.S.O.
Q.M.& T.O.

Howarth
Captain.
Adjutant.

OPERATION ORDER No.112

by

Lieut. Col. W.R. Peel. D.S.O. Commanding.

---

1. The Battalion will move tomorrow by march route to LEBUCQUIERE (I.30.a). and relieve the 13th R.B.

2. Route will be BAPAUME - FREMICOURT then road through I.25.a.& b - I.27.central, then to destination.

3. Order of march will be Headquarters, "C" "B" "A" "D" Coys. Head of leading Coy. will pass "C" Coy. Billets at 10 a.m.

4. Cookers. L.G.Limbers and 1 Pack Cob in rear of their respective Coys. Headquarters Transport with the exception of the L.G.Cart in rear of Battalion.
Water Carts to be filled before leaving.

5. Intervals of 200 yards to be maintained between Coys.

6. Location of Battalion H.Q. will be notified later.
Transport Lines will be at SLAG HEAP J.31.c.8.0.

7. All Billets, etc., will be left in a clean and satisfactory manner, before leaving.

8. ACKNOWLEDGE.

Howarth
Captain.
Adjutant.

19-9-18.

Distribution No.1. O.C."A" Coy.
               "B" "
               "C" "
               "D" "
               H.Q. "
      Lt.Col.W.R.Peel.D.S.O.
      Major L.C.Wilde.D.S.O.
      Q.M.
      T.O.
      War Diary.
      File.

ADMINISTRATIVE INSTRUCTIONS NO. 112

Issued in connection with OPERATION ORDER NO.112

by

Lieut.Col. W.R. PEEL. D.S.O. Commanding.

---

1. An advance party of 1 C.Q.M.S. or Sergt. per Coy. on bicycles under Lt. W. Schofield will rendezvous at the Guard Room at 8-45 a.m. tomorrow morning and proceed to LESOCQUIERE (I.29.A.) and take over all tents and trench shelters from 15th R.B.

2. An advance party for the front line of 1 Officer and 1 N.C.O per Coy. will rendezvous at the Guard Room at 8-15 a.m. tomorrow and proceed under charge of Capt.F.Hardman. M.C. to Cross Roads M.11.b. BAPAUME - ALBERT ROAD where they will pick up a bus at 9 a.m. This party will report to Headquarters 23rd Brigade PLACE MONTMARTE (Q.2.d.)
Bus should go as far as P.18.c.9.5.)

3. **Battle Surplus.** The Battle Surplus (less personnel for Signal Class) will parade at 12 noon tomorrow under Capt .G.B.Taylor , and will proceed by march route to Divnl Reception Camp MIRAUMONT .
This party will be rationed up to the 21st inst inclusive.
This party will clean up the Camp and hand over all tents and trench shelters for which receipts will be obtained.
Certificates of cleanliness will also be obtained, these will be sent to Rear Orderly Room as soon as possible.
DRESS :- Full Marching Order.

4. **Signal Class.** The Signal Class consisting of 11 O.R. under Sergt. Phillips will parade at 9 a.m. tomorrow morning at Battalion Guard Room . This party will be rationed up to the 21st inclusive and will report to R.T.O. ACHIET-LE-GRAND by noon tomorrow 20th inst. This party will detrain BEAUSSART and march to BUS.
DRESS :- Full Marching Order.

5. **Lewis Guns.** Lewis Gun limbers will be loaded tonight ready for the line of march. Magazines to be packed in Magazine boxes.

6. **Surplus Baggage.** Packs. Surplus Mess Stores,Surplus baggage of any description will be stacked opposite the Battalion Guard Room. Sergt.P.Healey will be in charge of this baggage.
This baggage will be taken to H.31.d. and unloaded by the Light Railway Siding.AT 10-20 a.m. tomorrow morning this baggage will be reloaded and taken by rail to LESOCQUIERE .
Sergt. Healey and 4 O.R. detailed by the Quartermaster will proceed with this baggage and act as unloading party.

7. **Ammunition party.** O.C."D" Coy. will detail 2 men to report to O.C. S.A.A. Section D.A.C. at H.31.d.2.4. by 4 p.m. tomorrow 20th inst. Names of men detailed to be sent to Battalion Orderly Room.
These men should have a good knowledge of grenades.
They should be rationed up to and including 21st inst.
They will proceed in Fighting Kit.

8. **Officers valises.** Officers valises will be stacked outside Battalion Guard Room by 7 a.m. tomorrow morning. Trench bundles will be made up by each Officer and loaded in the Maltese Cart by 8-30 a.m.

9. Coy. L.G.limbers and Coy.Pack Cobs will march behind their Coys. on the line of march tomorrow.

19/8/18.

Distribution as per O.O.No.112.

Howarth
Captain
Adjutant.

WAR DIARY

of

Officer Commanding (Lt Col w. R. Pol DSO)

1/10 Battalion Manchester Regiment

From October 1st 1918 To October 31st 1918.

Volume 39

Army Form C. 2118.

WAR DIARY
or
INTELLIGENCE SUMMARY.
(Erase heading not required.)

Instructions regarding War Diaries and Intelligence Summaries are contained in F. S. Regs., Part II. and the Staff Manual respectively. Title pages will be prepared in manuscript.

Place	Date 1918	Hour	Summary of Events and Information	Remarks and references to Appendices
HAVRINCOURT WOOD	Oct 1st		Battalion encamped in HAVRINCOURT WOOD	
	Oct 2nd		Battalion Training – Attack, leap frogging	
	Oct 3rd & 4th		Consolidation of practical	
	Oct 5th		Battalion training. A Coy gave demonstration of Company in the attack before Batt. Commandt and G.H.Q. representative. Afternoon:- Foot shooting and recreational training	
	Oct 6th		Brigade Church Parade. Reserve warning order that Battalion would be on 10 minutes notice after 8 am S.R. Chiroi	
	Oct 7th		Battalion in the attack. – leap frogging and consolidation practice. Preparing for move.	
HINDENBURG Support Line (Sheet 57c SE)	Oct 8th		Battalion moved forward from HAVRINCOURT WOOD with 1st Line Transport at 10 am and joined Brigade Column at METZ-EN-COUTURE Cross roads and marched via GOUZEAUCOURT LAVACQUERIE to R10 d Sheet 57c SE (HINDENBURG SUPPORT LINE)	
BRIEUX WOOD (Sheet 57b)	Oct 9th		Battalion moved out from Bivouacs at 7-15 am via LE QUENNET FARM – LES RUES des VIGNES – Canal due L'ESCAUT to LESDAIN arriving at 10 am. Bttalion moved forward again at 12-30 pm to BRIEUX Chateau – South of ESNES arriving at 2-30 pm. NZ Battalion encamped in the Brigade and Support to the NZ Division	
	Oct 10th		Battalion in bivouacs in BRIEUX WOOD (Sheet 57b N10c)	
FONTAINE-au-PIRE	Oct 11th		Battalion moved out of bivouacs at 7-15 am to FONTAINE-au-PIRE. – West of CAUDRY via ESNES – LONGSART	I

Army Form C. 2118.

WAR DIARY
or
INTELLIGENCE SUMMARY.
(Erase heading not required.)

Instructions regarding War Diaries and Intelligence Summaries are contained in F. S. Regs., Part II. and the Staff Manual respectively. Title pages will be prepared in manuscript.

Place	Date 1918	Hour	Summary of Events and Information	Remarks and references to Appendices
HERPIGNY FARM	Oct 12		Battalion moved to HERPIGNY FARM via BEAUVOIS-en-CAMBRESIS at 5 pm. 126th Brigade relieved NZ Division in the line. 126th Bde in support.	II
	Oct 13 14 15 16		Battalion at HERPIGNY FARM employed on digging defence WEST of QUIEVY. Practising forming up on tape and roads. Bathing etc.	
	Oct 17		Received Warning Order that the Brigade would relieve the 125th Inf Bde. in the front line on night 18th/19th inst. Practised the assembly and attack in the morning about the same evening after dark.	
BRIASTRE (East of)	Oct 18		Practised assembly and attack again in the morning. Lt-Col L.R. PEEL MC addressed the Battalion prior to going "Over the Top" Battalion marched out of HERPIGNY FARM at 18h45 and relieved the 17th Lancashire Fusiliers in the line in front of BRIASTRE. Relief complete at 19h45.	III
	Oct 19		Orders for attack on October 20th received. A Company moves from Support position to position of assembly at 11.00 pm. C Company " " " " " " 11.30 pm. B Coy to rendezvous moves — to position of assembly at 11.55 pm.	IV
	Oct 20		All troops in position of assembly at 1 am. At 1 am heavy shelling hit C.M. COOPER Killed and 27 other Ranks Casualties — 15 being of A Coy's left platoon details for final objective. Zero hour for the attack 2 am. Frontage and objective see map appendix. Front Coy's. A Coy on the left — tolls for green line. C Coy assembly killed for Blue line D Coy in rear of A Coy to leap frog. B Coy at Blue line and go to Yellow line. B Coy BHQ Makeshetort in rear of D Coy to position "X". S/C East known. B Coy to attack on the Right of the Battalion.	

Army Form C. 2118.

WAR DIARY
or
INTELLIGENCE SUMMARY.
(Erase heading not required.)

Instructions regarding War Diaries and Intelligence Summaries are contained in F. S. Regs., Part II. and the Staff Manual respectively. Title pages will be prepared in manuscript.

Place	Date	Hour	Summary of Events and Information	Remarks and references to Appendices
	Oct 20 1918 (cont)		On "A" Company reaching the objective 2/Lieut W.H. GREGORY took command all other officers in Company having become casualties. Owing to the enemy on the strip tanks of Rail Cutting, and the steps of the RAVINE – YELLOW LINE this Company had lost the Barrage. 2/Lieut W.H. GREGORY reorganised them and led them forward. The Company was not with Lewis M.G. fire before reaching the Green Line – this Officer became the Company became cut of practically until the first objective. After strong opposition with only of the enemy were killed and taken prisoner. 375837 Corpl W MARTIN did very good work on the left of the Company. Before the remainder he charged a large number of the enemy some of whom he killed, the remainder he captured. Before handling the Officer in charge of a Stokes mortar 3/Lieut Capt FISHER A (1st Lieut) whose action into a minenwerfer and brought this mortar to action against the enemy. After firing ten rounds, he, his men in this charge against the enemy successfully. The crew and Captain of the mortar were killed. The enemy final objective had been captured two trench mortars and Colonel "A" Coy (what deal of trouble from the left flank. Capt F.A.C TAYLOR D.S.O M.C obtained some rifle grenades and after these went forward killing two of the enemy, the remainder running away. This brought action cleared the situation and enabled a Sgt KILLEN of "B" Coy firstly shoulder "A" and for the Bandstation later. At this place some of the enemy were killed. Command that went had to hand fighting out a large number of the enemy were killed. 275179 Sergt VLEESS S.R. in command of the extreme left platoon had been detailed to get in touch with the 62nd Divn on his left. This he did in spite of a most back of the Railway from the left of the Battalion	

(49175) W. W335/1360 500,000 12/17 D. D. & L. Schr 52a Forms/C2118/5.

Army Form C. 2118.

WAR DIARY
or
INTELLIGENCE SUMMARY.
(Erase heading not required.)

Instructions regarding War Diaries and Intelligence Summaries are contained in F.S. Regs., Part II. and the Staff Manual respectively. Title pages will be prepared in manuscript.

Place	Date 1918	Hour	Summary of Events and Information	Remarks and references to Appendices
	Oct 2nd Cont'd		2/4 Y and 2/4 Division to attack on left of Battalion at Z + 30 Barrage came down at Zero hour 300 yards in front of Coverlly positions all troops immediately advancing to close under barrage but there getting their position up to Zero + 15. Barrage went 100 yards in 3 minutes then at 100 yards in 8 minutes. This attack was successfully covered by the leading Coy's immediately west of the Railway. The attack was successfully carried out cutting the wire so that good work in making exits in their barrel to let forward his ration through the wire was very strongly held by troops at that Red Railway. Heavy machine-gun fire indie brought to bear owing to the Division crossing the Railway entering and came up against C Coy on the right bank of the Railway. Heavy machine gun fire from enemy posts immediately back of the Railway. These posts were successfully dealt with by M.Z.M.S. JUPP. Commanding the Company himself with a few men charging the enemy and charging work with the rifle. This Company was able to take up the barrage before reaching the RAVINE or YELLOW LINE and they successfully kept up with it till the Final Objective was reached. At the Final Objective the Company had arrived in its correct frontage with the right of the Company in its correct position. The joint that direction was kept in touch. The right was intensely dark under the excellent leadership of Lieut. T.M.S JUPP and 2/Lieut. G O MORRIS. After the objective had been gained, supports were promptly pushed out on the ridge (sift) Lieut. T M S JUPP led to platoon against the enemy on his left flank and Newly greatly assisted 2/A Coyle John in left flank final objective forming the attack Sergt 375932 Sergt NEWTON. H did	

A Coyle John Mc. 375932 Forms/C2118/14

WAR DIARY
or
INTELLIGENCE SUMMARY.
(Erase heading not required.)

Army Form C. 2118.

Place	Date 1918	Hour	Summary of Events and Information	Remarks and references to Appendices
	Oct 20th cont		to this point - 1500 yards did some very good work. In the Railway Cpt. J.C.S. ROWBOTHAM ²/Lieut. T. AINSWORTH att⁴ 126 Gen.B. 3/5555 Corpl KEIGHLEY att⁴ 126 Gen.B. and ²/Lieut. T. AINSWORTH att⁴ 126 Gen.B. greatly assisted C Coy. D Coy detailed for the YELLOW LINE also with start Bivouacs in the Quarry line Lieut. J. F. BEVERIDGE did some very good work. A fatal shot was when 376731 C.S.M. TOOGOOD. K. to get in touch with the 52nd Division on the East of the Railway encountering a strong enemy Post. This they attacked killing 17 and capturing 12 of the enemy. Shortly after Zero hour the enemy barrage came down at BRIASTRE and went to any extent on the attacking troops. At 7 am the Bn. had reached 127 Bn. front through the Battalion. At this time the enemy sent down a heavy barrage on the Railway and on RAVINE later in the day all troops on the GREEN LINE. Casualties were as follows:— Lieut F E COOK and Lieut C M COOPER Killed. Lieut H B LAWSON Lieut C H COOPER and ²/Lieut W. WILLIAMS ²/Lieut R. A. HARROP & Lieut H J BANKES wounded. Other rank Casualties 18 Killed, 91 wounded, 1 Missing.	✗ ✗
	Oct 21		Front line Coys consolidated on their final objective. During afternoon the enemy counter attacked. The attack died down without event	✗ ✗
HERPIGNY FARM	Oct 21		Recd order that the Battalion would be relieved by the N.Z. Division. At 1700 the area was occupied by the 1st Canterburys with 1st and 2nd Otagos. Prior to the N.Z. Division attacking, the Battalion moved out and marched by WESLY to HERPIGNY FARM	V ✗

Army Form C. 2118.

WAR DIARY
or
INTELLIGENCE SUMMARY.
(Erase heading not required.)

Instructions regarding War Diaries and Intelligence Summaries are contained in F. S. Regs., Part II. and the Staff Manual respectively. Title pages will be prepared in manuscript.

Place	Date 1918	Hour	Summary of Events and Information	Remarks and references to Appendices
HERPIGNY FARM	Oct 23		The day was spent in cleaning up, taking over and reorganisation. The Commander-in-Chief in his despatch for the March operations mentioned the Battalion by name for the good work done at ESNIERES in repelling 8 enemy counter-attacks.	
BEAUVOIS-en-CAMBRESIS	Oct 24		The Battalion marched out of HERPIGNY FARM at 10.45am to BEAUVOIS-en-CAMBRESIS arriving about 12.30. Inspected on the line of march by Major General A. SOLLY-FLOOD. C.M.G. D.S.O. Batts. accommodated in billets.	VI
	Oct 25		Battalion settling down into billets. Cleaning up, inspections &c.	
	Oct 26		Coy's Stationary Coy and Platoon in the attack, training up to. Afternoon Recreational training	
	Oct 27		Battalion Church parade. Y.M.C.A. BEAUVOIS	
	Oct 28 29 30		Battalion Training - Coy in the attack - Musketry - Assembling prior to attack - Range practices &c	
	31		Presentation of Medal Ribbons to 128 Supple by Col. Roe M.C. Bar. Battalion lieutenants were Capt. J.A.Taylor D.S.O. Lieut. Major Butterworth and Lieut. Latham - M.C. Lieut. 376583 Sen. Sgt A.K. Dean, 250885 Cpl Riford Bar for DCM Ribbon 376329 Sgt. Brown S.D.M. Bar SR hun for 376386 Pte Broadhead tum 745377 Pte Adnett twn 376799 Sgt Law SR twn - 376386 Pte R.Taurens tim for MM sibbon, for MM Ribbon 376322 Pte R.Taurens Bar to MM sibbon 3/58714 Pte Whitetart R for Belgian Croix du Guerre Ribbon.	

Com/y/10 Lancashire Regt
W.C.

War Diary of the
1/0 Warehole Regt
Nov 1st to 30th 1918.

Vol no

Army Form C. 2118.

WAR DIARY
or
INTELLIGENCE SUMMARY

(Erase heading not required.)

Instructions regarding War Diaries and Intelligence Summaries are contained in F. S. Regs., Part II. and the Staff Manual respectively. Title pages will be prepared in manuscript.

Place	Date Nov. 1918	Hour	Summary of Events and Information	Remarks and references to Appendices
BEAUVOIS	1st		Battalion training. Company in the attack with without barrage	
-do-	2nd		Gas training. Received Warning order Prepare to move to SOLESMES night of 3/4 Nov.	
-do-	3rd		Battalion prepared to move. Received order that Division would attack through N.Z. Division about 5th or 6th inst. First objective to be goal EAST of FORÊT DE MORMAL. Battalion moved out of billets in BEAUVOIS at 1920 via BETHENCOURT – VIESLY – BRIASTRE – BELLE VUE – SOLESMES arriving at 2400.	
SOLESMES	4th		Battalion moved at mid-day to BEAUDIGNIES arriving there at 1600.	
	5th		Battalion moved from BEAUDIGNIES at 0900 marched to HERBIGNIES arriving at 1330. At 1515 Battalion moved to FORESTERS HOUSE to take over the night support Battalion position (1st Otago). The 5th EL Rgt. on the front line on the night, the 8th MANCHESTERS in the front line on the left. Great difficulty was experienced owing to several mine craters in the road. The men having to carry their gun over 6000 yards. The day was very wet. Relief was completed at 0200. Position of Companies as follows:– "D" Coy 027a; "C" Coy 027k; "B" Coy 033k, A Coy 025c. Owing to the dark, mud, rain it took Companies over 2½ hours to get into position from FORESTER'S HOUSE	

WAR DIARY
or
INTELLIGENCE SUMMARY

Army Form C. 2118.

(Erase heading not required.)

Instructions regarding War Diaries and Intelligence Summaries are contained in F. S. Regs., Part II. and the Staff Manual respectively. Title pages will be prepared in manuscript.

Place	Date November 1918	Hour	Summary of Events and Information	Remarks and references to Appendices
	6th		Rations could not be got up to Companies till 0900. On the situation on the right was not clear "A" Coy was moved to PETIT-RAVAY. Here they were able to get into action at mid-day. "B" Coy was sent up to 028a to make a defensive left flank at mid-day, they had 1 Officer (Lt G THORLEY) and 16 OR casualties. The enemy shelling was heavy all day. The day was very wet.	—
	7th		At 2400 an all out verbal orders received that the Battalion in conjunction with 2/MANCHESTERS would attack on the morning of the 7th. Objective given road 023a.6.7. 029.4.5.7. The Battalion concentrated in the BROWN LINE, the road immediately EAST of MORMAL FOREST and POLL HOU at CORISEAUX FARM. Great difficulty was experienced by Companies in getting into position owing to the darkness & the wet. At 0650 Zero hour what was to have been at 0100 was put off until 0845. Companies attacked as follows:– "A" Coy on the right, "D" Coy in support of "A" Coy. "B" Coy on the left, "C" Coy in support of "B" Coy. The objective was gained without opposition. Patrols were immediately sent forward by "C" Company who gained the right ground in (Sheet 51) P.25a1. Any Patrol going to MESNIL declared that villag in conjunction with "B" Coy1 during took the enemy to the EAST end of the village. At 1200 the Battalion was disposed as follows:– NORTH & SOUTH Road line through 19 & 25 Central – "B" Coy on left holding the outskirts of the village. "C" Coy on the right. A & D Coys near HOISIERES FARM in reserve. Battalion HQrs at the farm. At 1700 "B" Coy was moved up to MESNIL to form a defensive left flank on the 62nd Divisions had not come up further than HARGNIES. Heavy shelling of MESNIL – all day & night	—

WAR DIARY or INTELLIGENCE SUMMARY

Army Form C. 2118.

Place	Date	Hour	Summary of Events and Information	Remarks and references to Appendices
	1918 November 8th		At 0400 orders were received to continue the advance with the 5th E.L.Rgt. on the right, on HAUTMONT. "A" Coy pushed out patrols at 0530 to edge of Bois de HAUTMONT. "A" Coy advanced through "B" Coy. Joined "D" Coy on edge of wood. "C" Coy pushed under CPL. LANE had further forward & reached HAUTMONT at 0730. Vanguard of "A" & "D" Coys entered the Town at 1012. Main body at 1100. The van guard was under Lieut. STREET. Patrols were immediately pushed forward to the river SAMBRE. A footbridge was commenced by Captn. J.A.C.TAYLOR. D.S.O. M.C. and the leading Platoon moved over at 1130. Patrols were immediately sent forward where successfully drove the enemy rearguard to the eastern edge of the village. A "C" Coy followed the Patrols. Most of Battalion on following: P30 a.1.6. - P.24.c.o.4. - P.23.6.2.3. The 5th E.L.Rgt coming up later on the Right. The Brigade on the Left had not then reached the Railway. "D" Coy were moved up from MESNIL made a defensive left flank on the WEST bank of the river, facing NORTH. "B" Coy were also moved up from MESNIL. The enemy rearguards were occupying a line 200 yds in advance of our line. Artillery fire was brought to bear on them when their own Gun fire from loophole in allies forced them to retire to the N - S line between P.21.c & Q.19. At 1500 enemy shelled SOUTH of town intermittently keeping up their fire for several hours. The towns and TAYLOR'S BRIDGE were also heavily shelled. The enemy had a battery firing from Q.20. Artillery was put on to them. At 1600 orders were received that J.25 L.F.Rgts would take over the front line. This was completed at 0430 on the 9th inst. Contd—	

Army Form C. 2118.

WAR DIARY
or
INTELLIGENCE SUMMARY
(Erase heading not required.)

Instructions regarding War Diaries and Intelligence Summaries are contained in F.S. Regs., Part II. and the Staff Manual respectively. Title pages will be prepared in manuscript.

Place	Date 1918 November	Hour	Summary of Events and Information	Remarks and references to Appendices
	8th Continued		On the Battalion return to the Town great enthusiasm was displayed by the inhabitants. They greatly assisted in building the bridge. The leading patrols were received by the MAIRE and English Women who had been in German hands. Very great assistance was rendered by the inhabitants in giving positions of enemy machine guns, in the they displayed great bravery. Later in the day unfortunately many became casualties through hostile shelling. A. L.5 Howitzer old one 77 m.m; and numerous limbers, 1 motor lorry & one tractor were captured by the Battalion. Cpl LANE. "B" Coy did valuable work in leading forward the patrol of "C" Coy mentioned above. The Signal Communication namely visual was exceptionally well organised by Lieut SCHOFIELD. The advance of the Battalion was extraordinarily rapid, the ground being sodden with rain & the men having been exposed to the worst conditions for that day. The Battalion was visited by the Brigadier at 1130 in HAUTMONT	✗
HAUTMONT	9th	0630	The whole Battalion was in billets on the WEST SIDE of the Town. Every assistance was given by the inhabitants in making the men comfortable & preparing hot food. At 1000 the Battalion was visited by the Divisional Commander who expressed to the C.O his appreciation of the endurance the work the Battalion had performed in its rapid advance.	✗
-do-	10th		Battalion resting & cleaning up.	✗

Army Form C. 2118.

WAR DIARY
or
INTELLIGENCE SUMMARY

(Erase heading not required.)

Place	Date 1918 November	Hour	Summary of Events and Information	Remarks and references to Appendices
HAUTMONT	11th		At 0900. orders received that hostilities would cease at 1100.	
-do-	12th		Training.	
-do-	13th		Memorial Service for Privates of Allied Armies who died in HAUTMONT	
-do-	14th		Ditto	
-do-	15th		Rehearsal in square of ceremony to be held on 16th. Capt J.A.C. TAYLOR DSO MC. will act as 2nd in Command. Capt F. MERCER put in command of "A" Coy.	

-do-	16th		Whole Battalion represented all units of the Division formed up in the square. Lt Col W.R. Peel DSO. presented the L 5 Hon. W.M.; captured by the Battalion on the 8th inst, to the MAIRE & CITIZENS of HAUTMONT. The Mairie responded with an address. The Battalion then marched past the Div Commander & the MAIRE. Copies of Speeches etc attached. In the evening the Mairie presented a Bouquet to the Battalion. Officers in action from the 5th to 9th.
			
			Lieut Col W.R. Peel DSO. A Coy C Coy
			Capt J. Howarth MC Capt J.A.C. Taylor DSO MC Capt F. Mercer
			Lieut W. Selafield Lieut E.R. Sload 2/Lt F Mercer.
			Lieut Ams Smith 2/Lieut M. Bentley. 2/Lt. E Wintomleu.
			Revd. Matthews U.S.A. B Coy 2/- C.W. Wickler.
			    Lieut W.D Sloan, MC (killed) D Coy
			    " G. Thorley (killed) Capt A Rutherwort MC.
			    2/Lt W.L Griffith. Lieut E.O.M Harry
			    2/- S.G. Roberts. 2/- E.C Iriften MC
			        2/- E.W. Matthews.	

Army Form C. 2118.

WAR DIARY
or
INTELLIGENCE SUMMARY.
(Erase heading not required.)

Instructions regarding War Diaries and Intelligence Summaries are contained in F.S. Regs., Part II. and the Staff Manual respectively. Title pages will be prepared in manuscript.

1918

Place	Date November	Hour	Summary of Events and Information	Remarks and references to Appendices
HAUTMONT	14th		Relied Parade.	###
-do-	18th		Lieut Col W R Peel DSO assumed temporary command of 12th Lgt Bde, Capt J A C Taylor DSO M.C. took command of the Battalion.	###
-do-	19 20 21 22		Coy Training. Ceremonial Close Order Drill. Range Practices refitting & cleaning up etc.	###
-do-	23		Inspection by Brigade Commander Battalion in full marching order, billets, Transport, Lewis Guns, Orderly Room etc. Good report received after the inspection. Capt C H Cooper appointed Employment Officer. R C Tuttle M.C. Education	###
-do-	24		Church Parade.	###
-do-	25 26		Coy Training Ceremonial Close order drill etc.	###
-do-	27		Rode route march in the morning via NEUF MESNIL - LA LONQUEVILLE - HARGNIES - VIEUX MESNIL - BOUSSIERES - HAUTMONT.	###
-do-	28		Coy Training Close order Drill - Range Practices Lewis Gunade work etc.	###

WAR DIARY
INTELLIGENCE SUMMARY.
(Erase heading not required.)

Army Form C. 2118.

Place	Date	Hour	Summary of Events and Information	Remarks and references to Appendices
HAUTMONT	November 1918 29		Brigade took mark in the morning. – LOUVRIL – REMY – MAL-BATI– BOUSSIERES – HAUTMONT.	
–do–	30.		Battalion on salvage work, cleaning up Battalion area.	

Comdg 1/10th Londons to Captain
J.A.C. Tafer. Captain
Londons Regiment

Please quote
No. A150/16
1/10th Bn. Manchester Regt.

WR 23

WAR DIARY of

O.C. 1/10th Lancashire Regiment

from December 1st to 31st 1918.

VOLUME 41.

Original

Army Form C. 2118.

WAR DIARY
or
INTELLIGENCE SUMMARY.
(Erase heading not required.)

Instructions regarding War Diaries and Intelligence Summaries are contained in F.S. Regs., Part II. and the Staff Manual respectively. Title pages will be prepared in manuscript.

Place	Date	Hour	Summary of Events and Information	Remarks and references to Appendices
HAUTMONT	1/12/18		Battalion lined up on the MAUBEUGE — AVESNES RD and His Majesty the King walked through the ranks at 1110. Battalion then marched back to billets in HAUTMONT. The Rugby Team met the 2nd Devs. M.G.C. in the afternoon, winning the Divisional Rugby Cup by 13 — 3 points. Cups and medals presented by G.O.C.	#
	2/12/18		Battalion on Salvage work clearing up area round BOUSSIERES and roads to HAUTMONT.	#
	3/12/18		Battalion and Company training.	#
	4/12/18		Close order, Ceremonial and Arms Drill.	#
	5/12/18		Sports etc.	#
	6/12/18		Brigade Route March HAUTMONT — BOUSSIERES — VIEUX MESNIL — HARGNIES — LA LONGUVILLE — NEUF MESNIL — HAUTMONT.	#
	7/12/18		Commanding Officer inspected all Companies and Headquarters in full marching order.	#

WAR DIARY or INTELLIGENCE SUMMARY.

Army Form C. 2118.

Place	Date	Hour	Summary of Events and Information	Remarks and references to Appendices
	8/2/18		Brigade Church Parade.	
	9/2/18		Battalion Training and Baths.	
	10/2/18		M.O.C. 126 Inf Bde inspected the Battalion in full marching order on Parade. Returned himself well satisfied with the general turnout.	
	11/2/18		C.B.Y. and Close order Drill.	
	12/2/18		Company Training and Close order Drill.	
	13/2/18		Company Training Ceremonial.	
	14/2/18		Battalion leaves HAUTMONT and proceeds to GRAND RENG where Battalions were to Billet for the night.	
	15/2/18		Battalion continues march from GRAND RENG to BINCHE en route for CHARLEROI area.	
	16/2/18		Battalion leaves BINCHE by march route to FONTAINE L'EVEQUE and arrived in billets at 1200 hrs.	
	17/2/18		Battalion Resting at FONTAINE L'EVEQUE.	
	18/2/18		Battalion moves to GILLY nr CHARLEROI area reporting all in billets at 1700 hrs.	

Army Form C. 2118.

WAR DIARY
or
INTELLIGENCE SUMMARY.
(Erase heading not required.)

Instructions regarding War Diaries and Intelligence Summaries are contained in F. S. Regs., Part II. and the Staff Manual respectively. Title pages will be prepared in manuscript.

Place	Date	Hour	Summary of Events and Information	Remarks and references to Appendices
GILLY	19/2/18		Battalion Resting and cleaning equipment.	
"	20/2/18		Re-arranging Ration - training wfn	
"	21/2/18		Battalion Parade. 0930 Ft inspection by C.O.	
"	22/2/18		Church Parade	
"	23/2/18		C. O. D. Conference. Coy/Coyt Training	
			A. Coy. Infantry training	
			B. " Courses for NCOs	
"	24/2/18		Coyt Instruction. Lecture to Battalion by C.O. Following on	
			A.F.Z.10 by Corps.	
"	25/2/18		Demonstration Day. Voluntary Service	
			C. O. inspected all units transport.	
"	26/2/18		Regimental Holiday	
"	27/2/18		Bn. training. A Coy. fwd guard of 2 officers and 100 O.Cs. for duty at Montiques	

WAR DIARY
or
INTELLIGENCE SUMMARY.
(Erase heading not required.)

Army Form C. 2118.

Place	Date	Hour	Summary of Events and Information	Remarks and references to Appendices
	28/3/18		Sickness. 6 boys attached to foh. Montgomery apart for 6 days. Request made of 3 Munst. aut 100 other ranks speak by D Coy to return other rd Camp of Civilian riots.	
	29/3/18		Chemical Parade.	
	30/3/18		Regimental Fatigues.	
	31/3/18		Regimental Fatigues.	

h.R.Peel
LIEUT. COL.
COMMDG. 1/10TH MANCHESTER REGT.

1/10: Battalion Manchester Regiment.

WAR DIARY
FOR
January - 1919.

(Confidential.)

VOLUME No. 112.

Army Form C. 2118.

WAR DIARY
or
INTELLIGENCE SUMMARY.
(Erase heading not required.)

Instructions regarding War Diaries and Intelligence Summaries are contained in F. S. Regs., Part II and the Staff Manual respectively. Title pages will be prepared in manuscript.

Place	Date	Hour	Summary of Events and Information	Remarks and references to Appendices
GILLY	January			
	1		New Years Day.	füst
	2		73 Battalion on Education. 0900 - 1200 hrs.	füst
	3		Battalion Parade 0900 hrs.	füst
			0930-1200 hrs Training in Coy. Area.	füst
	4		Major. A. C. Booth joins unit.	füst
			Kit inspections - Recreational Training.	füst
	5		Church Parade.	füst
	6		73 Battalion Parade. 0900 hrs.	füst
	7		0930-1200 Coy. Training.	füst
			Educational Parade.	füst
			Major L.C. Wiles L.Co. Demobilised.	
	8		Battalion Parade 0900 hrs. A. Coy. firing on range. B.C.D Coy. Coy Training	füst
	9		Party of 22 men Proceed on demobilisation. - Educational Training.	füst
			Brigadier General inspected Transport & Cookhouse.	füst
	10		Battalion bathing at the Collery Baths.	füst
			Major A. E. Booth Proceeds to 263. P.O.W. Coy.	füst
	11		Battalion Parade. 0900 hrs. Education 1030-1200 hrs.	füst

Army Form C. 2118.

WAR DIARY
or
INTELLIGENCE SUMMARY.
(Erase heading not required.)

Instructions regarding War Diaries and Intelligence
Summaries are contained in F. S. Regs., Part II.
and the Staff Manual respectively. Title pages
will be prepared in manuscript.

Place	Date	Hour	Summary of Events and Information	Remarks and references to Appendices
GHHY.	12		Church Parade.	Appx
	13		Battalion for duty. A Coy & details from "D" Coy supply Montignies Guard.	Appx
			"B" Coy finds 1 Off + 30 O.Rs for NAMUR GUARD.	Appx
			"C" Coy finds 2 N.C.Os + 7 men for BOIS NOEL GUARD.	Appx
			"C" Coy finds 2 N.C.Os + 7 men for Divisional Guard.	Appx
	14		Battalion for duty. Guards, Fatigues, etc.	Appx
	15		Battalion for duty. Guards, Fatigues, etc.	Appx
	16		Battalion for duty. Guards, Fatigues, etc.	Appx
	17		Battalion for duty. Guards, Fatigues, etc.	Appx
			Lieut. Col. W.R. Peel. D.S.O Awarded 2nd bar to D.S.O.	Appx
			Capt. J.A.C. Taylor. 2nd Lt. M.C. Mentioned in Despatches	Appx
			375908 4/Cpl. Mellor. -do-	Appx
			14354 C.S.M. Ramsden -do-	Appx
	18		Battalion on duty. Guards Fatigues etc.	Appx
	19		Church Parade.	Appx
	20		Battalion Parades for Rehearsal of Divnl Medal Presentation - 0900 hrs.	Appx

Army Form C. 2118.

WAR DIARY
or
INTELLIGENCE SUMMARY.
(Erase heading not required.)

Place	Date	Hour	Summary of Events and Information	Remarks and references to Appendices
CINCY	21		Battalion Parade. 0830 hr. Presentation of Medal ribbons by Div. Commander.	
	22		Battalion Parade. 0900 hr. Lecture to all Officers by Lieut. E.O. Edwards on "Ceremonial Drill".	
	23		Battalion Headquarters, Transport & Quartermasters Personnel - bathing. Coy. Inspection. 0900 hr. Education. 0945 hr.	
	24		Battalion firing on Range. A + B Coys. Miniature Range. C + D Coys. Brigade Range.	
	25		B. Coy. Bathing. 1200 - 1300 hrs. Kit Inspection. Education. D. Coy. Bathing.	
	26		Church Parade.	
	27		Battalion Parade 0930 hr. Rehearsal for General Inspection.	
	28		Battalion on Educational Training.	
	29		Annual Inspection by G.O.C. 126th Bde. 0945 hr. on Place de la Gare.	
	30		Battalion on Education. Lieut. Col. W.R. Bell, D.S.O. Proceeds to U.K. on Demobilization.	
	31		Battalion firing on Range. A, B + C Coys. on Brigade Range. D. Coy. Battalion Range.	

Vol 25

1/10. Battalion. Manchester Regiment.

WAR DIARY.

For

FEBRUARY. 1919.

CONFIDENTIAL.

Volume No. 42.

WAR DIARY
or
INTELLIGENCE SUMMARY.

(Erase heading not required.)

Army Form C. 2118.

Place	Date	Hour	Summary of Events and Information	Remarks and references to Appendices
GULLY.	Feb. 1		Education Classes.	
	2		Lieut. Col. T.J. Kelly D.S.O. M.C. posted to command 10th Batt. Manchester Regt. Vice Lieut. Col. W.R. Pink D.S.O. demobilised 31-1-19.	
			Church Parade. Guard duty. C & D Coy. at MONTIGNIES Railroad.	
			A. Coy. flying picquet. B Coy. Namur Guard. Beir Noel Guard.	
			Bayo Guard. CHARLEROI. Refilling point Guard.	
	3.		Battalion on fatigue. Training. 1 officer & 118 men proceed on Demobilization.	
	4.		Education & Guard duties.	
	5.		Coy. Training. Guard duties.	
	6.		Education & Guard duties.	
	7.		Coy. Training & Guard duties.	
	8.		Education. Guard duties. 1 officer proceeded on Demobilization.	
	9.		Church Parade.	
	10.		Coy. Training. S.A.A. collected except 15 rounds per man. Lewis Gun Mob. Stores handed in to Quartermaster.	

Army Form C. 2118.

WAR DIARY
or
INTELLIGENCE SUMMARY.
(Erase heading not required.)

Place	Date	Hour	Summary of Events and Information	Remarks and references to Appendices
GIVRY	11.		Educational Classes.	
	12.		Coy. Inspection (Full Kit inspection).	
	13.		Educational Classes. 6 O.R's demobilized.	
	14.		Coy. Training.	
	15.		Educational Classes. Amalgamation of A & C Coys and B & D Coys to be known as X & Y Coys respectively.	
			1 Officer & 29 O.R on NAMUR Guard.	
			1 " " 25 O.R on ST. SERVAIS Guard.	
			1 " & 4 O.R on TAMINE'S Guard.	
			65. O.R's passed on demobilization. Church Parade.	
	16.		36. O.R's passed on demobilization. Coy fatigues. Reorganising billets & closing in on billets formed Battalion Headquarters.	
	17.			
	18.		Educational Classes.	
	19.		Coy. Training.	

Army Form C. 2118.

WAR DIARY
or
INTELLIGENCE SUMMARY.
(Erase heading not required.)

Instructions regarding War Diaries and Intelligence Summaries are contained in F. S. Regs., Part II. and the Staff Manual respectively. Title pages will be prepared in manuscript.

Place	Date	Hour	Summary of Events and Information	Remarks and references to Appendices
GHYY.	20.		Educational Classes. 63 ors proceeded on Demobilization.	MP
	21.		Coy. Training. 0900-1230 hr.	MP
	22.		Educational Classes. 34 ORs proceeded on Demobilization.	MP
	23.		Church Parade.	MP
	24.		Coy. Inspection 0900-0930. Training under Coy. arrangements 0930-1230 hr.	MP
	25.		Educational Classes. Lt. Col. T.J. Kelly D.S.O. M.C. joined Battalion from Leave & assumed Command.	MP
	26.		Coy. Training. 0900-1230 hr.	MP
	27.		Educational Classes.	MP
	28.		Battalion Bathing 1030-1130 hr.	MP

Nets Lt Col
Commanding 10th Manchester Regt.

No 26

10th Manchester Regiment.

WAR DIARY

FOR

MARCH 1919.

CONFIDENTIAL.

VOLUME No. 44.

WAR DIARY
or
INTELLIGENCE SUMMARY.
(Erase heading not required.)

Army Form C. 2118.

Instructions regarding War Diaries and Intelligence Summaries are contained in F. S. Regs., Part II. and the Staff Manual respectively. Title pages will be prepared in manuscript.

Place	Date	Hour	Summary of Events and Information	Remarks and references to Appendices
Givry	March 1st		The Battalion during this period was still in billets at Givry. Mobilization Stores, Transport, etc. were concentrated at the Cavalry Barracks, Charleroi	J.H.
	16	9k		J.H.
			About 60 OR's were demobilized leaving a strength of 24 Officers + 300 OR	J.H.
	10th		Battalion concentrated in billets to western edge of Givry in order to make way for the 5th Division.	J.H.
	11th to 14th		Concentration Stores + Transport at Barracks, Charleroi.	J.H.
	15th		Inspection of the Cadre by the Commanding Officer	J.H.
	16th to 21st		Battalion strength now 24 Officers + 260 OR's. All other ranks eligible for demobilization have been demobilized, the 260 OR's is made up of men for Army of Occupation "the Cadre".	J.H.
			Duties now are merely routine such as guards at NAMUR, or hospitals, settling of claims etc.	J.H.
	22nd		Inspection of Cadre by Commanding Officer	J.H.
	23rd to 27th		Routine duties such as Guards, Inspection of Mob Stores etc. During the last 10 days? date of embarkation of the Cadre for England has been repeatedly altered	J.H.

Army Form C. 2118.

WAR DIARY
or
INTELLIGENCE SUMMARY.
(Erase heading not required.)

Instructions regarding War Diaries and Intelligence Summaries are contained in F. S. Regs., Part II. and the Staff Manual respectively. Title pages will be prepared in manuscript.

Place	Date	Hour	Summary of Events and Information	Remarks and references to Appendices
	28th		The last order giving the date of April 5th.	##
			Orders received that Cadre of this Unit will entrain on April 2nd	##
			and personnel of Officers & other ranks not in Cadre are to concentrate	##
			at Jesuit College Charleroi under Command of Senior Claimant Officer.	##
			(Capt. J.M.S. Jopp. M.C.) on April 1st	##
	29th		Orders issued for Cadre. Boxing of Mob. Stores completed. Destination	##
			OSWESTRY. Parties on Transport and Stores.	##
	30th		8 O.Rs. Sent on train No 4 at 1900 hr 31/03 to ANTWERP.	##
	31st		Capt N Schofield with 1 NCO & 4 OR proceeded on No 4 train to ANTWERP.	##

Mowafford
Capt/Lt-Col.
Commdg "10th" Manchester Regt.

Apl 27

1/10: Battalion Manchester Regiment.

WAR DIARY

for

APRIL 1919.

CONFIDENTIAL.

VOLUME No 45.

Army Form C. 2118.

WAR DIARY
or
INTELLIGENCE SUMMARY.
(Erase heading not required)

Instructions regarding War Diaries and Intelligence
Summaries are contained in F. S. Regs., Part II.
and the Staff Manual respectively. Title pages
will be prepared in manuscript.

Place	Date	Hour	Summary of Events and Information	Remarks and references to Appendices
SHEY.	April 1st.		All Transport loaded with mobilization Stores & moved up to VILLENAUTE Station & fastened there.	
"	2nd		Transport entrained at 0900 hr. All officers & other ranks who are not marked for Army of Occupation on Cadre have been demobilised during the past two days. Officers include:— Capt. J.C.S. Newbotham M.C. Capt. J.F. Beveridge Capt. F. Mercer 2/Lieut. C.E.E. Thorne Lieut. F. Browne Lieut. G.O. Siniski, Lieut. B.E.W. Hughs. Lieut. A. Rowland 2/Lieut. J.T.D. Ramsden. The Cadre composed of Lt Col. T.J. Kelly, D.S.O. M.C. (Commanding.) Capt. F. Howarth, M.C. (Adjutant.) Capt. W. Schofield. (K.R. Offrs.) Capt. J. Derbyshire (Quartermaster.) Major J.AE Taylor, D.S.O. M.C. Lieut. S.G. Mally. (Colour Party) & H6 O.R.s with the Cadre of the 126th Inf Bde. L.T.M.B. attached (2 ORs) entrained at 1830 hrs. & the whole Transport train moved out from Charleroi at 1900 hr en route for ANTWERP. The remainder of the Battalion composed of about 8 officers & 108 ORs & 108	

Army Form C. 2118.

WAR DIARY
or
INTELLIGENCE SUMMARY.
(Erase heading not required.)

Instructions regarding War Diaries and Intelligence Summaries are contained in F. S. Regs., Part II. and the Staff Manual respectively. Title pages will be prepared in manuscript.

Place	Date	Hour	Summary of Events and Information	Remarks and references to Appendices
			OR. delivered under the command of Capt. Jones Supp. M.C. remained in	
			Billets at Silly awaiting orders to join the Army of Occupation.	
			All the Officers are volunteers & the others under 1916-17-18 category.	
ANTWERP.	April 3rd		The Cadre arrived at Antwerp at 0730 hours.	
			Transport was detrained & placed motor journey in large hangar on dock side.	
			Personnel marched to Embarkation Camp.	
	April 4th		Orders were received for Cadre to embark all vehicles at 1015 hours	
			"Cadre embarked on S.S. "MOGILOFF" at 1500 hrs.	
			The boat anchored off FLUSHING for the night. Proceeded to	
			SOUTHAMPTON. On arrival there the Cadre will proceed by train to	
			OSWESTRY.	

Alexander(?)
Capt.
Comndg. Hon. Lanchlin(?) Regt.